To Taffy & Uma,

With fondest greetings

Xmas 1980

If you cannot go maybe
this is the next best
thing

Wally

OMAN
& its Renaissance

Oman's achievement of grafting modern development upon a rich and traditional heritage is exemplified by Port Qaboos (partly seen on left) enclosing the ancient haven and entrepôt of Mutrah.

OMAN
& its Renaissance

Donald Hawley, CMG, MBE

STACEY INTERNATIONAL, LONDON

For Ruth, Sara, Caroline, Susan and Christopher, who was born in Oman in 1973

Oman and its Renaissance
Stacey International
128, Kensington Church Street, London W8 4BH
Telex 298768 Stacey G

© 1977 Stacey International
Reprinted 1978
Revised edition 1980

ISBN 0 905743 19 9

Art Director Anthony Nelthorpe MSIAD
Assisted by Keith Savage

Indexer Michèle Clarke
Editorial Assistant Hugo de Klee

Maps and diagrams specially prepared by Arka Cartographics Limited, London
Designer Le Roy-Chen
Cartographers Peter Arnold, Roger Bourne, Bob Brett, Lee Brooks, Roy Campen, Kevin Diaper, Allan Rees, Alan Tullett

Set in Monophoto Century by Tradespools Limited, Frome, England
Colour origination by Culver Graphics, High Wycombe, England and Dai Nippon Printing Company Limited, Tokyo
Printed and bound in Japan by Dai Nippon Printing Company Limited, Tokyo

Acknowledgements

I am grateful to many people for assistance and advice, in particular Miss Beatrice de Cardi, Professor Charles Beckingham, Professor Tom Johnstone, Professor Howard Bowen-Jones, Dr John Wilkinson, Dr David Harrison, Major W. Aucut and Miss Margaret Jones, who have very kindly read or helped over parts of the manuscript and made valuable suggestions. I have also relied considerably on published works, particularly those of Wilfred Thesiger, John Wilkinson, Ian Skeet and Alan Villiers, and most of the books mentioned in the bibliography have also been consulted at some stage.

I am also most grateful to my wife Ruth for her assistance over research and for doing much of the initial typing. I would also like to thank Mr Tom Stacey and Mr Raymond Flower for their advice in planning this book, and the staff of Stacey International, particularly Mrs Rosamund McDougall, Miss Charlotte Odgers, Miss Jane Rawlinson, Miss Angela Milburn and Mr Michael Bywater.   D.H.

Principal photographer: Peter Carmichael

All photographs in this volume, including the cover picture, were specially commissioned from Peter Carmichael, except as listed below. Page numbers and quantity of photographs, if more than one, follow the photographer's name.

Roger Bourne 189; Department of Manuscripts, British Library 181, 188–189; Anthony Buckley FIIP 11; Rosemary Drayson 71 (2); Robert Harding Associates 206–207; Dr David L. Harrison 70 (3), 71 (4); Donald Hawley CMG MBE 42, 106; Eric Hosking Hon FRPS, MBOU 191; Squadron Leader David Insall 184–185; Rudi Jäckli 14; Anthony James 164–165; A. M. Al-Khalifa, Aramco; Ray Lewellyn MBE, LRPS 192–193, 241, 243; James Mandaville Jnr. Aramco 71; The Mansell Collection 185, 189; Christopher Mitchell ARIBA, John R. Harris 47, 48–49, 66, 118 (2), 119 (2); Intercontinental Hotels 217; National Maritime Museum 186; National Portrait Gallery 26; Oman International Development Company Ltd and Taylor Woodrow Ltd 221; Mathias Oppersdorff 72–73, 74 (2), 78–79, 86 (2), 87, 88–89, 89, 90, 90–91, 96, 97 (2), 98, 99, 100–101, 101, 103, 104–105, 107, 124, 148–149, 152 (2), 224, 225; Peabody Museum, Salem, Massachusetts 186, 187; Photographers International 199 (2), 208, 217, 218, 222, 226, 230 (2), 233, 234; Michael Rice and Co Ltd 166, 195, 238, 241, 243, 244; Ronald Searight Collection 181; Shell International Petroleum Co Ltd 208 (2), 210; Roger Wood 16 (2), 17 (2), 30–31, 32, 33 (2), 34 (2), 35 (4), 36 (3), 37 (2), 116–117, 126 (3), 127 (5), 128–129, 146 (3), 147 (2), 160, 161 (2), 166, 196–197, 199, 200 (2), 201, 202 (2), 203, 204 (2), 205 (2), 208, 210, 211, 213, 214 (2), 216, 217, 220, 221, 222, 223, 227, 228, 229 (2), 231, 232, 233 (3), 235, 236, 237 (2), 241, 242, 243, 244; Dr C. Vita Finzi 52

The publishers gratefully acknowledge the help of the following organisations and individuals:

H.E. Shaikh Abdulla Ahmed Al-Ghazali; H.E. Shaikh Amor Ali Ameir; Anthony Ashworth; Asprey and Co. Ltd.; Air Commodore Erik Bennett; H.E. Shaikh Breik bin Hamood Al-Ghafiri; Dr D. Bosch; Richard Candlish; Richard Carrington; City Colour Ltd.; Colonel Malcolm Dennison; H.R.H. Sayyed Fahad bin Mahmood Al-Said; Sir William Halcrow and Partners; Dr David L. Harrison; Ian Henderson; The India Office Library; Rudi Jäckli; Peter Mason; H.E. Nasir Seif El Bualy and the staff of the Embassy of the Sultanate of Oman, London; Christopher Newall; Mr and Mrs W. Peyton; Chuck Pringle; Prospection Ltd., Toronto; H.E. Qais Abdul-Munim Al-Zawawi; Michael Rice and Co. Ltd. and Morison Johnston; Abdul Aziz Roas; Edward Stanford, Ltd.; Mr and Mrs David Tatham; John Townsend; the Wali of Sur; Anne Williams; the late Andrew Williamson

The publishers are grateful to the publishers of the following books for permission to quote from them: Ian Skeet *Muscat and Oman* (Faber and Faber); Wilfred Thesiger *Arabian Sands* (Longmans); Bertram Thomas *Alarms and Excursions in Arabia* (Allen and Unwin) and Alan Villiers *Sons of Sinbad* (Hodder and Stoughton).

Chapter 8 (Oman's Renaissance) has been written by the publisher's staff as Donald Hawley is, by the tradition of H M Diplomatic Service of which he is a serving member, precluded from writing on recent events in a country to which he has been accredited as ambassador.

Contents

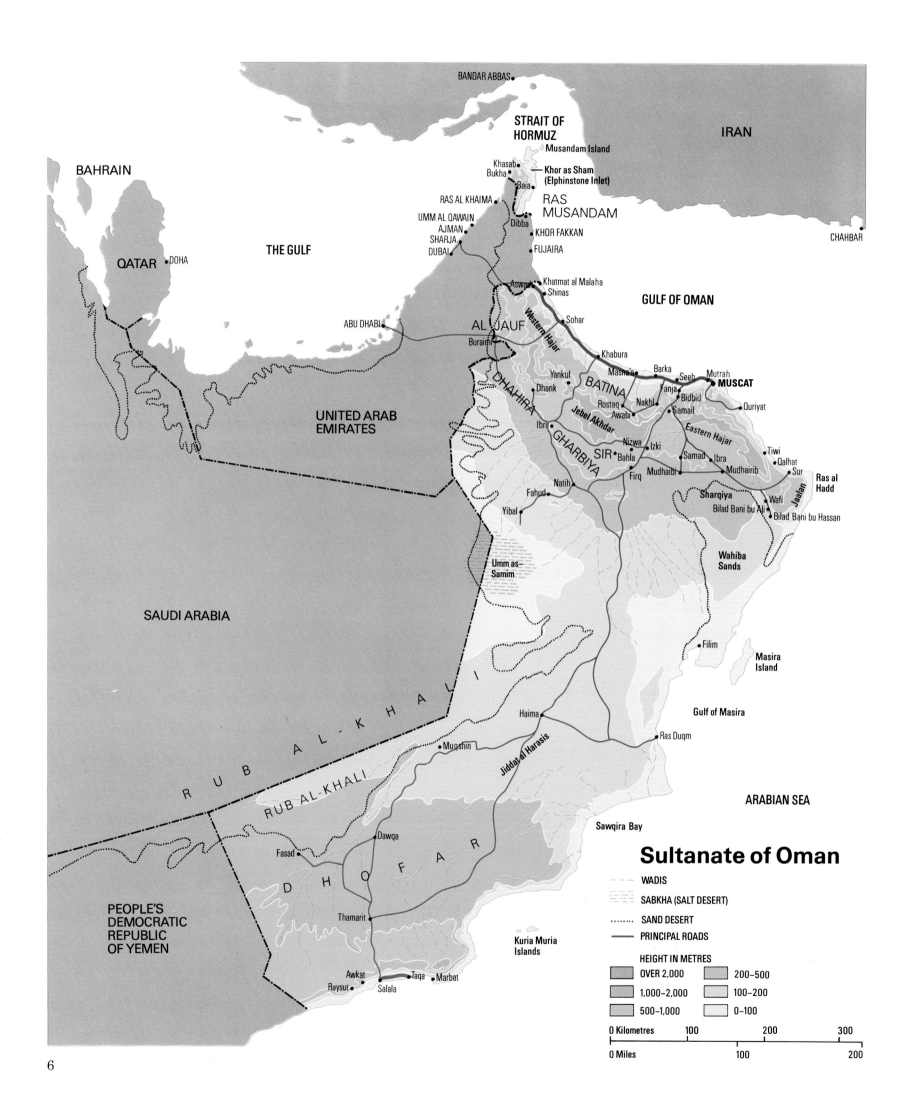

Sultanate of Oman

WADIS

SABKHA (SALT DESERT)

SAND DESERT

PRINCIPAL ROADS

HEIGHT IN METRES

OVER 2,000	200–500
1,000–2,000	100–200
500–1,000	0–100

0 Kilometres   100   200   300

0 Miles   100   200

Maps

Diagrams

Charts, diagrams and maps are based on the latest facts available at the time of their preparation, but subsequent developments may have superseded information contained therein.

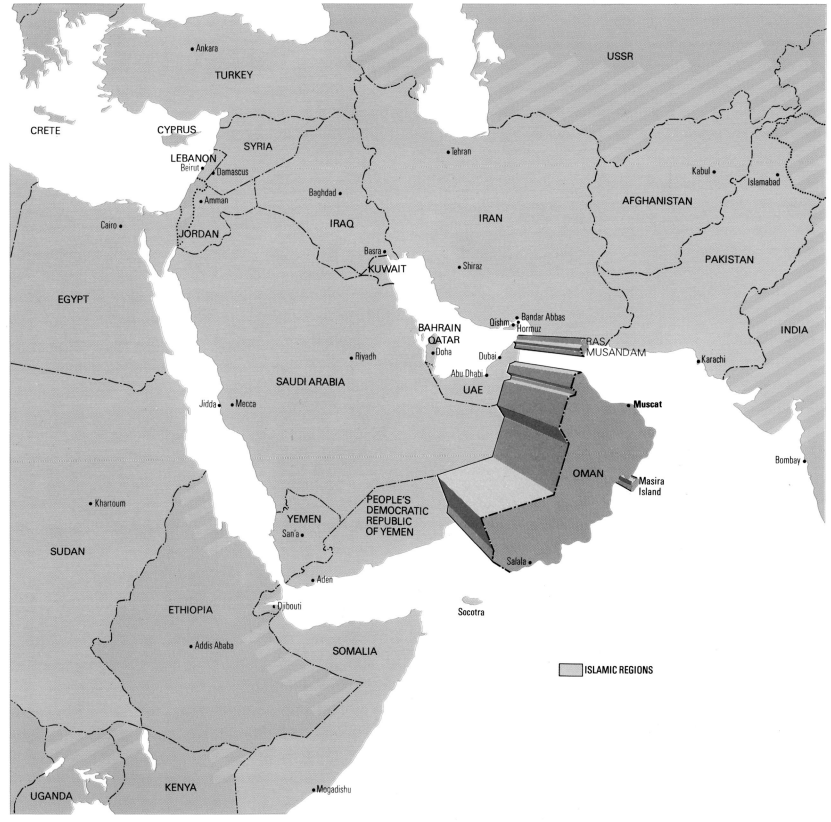

CRETE

TURKEY
• Ankara

CYPRUS

SYRIA
LEBANON
Beirut • • Damascus
• Amman
JORDAN

IRAQ
Baghdad •

Cairo •

EGYPT

USSR

Tehran •

IRAN

Kabul •
• Islamabad

AFGHANISTAN

PAKISTAN

Basra •
KUWAIT

• Shiraz

SAUDI ARABIA
• Riyadh

BAHRAIN
QATAR
• Doha

Qishm • • Bandar Abbas
Hormuz

RAS
MUSANDAM

INDIA

• Karachi

Jidda • • Mecca

Dubai •
• Abu Dhabi
UAE

Muscat

• Khartoum

SUDAN

YEMEN
San'a •

PEOPLE'S
DEMOCRATIC
REPUBLIC
OF YEMEN

OMAN

• Masira
Island

Bombay •

• Salala

ETHIOPIA

• Addis Ababa

• Aden

• Djibouti

SOMALIA

Socotra

ISLAMIC REGIONS

UGANDA

KENYA

• Mogadishu

8

Rulers of Oman

Reign begun (if known) AH	AD	Imams	Capital (if known)
135	751	Julanda ibn Mas'ud	—
—	—	Muhammad ibn Affan	Nizwa
185	801	Warith ibn Kaab	Nizwa
192	807	Ghassan ibn Abdulla	Nizwa
208	824	Abdul Malik ibn Hamad	—
226	840	al-Muhanna ibn Jaifar	Nizwa
237	851	as-Salt ibn Malik	—
273	886	Rashid ibn an-Nadhr	—
277	890	Azzan ibn Tamim	Nizwa
284	897	Muhammad ibn al-Hassan	—
285	898	Azzan ibn al-Hizr	—
286	899	Abdulla ibn Muhammad	—
287	900	as-Salt ibn al Qasim	—
287	900	Hassan ibn Said	—
292	904	al-Hawari ibn Matraf	—
300	912	Omar ibn Muhammad	—
—	—	Muhammad ibn Yazid	—
—	—	Mullah al Bahari	Nizwa
?328	939	Said ibn Abdulla	—
—	—	Rashid ibn Walid	Nizwa
400	1009	al-Khalil ibn Shadzan	—
?445	1053	Rashid ibn Said	—
445	1053	Hafs ibn Rashid	—
446	1054	Rashid ibn Ali	—
?549	1154	ibn Jabir Musa	Nizwa

Maliks of the Nabhan Period

AH	AD	Imams	Capital
809	1406	Malik ibn Ali	—
549	1154	al-Fallah ibn al Muhsin	Muqniyat
		Arar ibn Fallah	Muqniyat
		Mudhaffar ibn Sulaiman	—
809	1406	Makhzum ibn al Fallah	Bahla

Imams

AH	AD	Imams	Capital
839	1435	Abu'l Hassan	—
855	1451	Omar ibn al Khattab	—
896	1490	Omar as-Sharif	—

Reign begun (if known) AH	AD	Imams	Capital (if known)
—	—	Ahmad ibn Muhammad	Bahla
906	1500	Muhammad ibn Ismail	Izki
936	1529	Barakat ibn Muhammad	Nizwa
967	1560	Abdulla ibn Muhammad	Bahla

The Ya'ruba Dynasty

AH	AD	Imams	Capital
1034	1624	Nasir ibn Murshid	Rostaq
1059	1649	Sultan ibn Saif [I]	Rostaq
1079	1688	Bil'arub ibn Sultan	Jabrin
?1123	1711	Saif ibn Sultan [I]	Rostaq
1123	1711	Sultan ibn Saif [II]	al Hazm
1131	1718	Saif ibn Sultan [II]	—
1131	1718	Muhanna ibn Sultan	Rostaq
1134	1721	Ya'rub ibn Bil'arub	Nizwa
1135	1722	Saif ibn Sultan [II] (restored)	Rostaq
1137	1724	Muhammad ibn Nasir	Jabrin
1140	1728	Saif ibn Sultan [II] (restored)	Rostaq
1151	1738	Sultan ibn Murshid	Rostaq

The Al bu Said Dynasty
Elected Imams

AH	AD	Imams	Capital
1154	1741	Ahmad ibn Said	Rostaq
1188	1775	Said ibn Ahmad	Rostaq

Sayyids and Sultans

AH	AD	Imams	Capital
1193	1779	Hamad ibn Said (Regent)	Muscat
1206	1792	Sultan ibn Ahmad	Muscat
1219	1804	Said ibn Sultan	Muscat & Zanzibar
1273	1856	Thuwaini ibn Said	Muscat
1283	1866	Salim ibn Thuwaini	Muscat
1285	1868	Azzan ibn Qais	Muscat
1287	1870	Turki ibn Said	Muscat
1306	1888	Faisal ibn Turki	Muscat
1332	1913	Taimur ibn Faisal	Muscat
1351	1932	Said ibn Taimur	Muscat
1390	1970	Qaboos ibn Said	Muscat

Introduction

For thousands of years Oman lay along the sea trade routes between East and West. Oman was the link between Arabia and Africa. Oman's sailors were known in the ports of the world; her merchants to the world's seafarers. Then patterns changed. Steam supplanted sail. Oman slipped into neglect.

Yet the vigour and character of her people remained, as did their skills and the treasures of her heritage. By the 1960s the qualities of her people were under severe test, owing to a static policy at home and to armed insurrection inspired from across her southern borders.

In 1970 a new era dawned when H.M. Sultan Qaboos took over and introduced modern and enlightened government. Oman's new oil wealth was put to work for her people; military tenacity and courage brought the rebellion in Dhofar under control and finally to an end; relations with Arab and other friendly states were developed and Oman's isolation was ended. Once more ships queued at her ports and Oman moved back into her proper place on the world's stage.

H.M. Sultan Qaboos ibn Said

1 History

Influences from south and north Arabia and Yemen, from Mesopotamia and Iran, and from the Indian subcontinent and Africa, came together in the ancient past to form the Omani nation. But what has given to the dramatic history of Oman its special consistency? Perhaps it is above all the sea, bearing upon the lives of the people – as merchants, sailors, explorers, and missionaries of Islam, and the integrity of the Ibadhi Interior of the country against repeated assault from outside.

On a parapet beneath the Great Round Tower of the fort at Nizwa, stands the Wali and his entourage of Askars. One of Oman's larger castles, Nizwa was built in the seventeenth century AD by the Ya'ruba Dynasty. Nizwa has been Oman's capital at times and has always been an important administrative centre ever since.

From Prehistory to the Beginning of Islam

THE Omani, as befits an Arab people much concerned with genealogy, has a long pedigree, but it is not possible at present to trace it beyond about 12000 BC. Oman was then, towards the end of the last Ice Age, much wetter and greener than now and more populous. The people made their camps on the terraces in the *wadis* and hunted gazelle, oryx, wild goat, ostrich and the other animals which then abounded. Their diet was supplemented by berries and wild fruits but they had not yet learnt to harvest crops. Their stone tools and weapons – arrow heads, knives, scrapers and borers – were of high quality. Shisur in Dhofar was an important centre for flint production and stone age tools have also

Vigorous rock art – like this ferocious bull – has been a feature of northern Oman since prehistory.

been found in the Wadi Bahla, Ibri, Izki, and along the coast in northern Oman.

There follows a long gap in our present knowledge until the end of the fourth millennium BC, when light begins to appear, though little is known about the Omanis of that period. Few settlements have yet been discovered but burials of that date have proved informative. Distinctive jars deposited in tombs on Jebel Hafit near the Buraimi oasis and in burials to the west of Ibri were of a shape, and decorated in a style, closely resembling the Jemdet Nasr known in Mesopotamia from *c*.3000–2800 BC. Pottery with many similar features was also in use in southern Iran, notably on the settlement at Tepe Yahya in Kerman, and this raises the question as to the origin of the Jemdet Nasr influences

which penetrated Oman: were they the result of trade with Mesopotamia or of cultural contact with the adjacent areas of Iran?

Links with south-eastern Iran certainly became more evident during the third millennium. Current archaeological exploration is revealing the existence of a widespread but surprisingly uniform culture in Oman. This culture was first recognised on the island of Umm an-Nar off Abu Dhabi where both a settlement and burials were investigated. Comparable burials were later traced to Hili in Buraimi and more recently to Bat, 'Amla and other areas in Oman.

A feature of particular interest was the discovery in a number of these burials of exotic funerary vessels which had close counterparts on sites in southeastern Iran. Other objects of possibly foreign manufacture were carved stone bowls and small rectangular boxes deposited with the dead. Similar boxes are known from burials of the Kulli culture of southern Baluchistan at a time when that culture was strongly influenced by the Indus civilisation in the latter half of the third millennium, a period of considerable mercantile activity in the Gulf.

Then, for the first time, inscriptions refer specifically to the countries and commodities involved in this trade. Three names are mentioned repeatedly in this connection: Dilmun, Magan and Maluhha. Dilmun, which lay nearest to Mesopotamia, has now been convincingly identified with Bahrain and was probably the *entrepôt* for trade between Mesopotamia and the other countries. Maluhha, the furthest away, was possibly situated on the west coast of the Indian sub-continent in the region controlled by the Indus cities. Magan lay somewhere in between, but opinion remains divided as to its location. There are good grounds for identifying it with either the southern reaches of Baluchistan or Oman and it has even been suggested that the territory ranged across both shores of the Gulf. The issue is further confused by the fact that, while Old Babylonian and Sumerian references locate Magan and Maluhha

along the shores of the Gulf and the Indian Ocean, by the middle of the first millennium BC both regions had become identified with Egypt and Nubia/Ethiopia respectively.

There is, however, no doubt that Dilmun, Magan and Maluhha were all actively engaged in trade in the Gulf during the third millennium. King Sargon of Agade (2371–2316 BC) boasted that ships from Magan as well as Dilmun lay alongside his wharves. A century or two later Ur-Nammu (2113–2096 BC), famous as a reformer and prolific builder, claimed to have "brought back the ships of Magan"; perhaps by making trade with Ur more attractive or by re-opening silted canals. Magan and the Sumerian cities must, therefore, have had a mutual interest in close trade relations. However, Magan was, for reasons still obscure, conquered by Naram-Sin of Agade (2291–2255 BC) though the King of Magan, Manium, was duly honoured by having the Sumerian city of Manium-Ki named after him.

The various commodities which came from Magan were eagerly sought after in the luxurious cities of Mesopotamia. Gudea, Patasi or Prince of Lagash in about 2200 BC, claimed that Magan, Maluhha and Dilmun all brought tribute or gifts, and that the building material he imported for the god, Nin-Gir-Su, included wood and diorite from Magan. Lu-Enlilla, an agent of the temple of Nanna during the reign of Ibbi-Sin, the last king of the Third Dynasty in Ur (2029–2006 BC) had well-developed trading arrangements with Magan, and exported "merchandise for buying copper" from there. In the early centuries of the second millennium BC Magan lost its importance to Dilmun and references to its trade ceased by the old Babylonian period.

Magan denotes "a seafaring people" in Sumerian and its shipwrights were specifically mentioned in Sumerian inscriptions of 2050 BC. Omanis have throughout recorded history been seagoing people and Oman's periods of prosperity have stemmed from intelligent exploitation of its geographical position, seamanship and trading acumen. The

14

Arab geographer Mas'udi in the tenth century AD wrote of the shipwrights of Oman; the Omanis were ubiquitous on the seas then, and until the Portuguese arrived in the Indian Ocean in the sixteenth century.

Other points have been adduced to support the identification of Magan with Oman. Magan was called "The Mountain of Copper" and copper is recorded among the cargoes carried by its ships. This commodity was in great demand in the Sumerian cities where the coppersmiths had reached a high degree of skill. There are many ancient copper mines in Oman but most of them date only from the Early and Middle Islamic periods. Copper was, however, collected and worked during the third millennium and several settlements of the Umm an-Nar culture were engaged in smelting ores available locally. Analysis of copper found in Jebel Ma'adhan near Sohar showed a nickel content which suggested similarity to the copper implements found at Ur but a recent examination of slag from the Wadi Samad has shown no nickel in the copper from that area. As yet, there is no firm evidence for the export of copper from Oman as early as the third millennium.

Magan also exported stone and wood but while diorite is still to be found in Oman there are now insufficient trees for wood to be exported. However, Omanis persist in the belief that there were formerly forests in their country and it is possible that the rainfall was considerably heavier and the vegetation thicker in the third millennium BC. Research has, however, shown that the wood required by the Sumerian builders was the sissoo tree, indigenous to southern Baluchistan but not reported to grow in Oman. It is clear that, pending fresh archaeological discoveries, the identification of Magan with Oman must remain open.

The picture which is emerging of Oman in the protohistoric period is one of stable, relatively prosperous village communities living for the most part along the banks of *wadis* and relying upon flood irrigation for the cultivation of their wheat. Their houses were either stone-built or were less substantial structures comparable to present-day *barastis* but their public buildings included massive stone-walled enclosures and fortified watch towers. Their tombs were intended in some instances for multiple burials and some of the well

constructed circular structures were faced with carefully dressed and shaped ashlar masonry. Their pottery was wheel-made and sometimes painted with simple but effective designs. They also had beautifully fashioned bowls of stone and alabaster. They spun their cloth and wore jewellery.

There was considerable freedom of movement by donkey and perhaps camel, which was already domesticated, and the location of their settlements suggests that they used the land routes through the Buraimi and Ibri areas to the Oman coast through the Wadis Jizzi, Hawasina and Samail.

The Dark Ages

After the flowering of civilisation in the third millennium, there is another of those curious gaps which recur from time to time in any nation's history. So far there are few leads as to what happened in the second millennium BC. However, direct trade between the Mesopotamian cities and Magan and Maluhha came to a sudden end about 2000 BC, and thereafter merchandise from these places was landed for onward transit at Dilmun, the citizens of which grew temporarily rich on trade with Magan and Maluhha. Dilmun itself suffered a temporary decline about 1800 BC at roughly the same time as the Indus valley civilisation was wiped out by the Aryan invasion, but in the intervening period of two hundred years copper and diorite were no doubt the main commodities traded between Magan and Dilmun.

After about 1800 BC Dilmun ceased to be an international emporium for over a thousand years and its exports appear to have been confined to agricultural products such as dates. No doubt much the same occurred in Oman, for little is heard for a considerable time about any maritime activity in the Gulf and nothing about Oman in particular. Nonetheless certain finds at Buraimi indicate a connection in the thirteenth and fourteenth centuries BC with Luristan, and Oman may at this stage have come under some degree of Persian influence. It could possibly be that this decline of local civilisation caused the migration of the Phoenicians who may have originated in this area to the Levant.

Archaeological sites dated to the first millennium BC have been identified in Oman and a measure of prosperity returned to the area with the rise of the Assyrian Empire. By 700 BC an Aryan

prince in India had built up a civilisation once more and trade with India was re-established. The seafarers of Oman probably shared in this trade and also traded with Africa, carrying spices, perfumes and rare woods to Dilmun, as well as copper from Magan itself.

The Assyrian King Sennacherib (705–681 BC) attempted by destroying Tyre to resurrect the prosperity of the Gulf trade route which had suffered when the Phoenicians developed the Red Sea route for bringing oriental merchandise to the Levant and Mediterranean countries. However, it was not until the Persian Achaemenid dynasty united western Asia, when Cambyses (550–521 BC) conquered Egypt and his successor Darius I vanquished parts of India, that there was a revival of interest in sea routes and Darius commissioned a Greek seaman, Scylax of Caryinda, to explore the sea route between India and Egypt. Even this, however, did nothing to revive the Gulf route.

When Alexander the Great's admiral, Nearchos, sailed with a fleet of 1,500 vessels in 326 BC from India he referred in his journal to a Cape of Arabia called Maketa, which was probably Ras Musandam, "whence cinnamon and other products were exported to the Assyrians". This suggests that trade was continuing between Oman and Teredon in the Shatt al Arab at the head of the Gulf, which Nearchos described as "the emporium for the sea-borne trade in frankincense and all the other fragrant products of Arabia". Before his death Alexander despatched expeditions to explore the south and west side of the Gulf. Archias reached Bahrain, Androsthenes went somewhat further east and Hieron of Soli seems to have reached the Musandam peninsula without actually doubling it. These explorations, however, came to a sudden end with the death of Alexander himself.

Early in the third century BC there seems to have been sea-borne trade between the Gulf area and Ceylon, then called Taprobane, from which merchants in the Gulf also brought back cargoes such as gold from the Far East; and the Roman author Pliny (23–79 AD) in his *Natural History* later gives a detailed description of the Arabian shore of the Gulf mentioning Omana, Batrasave and Dabenegoris Regio as cities of Oman. Though these places have not been identified with certainty, Omana was probably in the region of Sohar, Batrasave was Ras al Khaima and Dabene-goris Regio, Dibba. At this time Pliny remarks that the planks of Arab ships were sewn together, as many of the small boats in Oman still are, and they made use of the north-east monsoon for trading with India. However, the seas were so infested by pirates that ships running to India from the Red Sea carried cohorts of archers. It may thus be that the mariners of Oman were among those who had been driven to piracy by a decline in legitimate trade.

Between the second and third centuries AD the Gulf was not subject to any single influence and piracy flourished periodically, but Trajan's expedition in 116 AD through Iraq to suppress the pirates did not reach as far as Oman. However, when the Sassanid King Shapur II (310–330 AD) mounted retaliatory raids on the Arab shore for acts of piracy committed during his reign, he seems to have sent a force at least as far as the Musandam peninsula.

The Earliest Arabs

Legends persist about the period between the prehistory which the spade has so far revealed and recorded history. Arab genealogists name Al-Ariba as the earliest inhabitants of the Arabian Peninsula and the Arabs, like most other peoples, have stories about ancient heroes of gigantic stature. Circles of great stones in several parts of Oman may date from these legendary days. The most famous heroes were Ad, who reputedly inhabited the sand-dunes between Oman and the Hadhramaut, and Thamud, both of whom gave their name to early Arab tribes. The Thamud tribe survived until classical times and were specifically referred to by such authors as Strabo. Two heroic sisters Tasm and Jadis also gave their names to tribes, suggesting that Omani society at one stage was matrilinear, and their descendants settled in the Buraimi area. Other ancient tribes which have influenced place names in Oman are the Sohar, who reputedly inhabited the Batina, the Obal or Wobal who are commemorated in two places, one in the Wadi Bani Ruwaha and the other near Rostaq, the Bahila, who gave their name to the town of Bahla, and the Akk, who gave their name to the Wadi Akk. Another tradition holds that Sam ibn Nuh – Shem the son of Noah – ruled the country from Hejaz as far as Oman and that the town of Sohar was founded by

his grandson, Suhail. Early connections between Oman and the Himyarite kingdoms of south Arabia and Yemen are also the subject of tribal tradition, which includes the story that the Queen of Saba in south Arabia – the Queen of Sheba – ruled the area.

There may have been a big invasion of Oman from south Arabia early in the eighth century BC. Ya'rub, a descendant of the patriarch Joktan – Qahtan as the Arabs call him – extended the rule of the Ya'ruba tribe, who gave a dynasty to Oman in the seventeenth and eighteenth centuries AD, all over south Arabia and Oman, and sent his brothers to govern Oman, Hejaz and Hadhramaut respectively. Ya'rub's successor Yashjab was weak and lost Oman but his son Abdul Shams, to whom is attributed the wonderfully constructed sluice dam at Marib in Yemen, regained Oman. Abdul Shams ruled the whole of south Arabia and founded two dynasties, the latter of which, the Himyarites – the Omeritae – ruled Yemen from 115 BC until nearly the time of the Prophet Muhammad.

Recent diggings at Samhuram in Dhofar have uncovered the relics and inscriptions of a sophisticated community whose wealth was based on the export of frankincense from before the time of Christ. Christian legend tells of the Wise Men of the New Testament meeting in Oman, a source of both frankincense and myrrh, before continuing their journey with their gifts for the infant Christ.

Beehive tombs – dated from the third millennium BC – were constructed for important people.

Himyar himself, so called because of the red robe he wore, was the son of Abdul Shams and his name is still used in Oman. Himyaritic rule may not, however, have lasted for long as Cyrus the Great, the founder of the Achaemenid dynasty, conquered Oman in about 563 BC.

The Coming of the Azd

Persian control of Oman probably persisted during the era of the Achaemenid dynasty founded by Cyrus – who reigned 550–530 BC – and it was during this time that many of the finest underground water channels, the *falajes*, were laboriously constructed. The course of events in Oman between the Achaemenid dynasty and the Sassanid (226–640 AD) is obscure, but at least part of the country probably remained Persian, as the author of the *Periplus of the Erythraean Sea*, writing in the first century AD, noted that Omana belonged to the Persians.

During the Sassanid period, however, Ardashir I (226–241 AD), the first of the dynasty, seems to have regained firm control over Oman and he sent a group of Azd tribesmen from Sohar to become sailors in Shihr in south Arabia. His involvement with the peoples of the Arabian littoral was probably aimed at controlling and expanding maritime commerce at a time when it was becoming possible for ships to sail out more boldly on the high seas using the prevailing winds and monsoons. However, his action in transplanting Azd sailors may well have been the beginning of the great maritime traditions of Mukalla and the people of Hadhramaut.

The Azd are the main tribal grouping in Oman. Arab sources clearly show that at the time of the first wave of Azd migrations into Oman led by Malik ibn Fahm – whether he was a historical personality or, as some people think, a heroic figure associated with the first of the migrations to be documented by Arab historians – the Persians were well established in the fertile agricultural areas. This wave probably came at the turn of the second and third centuries AD and Arab tradition generally associates it with the bursting of the great dam at Marib, though social disruption in the irrigated area of Yemen may rather have been the cause of this exodus.

Sirhan ibn Said, the eighteenth-century Omani author, may well have been giving a heroic account of early history of the Azd tribe but he tells the tale of Malik ibn Fahm in some detail.

17

Malik assembled a force of 6,000 men and placed his son, Honat – who may have given his name to the Bani Hina tribe and hence the great Hinawi faction of Oman – in charge of the vanguard. When Malik arrived in Oman he found the Persians holding the country for a Persian monarch called Dara – presumably not Darius the Great, as this would be a serious anachronism, while the Persian King's representative, the *Marzuban*, had his capital at Dastajird near Sohar, in the area the Persians called Mazun. Malik sent a messenger to the *Marzuban* requesting land for his people to settle, but the Persians decided that they "did not want this Arab to settle among us, that our land should be straitened unto us". The two sides, therefore, prepared to do battle on the plain near Nizwa. Malik, mounted on a piebald charger, wore a red robe over his armour with an iron helmet and

yellow turban on his head. The Azd, led by Malik, relied heavily on their cavalry while the Persians used elephants and the issue was decided only on the third day when Malik slew the *Marzuban* in single combat. Thereupon the Persians sued for a truce.

There has evidently been some telescoping of history here as the tribes associated with the Malik ibn Fahm incursions came in waves over several centuries. The main area of Arab settlement in the first instance was around Qalhat and in the Jaalan, but the Arabs later made much deeper inroads and a formal treaty between the Arabs and Persians was concluded during the reign of the Sassanid King Khusrau (Chosroes) Anurshirwan (531–578 AD). The terms provided that the Persians should withdraw their forces to Sohar and leave the western part of Oman within a year. As Awtabi put it "the Azd were kings in the

mountains, deserts and other parts of Oman". Under this treaty the Arabs were given a degree of autonomy and their ruler, known by the Sassanids as the Julanda – which later became a proper name used by the family of Azdi rulers of Oman – was officially confirmed by the Sassanids. According to some accounts the Persians were still in part of Oman at the dawn of Islam, for the Prophet Muhammad sent a letter to the local Persian ruler in Dastajird, calling on him to become a Muslim. The Persians' refusal to comply with this request eventually led to their being driven from Oman by the Azd.

Islam and the Early Imamate

THE call of the Prophet Muhammad in Mecca rapidly affected the immediate course of events and indeed the whole future of Oman. In about 630 AD (9 AH) Amr ibn al As arrived in Oman bearing a letter to Abd and Jaifar, the two sons of al Julanda ibn Mustansir who were then joint rulers of the Arab part of Oman. The Omanis did not take long to decide to embrace the new religion, despite an attempt at apostasy by a rival to the Julanda princes, Dhu't Taj Lakit, on the death of the Prophet in 632 AD (11 AH). His claim to be a prophet himself met with swift retribution and he and his followers were decisively beaten in a great battle at Dibba by the Caliph Abu Bakr's General, Hudhaifa ibn Muhsin and Abd and Jaifar's contingent, some time between 632 and 634 AD (11–13 AH). Hudhaifa remained for a while in Oman as governor. Then in 636 AD (15 AH) the second Caliph Omar ibn al Khattab (634–644 AD: 13–24 AH) appointed Othman ibn Abil Asi, who launched a great expedition against Sind from Omani ports, as governor of Oman. A governor appointed by the Caliph may have remained in Oman until the contest between Mu'awiya, the first Umayyad Caliph and Ali, the last orthodox Caliph (656–661 AD: 36–41 AH).

Omar showed some concern, after the defeat of the Persian army at the battle of Qadisiya in 636 AD (15 AH) that the

Oman, if properly identified as Magan, was already an important source of *copper by the third millennium BC and remained so during the Bronze Age.*

Persian King Yezdjird might ask for the help of the "King of Oman", which suggests that Islam had not yet been completely established in Oman at that time. However, the Persian population of Oman rejected the idea of conversion and this led the newly-converted Azd to attack them in their capital Dastajird, where they capitulated after the death of their leader, Maskan.

The Omanis played an important part in the early spread of Islam when Basra in southern Iraq became a dynamic centre for the Arab conquests of the vastly rich Persian Empire. The Azd and other tribes from Oman and Bahrain first started to move towards Basra to participate in the campaign against the Persian Province of Fars in about 637 AD (16 AH). The Caliph Omar appointed Kaab ibn Sur al-Laqiti of the Bani Hirth, a former Christian, *Qadhi* in Basra in 18 AH. The Azd were the largest single tribal grouping at the Battle of the Camel near Basra in 656 AD (36 AH) between Ali ibn Abu Talib, the fourth Caliph and husband of the Prophet's daughter Fatima, and a coalition of opposition elements of which the Azd formed part, led by Aisha, the Prophet's widow. Aisha's party was defeated, though she was given a residence at Medina, with all the honour due to her rank.

There were three clans of the Azd: Daws, Shanu'a and 'Imran, from which a distinctive "Azd Oman" grouping emerged. This group attained great prosperity in Basra between 665 and 683 AD (45 and 64 AH) on account of the favour they found in the eyes of Ziyad ibn Abihi, the Governor appointed by Mu'awiya, who was famous for re-organising the town into *akhmas*, "Fifths", and of his son Ubaidalla. The reorganisation had the effect of enhancing Omani standing by giving them leadership of a number of tribal groups and attracting, around 678 AD (59 AH), another wave of Omanis who left their homeland, rather as the Omanis were drawn to Iraq and the oil-producing Gulf states in the 1950s and 1960s AD.

Some sixty years after they had heard the call of Islam, the Azd reached the apogee of their power. Their leader, al Muhallab ibn Abi Sufra, gained control of Basra so effectively that it became known as Basra al Muhallab. The Omani contingent in his army was by far the largest, numbering some 3,000, and they fought against Khawarij fanatics as

Mediaeval Arab Cartography

Arab trade by sea increased rapidly after the establishment of Islam and, during the ninth century, Arab geographers under the Abbasid Caliphs in Baghdad began to take a keen interest in travel and sea routes. Ibn Khurdadhba described the route to China in about 850 AD and an Omani merchant made the voyage to Canton at about this time. Mas'udi in about 947 AD described personal experiences on voyages to India, Oman and east Africa. Such voyages, particularly in Sohar's heyday in the tenth century as the major seaport of Islam, gave rise to stories like *Sindbad the Sailor* and *Kitab Aja'ib al Hind* (*The Wonders of India*).

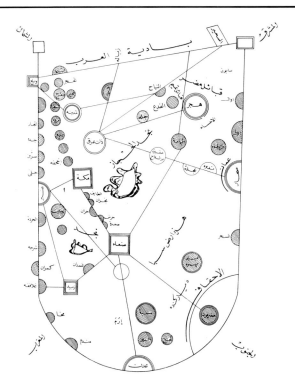

The earliest Arab maps showed Baghdad and Basra at the centre of things, but cartography became increasingly sophisticated as the centuries went by.

Oman and Sohar were marked on early maps in the ninth and tenth centuries. Omani seamen, such as Ahmad ibn Majid in the fifteenth century, made important contributions to navigation techniques and exploration.

well as in the conquest of Khorasan and Kerman, thereby gaining enormous wealth. Thus for a while the Azd became the most powerful group in the Eastern Caliphate.

After the death of al Muhallab in 702 AD (82 AH), however, their fortunes changed for the worse. Al Hujjaj ibn Yusif who was sent as Governor of Iraq by the Caliph Abdul Malik ibn Marwan (685–705 AD: 66–86 AH), had a profound distrust of the Azd, remarking sardonically during his early days as Governor, "O people of Iraq, you are slaves of al Muhallab." When his growing strength gave him opportunity, he set out to break this powerful clan and arrested Yazid ibn al Muhallab, who had succeeded his father as Commander and Governor in Khorasan.

This was part of a carefully laid plan to break all opposition to Umayyad rule. Al Hujjaj then attempted to deal with Oman which was becoming an increasingly important refuge for dissidents as the Azd returned home. He made several unsuccessful attempts and then conscripted an army of 40,000 from the Azd's tribal enemies and placed them under one of al Muhallab's former generals, al Khayar ibn Sabra ibn Dhuwaib al-Mujashi, and attacked the country, which was then ruled by Sulaiman ibn Abbad and his brother Said, grandsons of Abd al Julanda. One prong of the attack was on the Batina coast and the other through Julfar. Mujashi's land force was defeated by Sulaiman's army at Boshar but the sea force defeated Said at Barka, forty miles west of Muscat. Said fled to the Jebel Akhdar but Sulaiman swooped on Mujashi's fleet of 300 ships at Muscat and burnt it. Sulaiman then defeated Mujashi's land force at Samail causing it to fall back on Julfar. Mujashi thereupon requested reinforcements from al Hujjaj, who sent a fresh force. This was too much for Sulaiman and Said. When they heard from an Azdi well-wisher who had deserted from the Caliphate forces that reinforcements were on their way, they realised that further resistance was useless and departed to "one of the districts of Zanj" in east Africa.

Yazid ibn al Muhallab in Basra meantime found favour with later Caliphs but on Omar II's death in 720 AD (102 AH) declared war against the new Caliph Yazid II ibn Abdul Malik and occupied Basra. But his revolt was short-lived and he was defeated, dying with many of his Azd troops heroically in battle.

Parts of the vast castle at Bahla (right) *date from pre-Islamic times; and the seven-mile surrounding walls* (visible above) *conjure up Sumerian cities like Uruk, city of Gilgamish in Iraq, as a large cultivated area lies within them.*

The Azdis then returned home to Oman which had been handed back to its own people on Omar II's death and their victorious enemies sang "The fires of al Mazun (Oman) and its peoples are extinguished. They sought to kindle a revolt but you have left no standard for them to follow nor any soldier to al Muhallab's people." Thus ended an epoch of notable Omani achievement abroad.

The Early Imamate

The early Imamate in Oman arose out of idealism to create the true and ideal Muslim state; events, and doctrinal differences in Iraq affecting the Azd gave the necessary spur.

The first Imam was Julanda ibn Mas'ud, who – a strong proponent of the fundamentalist Ibadhi doctrine – was elected first of the "rightful Imams" in 751 AD (135 AH). His Imamate was, however, short-lived and he was slain in battle by an army sent by the first Caliph of the Abbasid dynasty, Abu'l Abbas as-Saffah. There followed a period of tyranny and confusion but in 801 AD (185 AH) Warith ibn Kaab was elected Imam and thereafter the Imamate was continuous for three hundred years or more.

In the ninth century AD, Bahla was the capital. By the following century Sohar had become the greatest sea port in all Islam, by some estimates the greatest in the world. Omani maritime power dominated the Gulf and the Indian Ocean, commanding the main routes of Far Eastern and African trade.

The Imams exercised spiritual, political and military functions in different portions according to the state of the country. As the name implies, the Imam was always spiritual leader, bound to lead the people in the Friday prayers, and the final judge of appeal on all religious matters. To the extent that he could impose his will, he also administered the secular government and imposed taxation. When necessity arose he acted, if he had the personality, as military governor as well. But his power was always limited in fact by the complicated tribal structure and this, combined with the general Ibadhi philosophy, ensured that temporal authority was seldom absolute. The isolation of the Omanis of the Interior in times past has centred round Ibadhism and to some extent this explains the dichotomy, so often apparent in Oman's history, between the Ibadhi Interior and the outward-looking coastal areas where the people are mainly Sunni and Shia.

The election of the Imam, Rashid ibn Walid, in Nizwa, was described by the Omani historian Salil ibn Razik in the tenth century and illustrates the generally approved method. Four eminent men of virtue and probity met under the presidency of Shaikh Abu Muhammad Abdulla in the house of the Imam to be. There the principles by which the country should be governed were agreed, and those assembled gave their allegiance to Rashid. A great crowd of people, representing many of the towns in Oman, were assembled on the plain of Nizwa. Shaikh Abu Muhammad addressed them, proclaiming Rashid as Imam, and called them to give him their allegiance, which they did by coming up to him singly or in pairs. The new Imam appointed governors over all the towns and districts, and collectors of *sadaqat* – voluntary alms for religious purposes – and led the next Friday prayers in Nizwa.

Between the beginning of the ninth century and 887 AD (274 AH) attacks by Caliphate troops were repelled and Indian pirates, the *Bawarij*, were successfully warded off by a fleet specially constructed in the time of the Imam

Ghassan ibn Abdulla (807–824 AD: 192–209 AH). However, severe disturbances followed the deposition of the Imam as-Salt ibn Malik which increased polarisation between the Nizar (northern or *Adnan*) and the Yemeni (southern or *Qahtan*) tribes. The Nizaris appealed to the Caliph al Mu'tadid (892–902 AD: 279–290 AH) and Muhammad ibn Nur, the Caliph's governor in Bahrain, collected a force of about 25,000 Nizaris clad in chain mail to march on Oman. In 893 AD (280 AH) the country was overrun. These were black days; as the Omani historian Sirhan ibn Said commented: "Thus Oman passed out of the hands of its inhabitants. It was not that God changed his grace which was in them, but they themselves changed the disposition of their souls by sin." The "bloody assize" of Muhammad ibn Nur – a reign of terror, during which the invaders cut off the hands, feet and ears of their victims and put their eyes out – has never been forgotten. It was a period of desecration during which the invaders blocked the *falajes* and burned the religious Ibadhi books. After Muhammad ibn Nur's invasion, eight Imams were elected in quick succession. It is not clear how firmly the Caliph's writ then ran, though coins were minted in Oman between 892 and 930 AD (279–318 AH) in the name of the Saffarids, who briefly controlled southern Iran. Ahmad ibn Hillal, who was left to govern Oman after Muhammad ibn Nur withdrew, identified himself with Omani interests, encouraging trade, particularly after he left his capital at Bahla for Sohar and defending Sohar's interests against the covetousness of the Caliph al Muqtadir (908–932 AD: 296–320 AH).

The opportunity for Oman to prosper arose with the weakening of the Caliphate's central authority during the ninth and tenth centuries AD (third and fourth centuries AH) when North Africa, Egypt and Syria broke away; local dynasties seized power in Khorasan, the lands beyond the Oxus and Sistan; Persia was partitioned; and the Carmathians occupied eastern Arabia. Circumstances became favourable for the development

of Sohar as the major *entrepôt* of the area when the Carmathians, followers of a movement which set out to achieve social reform and justice, conquered Oman shortly after they had sacked Mecca in 929 AD (317 AH). The Ibadhis found them moderate overlords and for some thirty-five years Oman remained under the control of the Wajihid family, independent of the Caliphate but paying tribute to the Carmathians. During this period the already great level of Omani maritime activity was expanded, Sohar became the greatest sea port in Islam, and Omani fleets traded with Africa and Madagascar. Twice Omani naval forces sailed to Basra, which had become the great commercial centre of southern Iraq, from which ships sailed even to the Far East. The Julanda family may have lost their control of Oman, but they were still firmly entrenched at Huzu on the southern Persian coast, where they exacted dues from all the ships entering and leaving the Gulf and between the years 950 and 960 AD (338–349 AH) Julandi coins were minted in the name of Radwan ibn Jaafar, "the Lord of the waters, ruler of the fortress of Huzu". The precise relationship between the Omanis and their cousins at Huzu may now be obscure but there is little doubt that in the tenth century AD (fourth century AH) it was the Omanis who ruled the waves in the Gulf and Indian Ocean.

The ramparts of Bahla's seven-mile wall (left) could be patrolled by soldiers. They protected what was at times the country's capital. The citadel itself is built of clay brick and palm trunk

woodwork as well as stone. Above: *The castle towers 150 feet above the surrounding plain, and overlooks neatly cultivated enclosures of palm trees, wheat and green fodder (lucerne).*

The inner stairways of the castle are built, like the walls, of clay, straw and dung plaster, and are of remarkable strength and durability.

Plastering the interiors of castles, houses and mosques became a craft quite early in Oman's history, as these geometric designs at Bahla, dating from two or three hundred years ago, indicate.

A Daylamite family, the Buyids, seized power in Baghdad making the Caliph virtually their prisoner, and by 980 AD (369 AH) they had brought Persia and most of the Gulf as well as Iraq back under the central authority of Baghdad. Sohar's naval power and mercantile customs revenues in Iraq and southern Persia – as well as its prosperity – attracted natural envy. Mu'Izz ad Dawla sent a fleet to Oman in 965 AD (354 AH) under Abu al Faraj Muhammad ibn Abbas. The expedition landed at Julfar, the present-day Ras al Khaima, and marched on Sohar, where they systematically destroyed property including seventy-nine ships, and massacred many people. Not long afterwards, the Julandid fortress of Huzu on the other side of the Gulf also fell to the Buyids. Sohar's glory was, however, not extinguished until 971 AD (360 AH) when the city which had been "the emporium of the whole world", was devastatingly sacked by the Buyids and most of its inhabitants killed.

Buyid domination of Oman was short, for their hegemony of the Gulf area lasted for less than a hundred years, their empire collapsing before the wave of Seljuk Turks from the steppes of central Asia in 1055 (447 AH). The first Seljuk Governor of Kerman, Qawurd Qara Arslan Beg, collected a fleet of transports at Hormuz and in 1064 (457 AH) invaded and occupied Oman, thus

Qalhat became Hormuz' twin

putting the finishing touches to an expansion south-westward from Transoxania which had been going on since the tenth century.

There followed almost three hundred years of disorder in the Gulf. The coast of Oman was held by the Seljuks only for some eighty years and then successively by the people of Basra and the Turkoman Ghuzz. The coastal towns were also raided by the Muzaffarid dynasty of Fars and people from the island of Qais as well as Omanis from the Interior, and Abul Fida, writing in the early fourteenth century, described Sohar as merely a village in ruins. Oman lacked unity and the Interior was ruled by Maliks of the Nabhan tribal dynasty. The Arab chronicler, Sirhan ibn Said, noted that he had not been able to find any record of Imams for over two hundred years, between 1153 (548 AH) when the Imam Musa ibn Abu Jabir died, and the reign of Imam Habis ibn Muhammad, who died in 1406 (809 AH).

After the fall of Sohar, Siraf was the first of three city states which successively grew rich on the Far Eastern and African trade. Siraf declined after the fall of the Buyids and its place was taken by Qais, which later vied with Hormuz for supremacy of the Gulf until the Hormuzis eventually came out on top. The fame of Hormuz spread to Europe and in "Paradise Lost", Milton wrote of Satan:

"High on a throne of royal state, which far
    Outshone the wealth of Ormuz and of Ind
Or where the gorgeous East with richest
    hand
Showers on her Kings barbaric pearl and
    gold."

The Amir of Hormuz, Mahmud ibn Ahmad al Kusi, established his authority by landing at Qalhat in the thirteenth century AD (seventh century AH) and summoning two of the Bani Nabhan Maliks ruling in Oman, after which he subdued part of the country. The Hormuzis were well established on the seaboard from the early fourteenth century (eighth century AH) and Qalhat served as the twin capital with Hormuz itself. Muscat was the other principal centre of Hormuzi power in Oman, though Sohar was also important to them. It is doubtful, however, if the Hormuzi writ ran far inland, for when the Portuguese Albuquerque arrived in 1507 he remarked that every house in Muscat

had a secret cupboard where valuables could be stored in the event of a raid from the Interior.

During this time the Bani Nabhan ruled central Oman mainly from Muqniyat on the Dhahira side of the Jebel Akhdar and though tradition may be unfair to them, they have not generally left a good name. There are, however, exceptions and Al Fallah ibn al Muhsin, the most famous of the Nabhan "Maliks", showed integrity, liberality and statesmanship. It was he who built the fine fort at Muqniyat – al Aswad – and he was also a patron of poets and a noted agriculturalist who introduced the mango tree into Oman. He was succeeded by his son, Arar, whose reputation was as good as his father's, and other Maliks won some renown for success in war and peace though this era is very sketchily chronicled. Nonetheless, the final verdict on the dynasty, at least by the Omani historians of the Imamate, is that their misrule caused widespread evils. On the death of Malik ibn al Hawari in 1435 (839 AH) the chief citizens assembled to appoint Abu al Hassan Abdulla ibn Khamis al Azdi as Imam, thus restoring the Imamate.

There is some confusion about where power lay during the next period, as the story of Sulaiman ibn Muzaffar al Nabhani and the Imam Muhammad ibn Ismail shows (1500–1529: 906–936 AH). Sulaiman, alone in his room in the fort at Bahla, heard a voice say, "Enjoy yourself son of al Nabhan a few more days. Your rule will soon be over. So prepare for death." It was shortly after this supernatural manifestation that, regarding the voice as a delusion of the devil, he set off with his companions by camel to Nizwa, where next morning he saw a woman going to bathe in the *falaj*. He attempted to molest her but she ran away and appealed to Muhammad ibn Ismail who came out of his house to protect her. Muhammad plunged his dagger into Sulaiman's heart and killed him on the spot, whereupon the people of the neighbourhood were so delighted that they elected him Imam. Thus, despite the renewed election of Imams, there were apparently also Nabhani Sultans, such as Sultan ibn Muhsin ibn Sulaiman al Nabhani, up to the time of Nasir ibn Murshid, the great Ya'rubi Imam whose reign began in 1624 (1034 AH).

European Powers in Oman

The Portuguese

Since the beginning of Islam the Arabs, despite internal quarrels and feuding and the rise of dynasties in rivalry with the Caliphate, had controlled the lucrative trade from the East. Arab seamen and merchants had a virtual monopoly of the spices which were increasingly sought after in Europe, and the Omanis, however severe their internal dissensions, had continued to profit. The prosperity of their coastal towns attested by the Portuguese at the beginning of the sixteenth century showed this very clearly. The Portuguese decisively broke this monopoly.

A combination of circumstances inspired the discovery of the route round the southern tip of Africa, the Cape of Good Hope, by Vasco da Gama in 1498 (904 AH). First, the Portuguese had been growing increasingly skilful as seamen and explorers since the time of Henry the Navigator in the early part of the fifteenth century. Second, they had become accustomed to oriental luxuries during the earlier Moorish occupation and hoped to capture a share in the spice trade. Third, Portuguese national consciousness had been moulded in their numerous battles against the Muslims and their ventures in the Indian Ocean were a continuation of Christendom's anti-Muslim thrust. This may explain, if not justify, the cruelty of Portuguese methods. Fourth, the Portuguese were determined to discover the mysterious land of Prester John, which at the time aroused great interest in Europe.

Vasco da Gama's voyage revolutionised the trade of Europe. The Portuguese increased their naval and military strength in the Indian Ocean and Portuguese ambitions in the area were proclaimed in King Manoel I's title "Lord of the Conquest, Navigation and Commerce of India, Ethiopia, Arabia and Persia". By one of the ironies of history, a famous Omani seaman, Ahmad ibn Majid, piloted Vasco da Gama from Malindi in east Africa across the Indian Ocean to Calicut thus unwittingly helping to bring about the downfall of Arab primacy on the seas.

It was perhaps King Manoel's predecessor, Joao II (1481–1495 AD) who first resolved to overthrow Arab commercial supremacy and in 1506 Afonso de Albuquerque set out for the East with a royal letter of appointment from King Manoel as Governor of India to supersede the Viceroy Francesco de Almeida. Clearly there had been some jockeying for position at King Manoel's court. Albuquerque arrived in the Indian Ocean in command of a fleet of five ships with instructions to blockade the Red Sea to the Eastern trade on which Egyptian and Venetian prosperity was based. The Venetians indeed were alive to this new menace to their trading position, and through the Consul which the Serenissima maintained in Alexandria, instigated the Mameluke Sultan of Egypt to petition the Pope to forbid all Christians to trade in the Arabian Sea and the Indian Ocean – the Venetians only came in on the act, of course, when the merchandise reached Egypt safely! Venetian diplomacy failed in this instance and the Portuguese pursued their conquests unmolested.

Albuquerque had personal ambitions as well as official instructions, and he hoped to establish a great empire in the East. After seizing Socotra as a base for

Cannonarchy

The arrival of cannon and gunpowder in the Indian Ocean in the late fifteenth century – in Portuguese ships – was to change the history of Oman. Portugal's ruthless empire-builder, Afonso de Albuquerque, sacked Muscat in 1507. Local vessels naturally had little chance of defending themselves against the heavy weaponry of the Portuguese. Albuquerque's aim was to protect the Portuguese eastern empire and control the trade routes by his well armed fleet and heavily defended coastal forts. From his time onwards the cannon became an essential weapon of war, both for Oman's defence from outside assault, and in the settlement of its internal quarrels.

Above: *An inscription on a Portuguese gun at al Hazm.*

The Portuguese coat of arms on the cannon (above) *indicates that it was captured by the Omanis when the Portuguese were driven from Muscat in the mid-seventeenth century.*

The muzzle-loading cannon (left) *in the castle at al Hazm is Portuguese.* Centre left: *A cannon bears Spanish arms.*

Muscat itself is guarded by the Portuguese-built forts of Mirani (left) and Jalali (right), completed in 1587

and 1588 when King Philip II of Spain (below), was at the same time King Philip (Felipe) I of Portugal.

the blockade of the Red Sea, he aimed to capture Hormuz which then controlled the lion's share of the Gulf trade. Albuquerque's objective was simple and strategically sound. He sought to dominate the two main channels through which the trade of the East had flowed for countless generations – the Red Sea and the Persian Gulf. It was natural, however, that he should first deal with the ports of Oman, which were not only subject to Hormuzi supremacy, but also important in their own right as harbours from which Omani fleets launched their operations all over the Indian Ocean.

Albuquerque, like Vasco da Gama before him, relied on Omani pilots but this did not predispose him in favour of the Omanis of the coastal towns, which he found in a flourishing state, supported by thriving agriculture in the interior. Even though he had come on a long sea voyage and Oman was by no means the first country he had visited – as he had called in at ports in east Africa *en route* – Omani agriculture left a deep impression on him. Of Qalhat, his first port of call, he wrote "All their supplies of corn, barley, millet and dates come from the interior, for there is plenty of these products there. This port is a great *entrepôt* of shipping, which comes thither to take horses and dates to India."

Muscat, he noted, was the principal *entrepôt* of the Kingdom of Hormuz, and he remarked "Muscat is a large and very populous city ... There are orchards, gardens, and palm groves, with pools for watering them by means of wooden engines. The harbour is small, shaped like a horseshoe and sheltered from every wind ... It is of old a market for carriage of horses and dates. It is a very elegant town with very fine houses and supplied from the interior with much wheat, millet, barley and dates for loading as many vessels as come for them." Sohar too he regarded as very beautiful with fine houses and he noted that the extensive land behind Sohar was all cultivated with wheat, maize and barley and that as the country was thickly wooded many cattle and horses were bred. He observed that the five hundred odd cavalrymen which the town boasted wore "steel armour covered with plates of iron, arranged after the manner of roof tiles with slates and strong enough to resist a shot from a crossbow", that ultimate weapon of the Middle Ages. The forequarters of their horses were similarly defended.

Khor Fakkan was equally prosperous. "In the interior are many estates with good houses, many orange trees, lemon trees, zamboa trees (*Pomum Adami*), fig trees, palms and all sorts of vegetables and many water pools, which they use for irrigation; in the fields is much straw stubble, as in Portugal, and there are many millet fields ... In the town there are large stables for horses and many straw lofts for their straw, for this port exports many horses to India."

On his way to Qalhat in 1507 (913 AH), Albuquerque destroyed every Arab vessel he came across, thus declaring total war on all those who opposed the Portuguese at sea. He left Qalhat, which accepted his overlordship, unharmed but later suspecting "disloyalty" pillaged it. Quriyat and Muscat were not so accommodating and were sacked and burned, the old men who were not put to death having their ears and noses cut off. Albuquerque again dealt out death and destruction at Khor Fakkan on his way to Hormuz where he quickly defeated the huge Hormuzi fleet. Albuquerque made the youthful Shaikh Saif al Din a vassal of Portugal and immediately built a fine fort – Nossa Senhora da Victoria, the first of a great chain of Portuguese forts on the Indian Ocean and in the Gulf.

Then followed an era of sea battles, with fighting between the Portuguese and the local people and later between other European powers as well, but the Portuguese never completely disturbed the pattern of Gulf life and trade. They

The Muscat that Albuquerque destroyed was "a very elegant town with fine houses ... with orchards, gardens, palm groves and pools".

attempted to control and profit from the traditional patterns though, locked up in their great forts, they remained remote and unsympathetic towards the local people. Relations between Oman and the Portuguese were never easy. The Portuguese attempted to secure the customs revenues of Hormuz and Portuguese officials were put in charge. This led to a general uprising in Hormuz and its dependencies on the coast of Oman – Muscat, Quriyat and Sohar, as well as Bahrain, in 1521 (927 AH). Nevertheless they held supreme, though not unchallenged, control of the Gulf and Indian Ocean for about a hundred years, preventing local vessels from trading without Portuguese passes.

The Ottoman Turks who took possession of Egypt from the Mameluke Sultan in 1517 (923 AH) reacted to the continued Portuguese blockade of the Red Sea by sending a huge fleet under Sulaiman

Pasha, the Governor of Egypt, against the Portuguese in the Indian Ocean in 1538 (945 AH). In 1550 (957 AH), Piri Rais, the Captain-General or Admiral of the Turkish fleet, made a further attempt to curb the activities of the Portuguese and with a large naval force swept the Gulf and parts of the Indian Ocean, capturing Muscat and temporarily deporting the Portuguese garrison there. For some reason not entirely plain the Ottoman Governor of Basra reported that the expedition had been a failure and Piri Rais was executed in Cairo on orders from Constantinople in 1551 (958 AH). In 1581 (989 AH) the Turks under the command of Ali Beg seized Muscat for the third time, and the Portuguese, who were caught unprepared, fled to the Interior until the Turks withdrew.

It was this disgrace to Portuguese arms which caused the government in Portugal to order increased fortification in Muscat and the construction of the powerful forts of Mirani and Jalali, but the Portuguese did not merely bequeath military architecture. They brought missionary zeal, expressed in bricks and mortar in three churches – a cathedral attached to an Augustinian Priory, another church somewhere near the present British Embassy at the foot of fort Jalali and the small chapel in fort Mirani which is the only one of the three still surviving.

The Dutch followed the Portuguese in search of the riches of the East and their first expedition round the Cape of Good Hope to Indonesia was sent out in 1594 (1003 AH). From here they were able to export valuable spices, including cloves and benzoin. They quickly realised that the Indian Ocean and the Gulf too were areas of crucial strategic and commercial interest and soon made their appearance there, trading with south India for peppers and Ceylon for cinnamon. The British and French had similar aspirations, and both were eventually to have closer contacts with Oman than the Dutch. John Newberrie of London arrived in Hormuz in 1580 (988 AH) and with another Londoner, Ralph Fitch, blazed the trail for British interests. When the Dutch shortly afterwards raised the price of pepper from three shillings a pound to eight shillings, the merchants of London, who had already been stirred by reading of the Londoners' travels, published in 1598 in Hakluyt's *Voyages*, founded the English East India Company in 1600 (1006 AH).

The activities of two other Englishmen, the Sherley brothers, gave the British the edge in acquiring influence at the court of Shah Abbas I, "the Great", who came to the throne in 1587 (985 AH) and, reigning until 1629 (1038 AH), restored the fortunes of Persia. Shah Abbas had for some years aimed to drive the Portuguese, whose general position had been weakened by their expulsion from Bahrain in 1602 (1011 AH) at his hands, from Hormuz itself, their main stronghold. For a while his interests coincided with those of the English traders, whose ships joined in a successful attack on the famous *entrepôt* in 1622 (1032 AH). Shah Abbas was quick to follow up his success at Hormuz and temporarily drove the Portuguese from Sohar, which they had occupied in strength in 1616 (1025 AH) and Khor Fakkan.

Persian success was, however, short-lived and Ruy Freire de Andrade, commander of the forts at Muscat, whose name was dreaded throughout the area, recovered both places. The Portuguese held Sohar until 1643 (1053 AH), when the Imam Nasir ibn Murshid finally drove them out, but Portuguese hold on the Arabian shore was weakening all the while as the century wore on, despite such measures as the strengthening in 1649 (1059 AH) of the Fort at "Cassapo" – Khasab at the tip of the Musandam peninsula.

The Imam Nasir had succeeded in weakening the grip of the Portuguese in Oman but they still retained Muscat, and it was left to his cousin and successor, Sultan ibn Saif, who succeeded him as Imam in 1649 (1059 AH), to administer the *coup de grâce*. It is generally agreed that Muscat's nearly impregnable defences fell as a result of a "stratagem" which deprived the Portuguese of supplies and enabled the Omanis to attack the forts successfully. When the Portuguese commander of the Mutrah fort subsequently surrendered to the Imam, Portuguese influence in Oman came to an end but naval warfare between Omanis and Portuguese continued to the end of the seventeenth century even as far away as the coast of east Africa.

The British
The long association between Oman and the British commenced in the middle of the seventeenth century when in 1645 (1055 AH) the Imam Nasir wrote to the English East India Company offering

them trading facilities at Sohar. The company responded quickly and in 1646 (1056 AH) their representative Philip Wylde arrived to negotiate a treaty, which was duly signed in February. It granted the English a trading monopoly, the freedom to practise their own religion and extraterritorial jurisdiction. How long it in fact remained in force is not clear, but it was the forerunner of numerous treaties of friendship with Britain over the following three centuries.

The English had been giving the Imam discreet help against the Portuguese, and when the *Fellowship* called at Muscat in 1650 (1061 AH) the captain was offered "the best house in the town", if the company would establish a trading factory there. So well disposed was the Imam in fact that in 1659 (1070 AH) he negotiated a treaty with Colonel Rainsford of the East India Company, providing that the English should have one of the forts, be given part of the town for residence, provide a garrison of one hundred soldiers and share the customs with the Omanis. However, the death of Colonel Rainsford caused the Imam to have second thoughts, possibly at the instance of the Dutch, who were becoming strong and successful rivals for the trade of the area. Nonetheless the English were again invited to trade in Muscat and open a factory and, though this was never established, the East India Company's ships from then on visited Muscat regularly.

The Dutch
The Dutch East India Company established a factory at Bandar Abbas shortly after a joint action with the British against the Portuguese commander Ruy de Andrade off Bandar Abbas in 1625 (1035 AH) which enabled them to gain their initial foothold in the Gulf. This led Ruy de Andrade to retire with some of his vessels to Khor Kuwai on the opposite shore on the Arabian coast where he established a temporary base.

Although relations between Dutch and English were initially cordial, the Dutch, who were able to trade spices from the Far East to which the English had not yet obtained access, were for a while the more successful. The English silk monopoly granted by Shah Abbas lapsed on his death in 1629 (1039 AH) and the Dutch company received substantial help from their home government, while the English had to fend for themselves. The Dutch held political and commercial supremacy for the greater part of the century. In 1670 the Dutch East India Company leased an office in Muscat mainly to facilitate their mail service and a commercial mission arrived there in 1672 (1083 AH). By 1680 (1091 AH) they were firmly established both at Basra and Bandar Abbas but with the decline of metro-politan Holland in the eighteenth century, Dutch influence was gradually eclipsed by the British and French. In 1759 (1173 AH) they had to abandon Bandar Abbas and in 1765 (1179 AH), when they abandoned their last settle-ments at Kharg Island, Dutch influence in the area virtually ceased and the field was left open to the ever sharpening rivalry between British and French.

The French

The French as well as the English and the Dutch were eager to supplant the Portuguese. The French East India Com-pany was founded in 1664 (1075 AH) and as early as 1667 Muscat featured in their strategic thinking, de Lalain, the French Ambassador to Persia, advocating that it should be seized and turned into a French naval base. Between 1699 (1111 AH) and 1719 (1132 AH) French repre-sentatives in Persia pored over their maps, and several paper schemes, all of which envisaged French troops in forts Jalali and Mirani, were hatched with the intention of extending their influence to Muscat in collaboration with the Persians. It was not, however, until 1749 (1163 AH), when French privateers attacked British vessels in Muscat har-bour, that there was any direct French contact with Muscat.

The French Company like the English and the Dutch established a trading factory at Bandar Abbas, though it was closed comparatively early in the eighteenth century. In 1759, during the Seven Years' War, a French naval squadron under Count d'Estaing cap-tured and nearly destroyed the English East India Company's property at Bandar Abbas and, with the Dutch virtually removed from the scene, Anglo-French rivalry grew in the area generally over the next few decades. This was naturally not without its effect on Oman, particularly when Napoleon's star rose towards the end of the century and he revived French ambitions for a great Empire in the East.

The Ya'ruba Dynasty

THE first two Imams of the Ya'ruba dynasty, as we have seen, managed to dislodge the Portuguese from their strongholds in Oman. From then until now Oman has never been occupied by any foreign power except between 1737 and 1747 (1150–1160 AH), when the Persians, who became involved in the great Omani civil war between Ghafiris and Hinawis, remained for a while on part of the coast. Instead Oman's relations with the larger powers has been regulated by treaties of friendship and commerce and specific understand-ings. Even when the British Empire was at its zenith Oman, though within the British zone of influence, retained its independence despite Lord Curzon's remark in 1903 (1321 AH) "I have little doubt that the time will come . . . when the Union Jack will be seen flying from the castles of Muscat." This Ya'rubi action was, therefore, an early success for Omani nationalism.

The reputation of the Ya'ruba dynasty did not depend on this alone, and the best of their rule is still associated, historically as well as in the popular mind, with a period of renaissance. The unification of the country under strong rulers led to a revival of naval and military prowess, to commercial pros-perity, to the encouragement and flowering of learning and the erection of buildings of strength, beauty and elegance. According to Omani chroni-cles, the first Imam of the dynasty, Nasir ibn Murshid, made the "sun of salvation" shine on the long-afflicted people of Oman.

Nasir lived near Rostaq at a time of contention and strife. Tiring of this, seventy of the *Ulema* met together in the year 1624 (1034 AH) and urged him to accept supreme power as Imam. This after some demur he did and, starting from his base at Rostaq and Nakhl, Nasir began the task of uniting the country. The people of Nizwa early sent word inviting him to take over. Samail and Izki quickly followed suit and, with the possession of these key towns in the heartland of Oman, he moved against the Dhahira taking the towns of Dhank, Ibri, Ghabbi, Muqniyat and Bat in quick succession. Despite backsliding, treachery and setbacks, Nasir was able

The map shows the principal castles which dot the landscape of interior Oman.

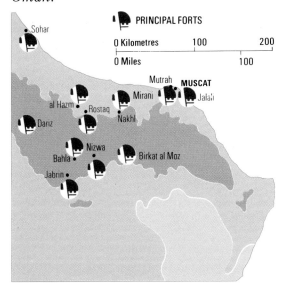

to move on and obtain control of Tuam – the old name for the Buraimi al Ain oasis complex in the area then known as al Jauf. With these successes behind him, Nasir turned his attention to the coastal area. The Portuguese in Muscat and Mutrah sued for peace, and an agreement was reached that they would surrender their possessions at Sohar, pay an annual tribute to the Imam and allow Muslim Omanis to visit Muscat without let or hindrance.

However, when Nasir later sent messengers, the Portuguese in Muscat treated them harshly and refused to pay the tribute agreed. One of Nasir's chief supporters – a successful general, Qadhi Khamis ibn Said al Shaksy – was sent to Muscat and a further agreement reached by which the Portuguese agreed to pay the tribute due, to restore the fortified posts at Mutrah recently seized, to permit Omanis to trade freely and to abstain from acts of war. This agreement was enough to make Nasir suspend further hostilities against the Portuguese, but not to prevent him later recapturing Sur and Quriyat which the Portuguese still held. After this he turned his attention to the Sharqiya thus concluding the process of internal unification.

The rest of his reign was not entirely free from attempts at rebellion. How-ever he was clearly an outstanding personality both as ruler and military

commander and the Omani historian, Salil ibn Razik, epitomises the regard in which he was held: "He was a man of perfect integrity and an eminent example of justice personified." This, judging by Omani written and oral tradition, was not merely a eulogist's phrase, for a number of exceptional powers were attributed to him and he was even credited with miracles.

On Nasir's death in 1649 (1059 AH) his cousin Sultan ibn Saif, who had already acquitted himself well in war at the capture of Sur and Quriyat from the Portuguese, was elected Imam. His first act was to oust the Portuguese from Muscat, thus greatly enhancing his prestige, and he then ordered a *jihad* – or holy war – against the Portuguese, sending ships to attack their stronghold on the coast of Gujerat.

It was Sultan who built the great round fort at Nizwa, which took some twelve years to complete, and he renewed the aqueduct between Izki and Nizwa. He also fostered trade, attaching particular importance to the export of horses, for which Oman was then noted, and furthered Oman's external relations by sending emissaries to India, Persia, San'a in Yemen, Basra and Iraq. The historian Salil ibn Razik sums up his accomplishments: "Oman revived during his government and prospered and the people rested from their troubles. Prices were low, roads were safe, merchants made large profits and crops were abundant. The Imam himself was humble towards the one Almighty God and compassionate towards his subjects, condoning their offences when such condonation was lawful and never keeping himself aloof from them. He went about without an escort and would sit and talk familiarly with the people, saluting great and small, freeman and slave."

Sultan's son Bil'arub, who succeeded him in 1668 (1079 AH) began his reign well, following the good example of his immediate Ya'ruba predecessors. He built the great fort at Jabrin and renewed the water supply, after which he moved the capital there from Nizwa. The college he established there, for which he paid masters' salaries and pupils' expenses, produced many learned theologians and famous scholars. His reign was, however, later marred by serious differences between him and his brother Saif ibn Sultan and constant family feuds. These led even the learned and devout shaikhs of Oman to follow "the counsel of the

Beneath the stark cliff face the castle at Birkat al Moz controls one access route to the heights of the Jebel Akhdar. Below: *The tower of the great castle at Jabrin, another former capital, soars skywards.*

demented" and in their divisions they brought great disaster on the country. It was, of course, the ordinary people who suffered most and thinking "a plague on both your houses" nicknamed Bil'arub "the calamity of the Arabs" and his brother Saif "the scourge".

It was Saif who proved the stronger and obtained control of all the major forts. This gave him sufficient power to procure his own election as Imam, even during his brother's lifetime. Some people maintained that Bil'arub was still the rightful Imam, whilst others reckoned that Saif's election was justified but eventually the hapless Bil'arub was besieged at Jabrin by Saif and a large army. Losing all hope Bil'arub prayed for death and, as the chronicles relate, "God granted his petition". He was buried in his own splendid and beautiful fort at Jabrin.

Saif's motives and methods may not have been unexceptionable, but after the death of his brother no one contested his earlier election as Imam. He proved a strong ruler, carrying the war against the Portuguese even to their settlements in east Africa and India. Saif's strength impressed the Arabs in east Africa, and in 1698 (1110 AH) the Omanis of Mombasa, which had been in Portuguese hands since 1503 (909 AH), sent a delegation, requesting his assistance in ousting the Portuguese. Saif responded by sending a naval force, which not only

31

By the end of the seventeenth century Omanis had dislodged the Portuguese from east Africa.

captured Mombasa but also Pemba – called the "Green Island" by the Arabs – Kilwa and other places, thus effectively driving the Portuguese out of all their settlements north of Mozambique.

Earlier, in about 1694 (1106 AH) the Omanis attacked the Portuguese position in Salsette Island near Bombay, plundering and burning it. At this time they also turned to privateering on the high seas and to naval warfare. In this they had no monopoly, for Europeans such as the "Feringhis" and the "Muggs" engaged in it in the Gulf and Indian Ocean so wholeheartedly that the British and other Europeans were black-balled at the Court of the Great Mogul! To combat lawlessness at sea the principal European nations agreed in 1698 that the British should police the southern waters, the Dutch the Red Sea and the French the Gulf – theoretically a

splendid early example of European cooperation but unfortunately still-born.

The Imam Saif benefited from Omani naval expeditions, acquiring great wealth and owning seven hundred male slaves. This enabled him to promote agriculture by building new *falajes* and repairing others, for example at Rostaq, al Hazm and al Bazili in the Dhahira. He planted so many trees that he was reputed to own a third of all the date palms in the country, and in Barka alone he planted 30,000 young date trees and 6,000 coconuts. He was, according to some accounts, also the Onassis of his time, owning twenty-eight ships, of which one, *al Falak*, was armed with eighty large guns. According to European accounts, the Omani fleet in 1715 consisted of one ship of 74 guns, two of 60, one of 50, eighteen of between 12 and 32 guns and a large number of *trankis* or

rowing vessels, each carrying from 4 to 8 guns. On his death in 1711 he was buried at Rostaq, and his son who succeeded him as Imam, Sultan ibn Saif II, built a fine dome over the tomb which was, however, destroyed in the nineteenth century by the Wahhabis.

Sultan ibn Saif II also continued the warfare against the Portuguese. He moved his capital from Rostaq to al Hazm where he built the fine fort, spending all he had inherited from his father as well as borrowing from the religious endowments – *awkaf*. His reputation for power and justice was formidable and on one occasion when he was masquerading as an ordinary Arab carrying a water skin – a habit which several Omani rulers have shared with the famous Caliph Haroun ar Rashid – an Arab menaced him with a sword and demanded water. "And what if I refuse?" said the disguised Imam. "Why", came the response, "I would smite you with this sword, if it were not for Sultan ibn Saif!"

The Civil War

ON the death of the Imam Sultan ibn Saif II in 1718 (1131 AH) at al Hazm, where he was buried, the unity which Oman had known for the greater part of a century came to an end and a period of civil war, comparable with the Wars of the Roses in England, followed. The trouble began over who should succeed Sultan as Imam. After so long and successful a period of dynastic rule the tribal leaders and ordinary people thought that Saif, the young son of Sultan, was the natural successor, even though he had not yet reached puberty. The *Ulema*, the learned men, favoured Muhanna ibn Sultan, whom they thought had all the necessary attributes for the office. The legal argument they deployed against Saif's appointment was that as a minor he was not entitled to possession of his own property and *a fortiori* he could not, as required of the Imam, take charge of property belonging to the State or to orphans.

However, the *Ulema* knew that popular sentiment ran in favour of Saif and did not dare to press Muhanna's case openly. They therefore resorted to a political ruse and, producing the young Saif before the assembled people, made an announcement capable of *double entendre* in Arabic; either "Your Imam is Saif ibn Sultan," or "It is Saif ibn Sultan who is standing before you." He was nonetheless proclaimed Imam and the guns were fired as an act of traditional recognition. In May 1719 (1132 AH), however, after the original tumult over the succession had died down, the *Ulema* felt strong enough to come out into the open. They therefore smuggled Muhanna into the fort at Rostaq and proclaimed him Imam from there. Muhanna took effective control and started his reign well, abolishing the customs at Muscat and thus enabling large trading profits to be made. Prices were low and the harvest good, but despite these promising auguries, his reign was in the event to be very short and under him the country enjoyed tranquillity for the last time for many years.

Even the people of Rostaq itself remained hostile to him and Ya'rub ibn Bil'arub, the son of the Imam Bil'arub, added his influential weight to the opposition by besieging him in Rostaq fort and demanding his surrender. Muhanna was tricked by a promise of safe conduct to come down from the fort, but Ya'rub broke his word and ordered Muhanna and his supporters to be bound and flogged, after which Muhanna was imprisoned and murdered. Ya'rub's intervention had perhaps not been entirely selfless and he was himself elected Imam after expressing pious contrition for the death of Muhanna. He then moved to Nizwa taking the boy Saif with

Approach to Jabrin

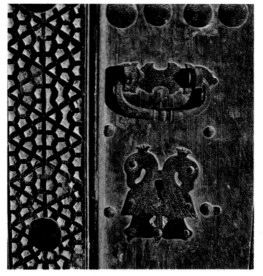

Built in the late seventeenth century, Jabrin is the finest of Oman's castles, and became a seat of Omani learning. The arched entrance (*left*) suggests general Mogul influence, but the carving on the door (*above*) is in the true Omani tradition. Steps have been taken recently to restore Jabrin.

him but, in doing so, incensed the tribes who thought that the Imamate should be preserved for Saif when he came of age. Another rebellion broke out, this time led by Bil'arub ibn Nasir al Ya'rubi with the support of the Bani Hina tribe who captured Rostaq, thus dominating the trade routes from the Interior to the coast. The revolt spread like wildfire, Ya'rub was compelled to stand down, and the boy Saif was elected Imam for the second time.

This might have led to a period of stability, but in fact the reverse was the case. A long civil war was sparked off by an incident at Rostaq, where the tribesmen had gathered to swear their allegiance to Saif. Bil'arub, who had played so large a part in Saif's restoration, was not unnaturally appointed regent to the boy, but for some unknown reason he used on the occasion of this gathering threats of such severity against the Bani Ghafir tribe and their leader, Muhammad ibn Nasir al Ghafiri, that they were provoked into immediate opposition.

Muhammad may have felt that the second formal election of Saif had been something of a sham and that Bil'arub would in fact wield power in a manner favourable to the Bani Hina and detrimental to the Bani Ghafir. At all events he wrote to the former Imam, Ya'rub, and urged him to raise his standard again, turning at the same time to the tribes of the Shamal, the present Union of Arab Emirates, for support. This was in fact forthcoming from the Bani Yas, the Bani Qitab and the Naim of the Buraimi area. The force which Muhammad mustered marched to Nizwa, and having consolidated there attacked Bil'arub's army at Firq. Bil'arub surrendered and Saif, who had by now reached puberty, was proclaimed Imam yet again, this time under the auspices of Muhammad ibn Nasir and the Bani Ghafir. Ya'rub died shortly afterwards, on 21st March 1723 (1136 AH) and thus one of the rivals for the Imamate was removed from the scene.

Fighting over the succession had led

to increasing tribal enmity and the whole of Oman then became engulfed in desultory warfare between two factions – the Hinawi, based on the Bani Hina tribe and the Ghafiri, based on the Bani Ghafir. After the death of the former Imam, Ya'rub, the Hinawis rallied to a new leader – Khalf ibn Mubarak al Hina'i, nicknamed "Tiny". Endowed with skill and determination he responded to Muhammad ibn Nasir's "capture of the King" by seizing the coastal towns of Muscat and Barka.

Muhammad meanwhile appointed *Walis* in the boy Imam's name over the different districts of Oman and assembled a force of some 15,000 men who included the Bani Riyam and a considerable force from the north led by Rahma ibn Mattar al Hawali, the Amir of Julfar – Ras al Khaima – with which he attacked the Hinawis at Barka. The result was inconclusive, but Khalf and the Hinawis turned the tables by instigating countermoves in the Dhahira and by capturing Rostaq and Sohar. Khalf

Jabrin: interior aspect

The inscriptions above the entrance to the tomb of the Imam Bil'arub ibn Sultan (*above*) refer to his reign. Various Arabic scripts are represented in the wall and ceiling decorations (*right*). The Ya'ruba dynasty, which ruled from 1624 until 1748, gave strong central government to Oman. Jabrin was built at the apogee of the Ya'ruba period around 1670 by the Imam Bil'arub, whose father had expelled the Portu-

then had the advantage of holding the important passes and the richest ports, but Muhammad had the advantage of larger forces. However Muhammad's reliance on tribesmen from the Shamal may have accentuated animosities as the Hinawis could not forgive him for introducing Sunnis into an internal Ibadhi quarrel about the succession to the Imamate.

Muhammad then obtained control of the Sharqiya, where the Hinawi faction were won over by force of arms. This success enabled him to attack the Hinawis in their area of strength on the Batina coast. But in 1724 he took an unexpected step. Summoning the tribal chiefs and *Ulema* to Nizwa he expressed a wish to give up responsibility for waging wars and administering Ibadhi affairs and suggested that another regent for the young Saif should be appointed. His motive is obscure. Possibly he had had enough, or his health was under strain. Possibly he was sufficiently patriotic to ask himself where the civil wars were

leading Oman, for he had all along positively identified himself with the Ya'ruba dynasty and he was perhaps at heart more sympathetic to them than to Bani Ghafir tribal factionalism. It could, however, be that his purpose was more Machiavellian and that he was angling for the Imamate. However this may be, the shaikhs and *Ulema* would not accept his resignation but instead proclaimed him Imam. Unfortunately for Oman his appointment did not end the civil war which continued for another four years. He built up his control over much of the country in the next year or two and then attempted to attack Khalf's forces at Sohar. This move brought the end which, like the final act of a Shakespearean tragedy, resulted in the death of both leaders in the fighting under the walls of the great fort.

Before this, however, Muhammad sent a message warning the Hinawi garrison of Sohar not to resist. The messenger treacherously changed sides

and remained with the Hinawis, who though prepared for Muhammad's army nonetheless lost the battle. The townspeople of Sohar then submitted to the Imam Muhammad. Khalf was meanwhile in Muscat where he gathered a force to march against Sohar. But realising that the odds were against him, unless he could detach from Muhammad's forces the contingent from the Shamal, he resorted to a stratagem inducing the owner of a field of standing millet to destroy it and to complain to the Imam Muhammad that the damage had been done by Arabs of the north. Muhammad, having heard the case, gave judgement that damages should be paid to the plaintiff. But the latter, acting at Khalf's instigation, refused the damages and demanded that the "offenders" should be punished. Muhammad then ordered that the "offenders" should be bastinadoed, even though their own chiefs asserted their innocence. This so incensed the northern tribesmen that they quitted their camp

guese. Designed as an elegant country home, it became for a while the Imam's capital; an important school was also founded there by the Imam. Bil'arub himself was eventually supplanted by his brother Saif and buried in this fine tomb beneath the Jabrin fort.

The interior courtyard is overlooked by the verandahs (far left above). Restrained elegance is the hallmark of the arches (above centre) and the screens and niches (above right). The inscriptions (left) are from the tomb of the Imam Bil'arub.

and returned home. Khalf's ruse had worked and seizing his opportunity he attacked at once but only to face defeat and death. Fate was, however, to deal impartially with the two great protagonists and Muhammad was struck by a bullet fired from the fort when in hot pursuit of the Hinawis.

The Hinawis thereupon surrendered to Saif ibn Sultan who was once again proclaimed Imam in Nizwa in March 1728 (1140 AH). At last, one might have thought, peace must return to Oman, but internal divisions and dissensions remained so severe that in 1733 (1146 AH) yet another Ya'rubi contender for the Imamate, Bil'arub ibn Himyar, was elected and Oman again had a split Imamate. The situation had gone from bad to worse, but blacker days were still to come. When Muhammad and Khalf died the Ghafiris held Nizwa, most of central Oman, the Dhahira and the Sharqiya. The Hinawis held Rostaq, the Batina area and Jabrin. Saif then took over these Hinawi territories in-cluding Muscat and Bil'arub the area held by the Ghafiris.

Saif, however, judged that he was not strong enough on his own and brought in Baluch mercenaries from Makran, the first recorded instance of Baluchis coming to Oman for military service. Later, when defeated even with their help, he wrote to Nadir Shah of Persia requesting assistance. Tradition relates that the Shah in reply sent a very powerful and restive horse with the message that, if Saif could maintain his seat on it, the Shah would send as many soldiers as he desired. Saif had it saddled and managed to master it riding furiously through the Wadi al Kabir in Muscat, with the stones flying up behind in every direction. On reaching the Bab al Mitha'ib the horse leaped the wall on the top of which Saif landed safely on his feet. This display of horse-manship sufficiently impressed the Shah's messenger, but unfortunately the horse broke its legs and was killed. It is a tribute to Saif's character that he "greatly regretted the death of the horse".

The Safavid dynasty had virtually come to an end with the abdication of Shah Hussain after the Afghans had invaded Persia in 1722 (1135 AH) and the country remained unsettled until a leader of genius, Nadir Quli who came to the throne as Nadir Shah in 1736 (1148 AH), expelled them. He ruled for only eleven years, but in this short time managed not only to restore order but also to pursue an expansionist policy. In response to Saif's appeal he sent 500 men and 1,580 horses, with the help of Dutch transports – the British were unwilling to become involved – to Julfar and Khor Fakkan. The local Arabs submitted and Saif's forces, join-ing those of Latif Khan, the Persian "Admiral of the Gulf", advanced to engage and defeat Bil'arub's army at Falaj Sumaini near Buraimi in 1736 (1149 AH). But Bil'arub recovered and in the following year (1150 AH), a fresh Persian force of some 6,000 arrived in

Jabrin: ceiling decoration

The painting of house ceilings is a feature of central Oman. Even relatively modest houses have ceilings gaily painted in different colours with typically Islamic designs, such as geo-metrical patterns, flowers, and sometimes verses from the Qur'an. The finest examples are found in the great fort at Jabrin. This massive building nonetheless has decoration executed with great sensitivity. A sense of elegance and beauty inspires the carving of the doors and painting of the ceilings, and the colours are subtle and well-blended. The Imam's room and the mosque are the finest examples of this delicate work in the fort.

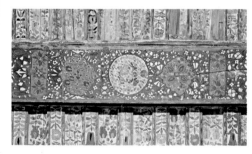

The ceiling of one of the principal reception rooms at Jabrin (right) shows the highest achievements in Omani ceiling-painting. The design resembles the Iranian/Mogul style, with its flowing curves and flower patterns.

Julfar. Saif by now regretted his invitation to the Persians, realising that their ambitions extended beyond merely helping him. It was, however, too late and the Persians reduced the Dhahira area to submission and started to levy taxes. In view of the heavy fighting between Omanis and Persians, Saif went to the Wadi Bani Ghafir to meet Bil'arub and the Bani Ghafir agreed that, in order to heal Omani divisions and enable both factions to join against the Persians, Bil'arub should stand down from the Imamate in favour of Saif. All went well for a time and Saif relieved the people of tax imposed by the Persians. However things again turned sour for him in 1741 (1154 AH) when the *Ulema* and tribal chiefs, who were dissatisfied with him – the reason is not clear, unless it was divinely ordained, as Salil ibn Razik the Oman historian suggests, that "the people of Oman had to undergo the consequences of their fickleness and love of change" – conferred the Imamate on Sultan ibn Murshid al Ya'rubi.

War broke out between rival Imams, whose fortunes ebbed and flowed until Saif lost Muscat to Sultan and, despite earlier disenchantment, again turned to the Persians, who still maintained a garrison at Julfar, for help. Saif offered to give the Persians the fort at Sohar – the centre of their influence in Sassanid times – in perpetuity. They replied somewhat loftily that Saif was a sincere friend and ally and they did not need such a gift as they had everything in abundance! Nadir Shah assembled another fleet, which sailed for Julfar in June 1742 (1155 AH) and Saif and Taqi Khan the Persian commander, who was also *Beglarbegi* of the province of Fars, met there to sign a treaty, by which the Persians agreed to restore the Imamate to Saif in return, despite their earlier reticence, for recognition of Persian suzerainty over Oman. Persian troops then marched down the Batina and attacked Sohar, where the fort was held by Ahmad ibn Said who later became the first Imam of the Al bu Said dynasty. He

successfully withstood their siege, but the Persians took Muscat and Mutrah. They then redoubled their efforts to take Sohar, but Ahmad, even though his own supplies were very short, sallied forth every day to attack them.

In 1743 (1156 AH) one of the complications of the Omani scene was removed with the death of the Imam Sultan. The unfortunate Saif again became disillusioned with the Persians when they refused to hand over the forts at Muscat and Mutrah to him and he slipped away from their camp, as they were encircling Sohar, to the fort of al Hazm. There he died of a broken heart shortly after hearing of the defeat and death of his rival the Imam Sultan in a cavalry engagement near Sohar with the Persians. What a strange mixture of feelings must have assailed him towards the end of his tragic life! He said to one of his officers just before his death: "This is my castle and my grave. I am become a eyesore to every one, and the quiet of death will be preferable to any happiness

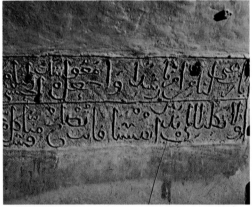

Inscriptions from the Qur'an are frequently a feature of interior decoration. The ceiling (left) bears a fine medallion enclosing an example of this style. A variant (top) is relief-work on plaster. Wood-carving, too, was beautifully executed at Jabrin; the door (above) bears evidence of the carver's skill.

The face of Nizwa has, until recently, changed little since the Arabs fought against the Persians nearly two thousand years ago. Many of the streets are too narrow to permit any form of transport other than a donkey or camel.

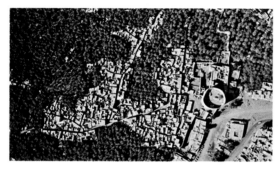

From air and ground, the city is dominated by the great tower of Nizwa fort.

which dominion has afforded me."

With the death of Saif and Sultan no other member of the Ya'ruba came forward, but Ahmad ibn Said continued the fight against the Persians single-handed. The Persians maintained the siege of Sohar for nine months in all but after Saif's death agreed with Ahmad to withdraw from there whilst retaining Muscat. Ahmad was not slow to find a means of exerting further pressure on them and he established a thriving market at Barka, which diverted imports and trade from the Interior away from Muscat. Ahmad then made up his mind to get rid of the Persians once and for all. He invited them to a vast gathering at Barka, for which the preparations were so lavish that local people began to complain. Great dishes of meat were sent to the tents which the Persians had pitched on the plain, whose fifty officers were invited to a banquet by Ahmad. His undisclosed object was similar to the ruse by which Muhammad Ali Pasha later ended the influence of the Mamelukes in Egypt in 1811 (1226 AH). When all the guests were at dinner, the drum of the fort was sounded and the crier proclaimed "Anyone who has a grudge against the Persians may now take his revenge." This was the signal for a wholesale massacre which only 200 odd Persians survived. Thus in 1747 (1160 AH) their adventure in Oman was ended – although a garrison remained in Julfar until 1748 (1161 AH) – and Ahmad ibn Said who became a popular hero was elected Imam.

The Al bu Said Dynasty

The Great Fort at Nizwa was built by Sultan ibn Saif over three hundred years ago, and took twelve years to complete.

From the high windows of the fort (top) *the sentries on guard had a view over the whole town and beyond. The round tower has a diameter of 120 feet, and contains dungeons and oubliettes* (above) *into which prisoners could be thrown.*

AHMAD ibn Said was a man of outstanding courage, vigour, enterprise, generosity and personality, and all these qualities were as much needed after he became Imam as before. The factionalism of the civil war did not disappear overnight and it was not long after he was elected Imam that the Ya'ruba family started intriguing with the support of the Ghafiri faction. Bil'arub ibn Himyar, the former Imam – Saif ibn Sultan's rival – was induced to show his hand by a report that the Imam Ahmad ibn Said was dead. Ahmad had in fact only gone into hiding in Yankul and, hearing of Bil'arub's action, he emerged and raised the Hinawi tribes. Setting off through the Wadi Samail, and gathering increasing strength, he defeated Bil'arub's army at Firq near Nizwa. Bil'arub himself was killed and Ahmad punished those who had joined Bil'arub against him, though he later showed his magnanimity by pardoning them.

Thereafter Ahmad's difficulties lay nearer home for his two sons, Saif and Sultan, led him something of a dance and at one time seized the two forts in Muscat. Ibn Rahma al Hawali, the Amir of Julfar, seized the opportunity provided by their family dissension to besiege Rostaq with some 30,000 men, but this only caused family solidarity and patriotism to reassert itself. Father and sons were immediately reconciled and ibn Rahma, who had previously fought an inconclusive battle with Ahmad's forces at Bithna in the early 1750s (1160s AH), withdrew.

Another threat in the early days of Ahmad's reign came from Nasir ibn Muhammad ibn Nasir who led a faction of the Ghafiris in opposition until he and Ahmad were reconciled by a marriage, which made them brothers-in-law.

Though Ahmad had his early difficulties in securing internal peace after the civil war, Oman in his day was an important power to be reckoned with externally. By 1775 (1189 AH) his fleet consisted of thirty-four warships – four of 44 guns, five frigates mounting 18–24 guns and the rest ketches or galiots mounting from 8–14 guns. The British were involved militarily with Oman even at this stage, and in 1758 (1172 AH) the captain of an English ketch hired her to the Imam for a naval expedition against the people of Ras al Khaima. Seapower enabled Ahmad to assert Omani influence abroad and to carry the war against the Persians further afield. In 1756 (1170 AH) the Persians besieged Basra and, when the inhabitants wrote to Ahmad seeking help, he himself led an expedition of ten large ships, a number of smaller ones and a force of 10,000 men. He drove the Persians out after his ship, *Ah-Rahmany*, had managed to break the iron chain which the Persians had stretched across the river. So delighted was the Ottoman Sultan, within whose jurisdiction Basra then fell, that he ordered the Governor of Basra to pay the Imam *kharaj*, or a subsidy, which continued until the reign of Said ibn Sultan ibn al Imam Ahmad (1804–1856: 1219–1273 AH).

The Mogul Emperor, Shah Alam, was grateful too for the cooperation of Ahmad's fleet against pirates on the west coast of India. He therefore sent an envoy to Oman to make a treaty agreeing to aid Ahmad with money and men against his enemies and to establish a resident mission in Muscat in premises which came to be known as "the Nawab's house".

At home Ahmad proved a good administrator of a generally strong central government and gained a reputation for liberality. On his way from Rostaq to Muscat he used to distribute sweets to the children of the poor. Though he was always accessible to his people, he kept some state and had a personal bodyguard, which included a thousand free men, a thousand Zanzibaris and a hundred Nubian slaves. When on the march, his retinue carried four banners, attached to staffs, two with gold at the head and two with silver. He also included in his retinue *Qadhis*, scholars, notables and even executioners – described by Salil ibn Razik, the Omani historian, as a "brave set of fellows"! He was assiduous in attention to administrative detail and visited Muscat, which yielded a very good income from customs; revenue from this source alone was from at least one *lakh* of rupees and perhaps as high as three or five *lakhs*. These visits from Rostaq were usually of twelve days' duration and on the eleventh day, when he inspected

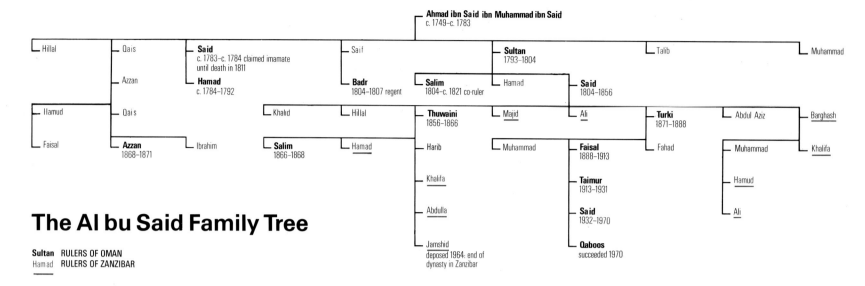

The Al bu Said Family Tree

Sultan RULERS OF OMAN
Hamad RULERS OF ZANZIBAR

fort Mirani, all dues on goods then deposited in customs were remitted. Curiously, Ahmad never succeeded in obtaining the Ya'ruba fort at al Hazm and this remained in the hands of the Ya'ruba family until 1861 (1278 AH).

Ahmad died in Rostaq in 1783 (1198 AH) and his son Said was elected Imam, despite a general desire that the older and most intelligent son, Hillal, should succeed. Hillal, who suffered from cataract, had gone to Sind for a cure and never returned to Oman. On such slender threads do the succession of kings and the fate of nations depend. For Said was not a popular ruler. As *Wali* of Nizwa he had earlier antagonised the local population by establishing a personal monopoly of indigo dyeing, and this as well as other measures alienated him from the people. Efforts were consequently made to appoint first his brother Qais and later his son Hamad as Imam in his place. Hamad in fact later became *de facto* ruler of Oman, residing in Muscat whilst his father remained at Rostaq, thus beginning the dichotomy between Sultanate and Imamate which so bedevilled internal politics later.

Hamad, who was perhaps the first of the family to be formally designated Sayyid, surrounded himself with men of learning and piety and gained a reputation for justice. His reputation for bravery was only equalled by that of his uncle Sultan, who later assumed the rule, and he added a tower facing the Mukalla cove to fort Mirani in Muscat which he armed with great guns. A man of determination, he built forts in Ruwi and Barka, and had a ship called *Ar-Rahmany* built for him at Zanzibar. He acquired Lamu in east Africa and

had designs on Mombasa and even Bombay.

During Hamad's administration there was a severe drought, but after he had led the people in prayer in the Wadi al Kabir at Muscat, rain, accompanied by thunder and lightning, came in abundance. The valleys ran with water and a period of prosperity followed. After mustering a large army – whether to reduce al Hazm, to attack his uncle Qais at Sohar, to make war on his father or to attack Mombasa, is still a matter of speculation – Hamad died suddenly in 1792 (1206 AH). He was buried in Muscat and his father the Imam Said made a funeral feast in fort Jalali after which he returned to Rostaq and thereafter neglected the administration of his subjects utterly. As a result of his indolence the reins of government were taken up by his brother Sultan, another son of the Imam Ahmad ibn Said, and it was not long before Sultan had effective control of Muscat and the greater part of the country.

Sultan was tall in stature, of noble countenance, and brave; and his reputation in Oman was second to none. In taking Muscat from the representative whom the Imam Said had put in to succeed Hamad there, Sultan and his men sang, as they came down the *wadi* with drawn swords, "The right has overcome and has overthrown the wrong!" But he was practical as well as idealistic, and realising the importance of stability to Muscat's trade he hastened to assure the merchants and notables of immunity for themselves and their property.

During the latter half of the eighteenth century goods were carried between the Gulf and India by both European and Arab vessels and the merchants of

Muscat had a lion's share of this trade. Sayyid Sultan had fifteen ships of between 400 and 700 tons and three brigs based on Muscat alone, whilst at Sur there was a fleet of 100 or so sea-going vessels of various sizes. Import duties at Muscat amounted to 6 or 6½ per cent *ad valorem* on merchandise of all kinds and about five-eighths of the whole Persian Gulf trade passed through this port from which ships sailed to Batavia, Bengal, Malabar, Malaya, Zanzibar and Abyssinia to trade.

Sayyid Sultan claimed the exclusive right to protect navigation in the Gulf and at this time indeed Oman controlled both sides of the Gulf, as parts of southern Persia had been leased from the Persians. He tried – though without ultimate success – to make a preliminary visit to Muscat obligatory on all vessels proceeding up the Gulf, a stratagem which had made earlier *entrepôts* in the Gulf area prosperous in their own heydays.

Sultan's grip on Oman itself was so firm that the European powers – particularly the British and French, whose interests began to conflict in the East as well as in Europe – dealt with him as the effective ruler and both powers formally addressed him as if he were the elected Imam. The dim existence of the Imam himself in Rostaq was of little political consequence.

The French base in Mauritius, the Ile de France, became a flourishing colonial possession, whose Governor maintained contact with the rulers of Oman, and well chosen gifts were from time to time exchanged. Even earlier the French Consul in Basra had struck up a personal friendship with Ahmad ibn Said and in 1785 (1200 AH) the French sent a mission under the Comte de Rosily to Muscat seeking permission to set up a factory and a consulate, though this in fact came to nothing.

Rivalry between the British and the French grew in intensity with the rise of Napoleon's star. His ambitions for a vast eastern empire alarmed the British, who had been consolidating their power in India since the Seven Years War and were very sensitive about their communications with home. Napoleon's arrival in Egypt heralded a diplomatic struggle for influence in Oman between the two powers. Despite an earlier incident when they had seized an Omani frigate, the *Saleh*, off Sohar, the French were well thought of in Muscat and in 1799 (1214 AH) Napoleon addressed a letter to Sultan which read:

"A L'Imam de Muscat –
Je vous écris cette lettre pour vous faire connaître ce que vous avez déjà appris sans doute, l'arrivée de l'armée française en Egypte. Comme vous avez été de tout temps notre ami, vous devez être convaincu du désir que j'ai de protéger tous les bâtiments de votre nation et que vous engagiez à venir à Suez, où ils trouveront protection pour le commerce. Je vous prie aussi de faire parvenir cette lettre à Tippoo-Saib par la première occasion qui se trouvera pour les Indes."

The British had been off the mark even earlier and had decided to forestall the French. Their suspicions had already been aroused by the activities of two eminent French naturalists, Messieurs Bruguière and Olivier, who made journeys to the Gulf area, and thus Napoleon's letter was intercepted by a British agent. The reference to Tippoo Sahib who was in rebellion against them in India particularly alarmed the British authorities.

In 1798 (1213 AH) Sir Harford Jones, who later led a mission to Persia, was appointed Resident at Basra to forestall French influence with the Pasha of Baghdad. In the same year the British Government in Bombay sent Mirza Mahdi Ali Khan, one of the Persian gentlemen of good family who were employed in the British service at the time, to Sayyid Sultan of Muscat. A treaty in the form of a *Qaulnameh* was signed, by which Sultan bound himself to take the British part in international matters; to deny the French or their allies the Dutch "a place to fix or seat themselves" whilst warfare between them and the British continued; to

dismiss from his service a Frenchman who was commanding one of his vessels; to exclude French vessels from the inner cove at Muscat; and to permit the British to garrison Bandar Abbas which Sultan then claimed – an offer which was not in fact taken up.

The Governor-General in India and his brother, Sir Arthur Wellesley, who later became the Duke of Wellington, feared that the French might attempt to invade India through Persia and doubted the strength of Sultan's commitment. They therefore sent an impressive mission in 1800 (1215 AH) under Captain John Malcolm – one of the East India Company's most able young officers, who later became General Sir John Malcolm, Governor of Bombay – to conclude political and commercial treaties with Fath Ali Khan, the Shah of Persia. "Boy" Malcolm – his nickname through life – also called at Muscat on the way to negotiate a more formal treaty with Sultan. This reaffirmed the earlier treaty and provided that "an English gentleman of respectability should always reside in the port of Muscat" and that the friendship of the two countries should "endure till the end of time or the sun and moon cease in their revolving careers". Sayyid Sultan found no difficulty in agreeing the terms. He was however somewhat upset at having to dismiss his French surgeon and for this reason the first British representative appointed to reside in Muscat was a doctor, Assistant-Surgeon A. H. Bogle.

The British recognised the Omanis as the predominant power in the area and calculated that alliance with them would help contain the growing power of the Qawasim of Ras al Khaima who were beginning to harass British as well as local shipping. Anxieties had been aroused by an incident in 1797 (1212 AH) when the *Viper*, a 14-gun cruiser of the Bombay Marine was lying off Bushire.

Shaikh Salih, one of the Qasimi shaikhs, who was also there planning to intercept Omani ships sailing from Basra to Sur, called on the British Resident with professions of friendship and requested that the British should neither give protection to Omani ships nor despatch any goods in them – an interesting request, suggesting that the British were already doing this. His plea for ball and powder was met by the captain of the *Viper*, but the Shaikh

nevertheless suddenly attacked the British ship, perhaps having received no firm assurance about the British attitude over Omani ships.

During the latter part of the eighteenth century there was constant warfare between the Omanis and the Qawasim, who sought a greater share of the Gulf, Indian and African trade enjoyed by the Omanis. These wars also had roots in tribal and factional considerations, arising from the direct involvement of the tribes of Shamal in the Omani civil war. Ahmad ibn Said had tried in 1758 (1172 AH) to reduce the tribes of Sir – the Ras al Khaima area – and in 1762 (1176 AH) obtained recognition of his authority from all the tribes but not from the historical port of Julfar, whose Amir, Shaikh Saqr, invaded Oman in 1763 (1177 AH) and even threatened Rostaq. Niebuhr, however, who visited the Ras al Khaima area in the 1760s, commented that though these tribes recognised the overlordship of the Imam they were in fact independent and often at war with their former masters.

Meantime a new element appeared on the already complicated scene. A boy born in Ayaina in Saudi Arabia in 1703 (1115 AH) was to have a great influence on the fortunes of south-east Arabia. As a child Muhammad ibn Abdul Wahhab showed unusual religious fervour and as a man became a formidable fundamentalist reformer, preaching the oneness of God and a return to God's word as revealed in the Qur'an. The Al Saud shaikhs of Dara'iya and Najd were won over, and by the last quarter of the eighteenth century the tribes of Najd were welded together under the leadership of the Shaikh of the Al Saud who, after the death of the founder, became Imam of the new movement. This by then had become a religio-military confederacy of desert people and common cause was maintained by keeping fanaticism at white heat. The fuel required was constant expansion and this had important consequences for Oman in the nineteenth and twentieth centuries. In 1800 (1215 AH) the Wahhabis arrived in Buraimi, which had been indisputably part of Oman throughout countless generations, and the alliance which developed between Wahhabis and Qawasim involved Oman in warfare on land and sea for several decades.

Meantime, however, the French made further attempts to win influence in Oman despite the treaties made with

Recognising Oman's power, Britain sought an alliance in the seventeenth century.

Britain. Talleyrand advised Napoleon in 1803 (1218 AH):

> "Mascate est une place importante. L'Imam qui y gouverne, et dont la domination s'étend fort avant dans l'intérieur des terres et même sur quelques districts de la côte de Mozambique, est un prince indépendant sous tous rapports."

This led Napoleon to appoint M. Cavaignac as Consul, and he arrived in Muscat on 3rd October 1803 (1218 AH) with his baggage, clearly expecting to set up house. Sultan, however, honoured his treaties with Britain by firmly refusing to accept Cavaignac. No doubt the "English gentleman of respectability" had been earning his keep, though he kept up no grand style locally and lived in a "miserable house". Sultan no doubt realised that the British were the only power who could and might help him against the Wahhabis and he did not want to antagonise them for the sake of the French. It was no doubt sour grapes which made Cavaignac comment: "Ce pays et ses inhabitants sont tout à fait misérables" and that all that Muscat needed in the way of representation was "un agent commercial de la dernière classe".

Sultan was at the time involved in hostilities against the Wahhabis, who had reached Barka on the Batina coast, and the Qawasim. A man of courage and decision, he swept the whole Gulf in 1804 (1219 AH) with fourteen warships and visited Basra to seek aid from his Turkish friends. On the return voyage he transferred to a smaller vessel near Lingeh to cross to Oman, but when the rest of the Omani fleet was not sufficiently close to give protection his vessel was attacked by the Qawasim. Sultan was shot through the head and buried at Lingeh.

The Qawasim attack on two British brigs in 1805 (1220 AH) and renewed fears of French involvement in Muscat aroused fresh concern in Bombay and consequently Captain David Seton who had been Political Agent in Muscat for a short time in 1801 (1216 AH), was sent back to the Gulf to report. He recommended that the East India Company's cruisers should be sent to assist the fleet of Badr ibn Saif who had succeeded Sultan in Oman against the Qawasim. The Council at Bombay approved his

This watercolour was painted by Major C. F. Hinchcliffe in 1857.

recommendation, though with considerable apprehension, for it involved taking sides and abandoning the traditional policy of standing aloof from Arab wars. Seton was, therefore, sent fresh instructions, while still in the Gulf and told to act "with the greatest of moderation, to aim at pacification by means of negotiation, and to avoid hostilities, at all events with any classes of armed boats belonging to either side of the Gulph . . . which may have respected the British flag". At the same time cruisers of the Bombay Marine were strictly forbidden to fire on Arab ships unless fired on themselves.

The internal Omani scene again became complicated on Sultan's death. The family was divided about the successor and though the British dealt with Badr, presumably because he was *de facto* ruler on the coast, Omani historians reckon that the rule passed jointly to Sultan's two sons, Salim and Said until Salim died of paralysis in Muscat in April 1821 (1236 AH). But Qais, the ablest surviving son of the Imam Ahmad who still held Sohar also had aspirations, supported by the shadowy Imam Said in Rostaq. Badr, who had initially supported the cause of Said and Salim, was killed by Said in somewhat strange circumstances when they were playing with arms in the fort at Nakhl.

The Reign of Sayyid Said ibn Sultan

The nineteenth was a century of long reigns and Sayyid Said who was born in Samail in 1791 (1206 AH) reigned for fifty-two years from 1804 to 1856 (1219–1273 AH) – an era during which Britain's paramountcy in the area was being consolidated. Said came to be preferred over Salim with the latter's consent, principally because of the influence of his aunt, Moza the daughter of the first Imam Ahmad. Said concluded a treaty of Amity and Commerce in 1807 (1222 AH) with de Caen, the French "Captain-General of the East" but it was short-lived as he and the French were driven out of the Ile de France, Mauritius, by the British with whom Said maintained close relations for the rest of his reign. Their direct involvement against the Qawasim and indirect support against the Wahhabis stood him in good stead, though initially, as we have seen, there were doubts amongst some British officials.

Qasimi attacks on British ships led the Governor-General of India, Lord Minto, to write that the independence of Oman was an important interest which involved British cooperation "against the Joasmee pirates". Joint operations with Said were undertaken

The great-grandfather (Sultan Faisal) (far left) and grandfather (Sultan Taimur) (left) of the present Sultan. Above: Oman's coronation gift to King Edward VII of England.

but Said's final triumph did not come until 1820 (1236 AH), when Qasimi power was finally destroyed and treaties were signed with the shaikhdoms which later came to be called the Trucial States.

Wahhabi influence on the Bani bu Ali and this tribe's piracies prompted Said to prevail on Captain T. Perronet Thompson, who was left as Political Agent in Ras al Khaima after the 1820 treaties, to launch a British expedition against them. It was an unsuccessful and illfated venture which resulted in Captain Thompson's court martial though he survived it to become a full general in the British Army. A second and successful expedition was sent in 1821 (1237 AH) under the command of General Sir Lionel Smith.

Sayyid Said was a great ruler who had stamped his personality on affairs long before the death of the pathetic Imam Said in about 1821 (1237 AH). His biographer Salil wrote to him "Praise be to God through whom Said, the happiest of rulers, attained quiet prosperity and perennial glory, decreeing to him sublime eminence in the sphere of happiness and renown, insomuch that by the Divine aid vouchsafed to him he subdued the sovereigns of his time, acquired dignity by the battles which he fought with his enemies, conquered with the sword hitherto unknown countries and made a straight road over the dissevered

necks of the rebellious." Said, however, did not rule a universally tranquil country even after acquiring ascendancy over his rivals. The scene was perhaps somewhat comparable with England in Henry II's time when those who held the great castles were often in rebellion. The Wahhabis too ate into Said's territory to a greater or lesser extent throughout his reign. Nonetheless there was never, after the first few years, any real doubt about his authority. The character of the "Imam", as he was inaccurately called by Europeans as he was never formally elected, impressed many travellers who described his liberality, charm, and ease with his people. For instance Lieutenant J. R. Wellsted wrote in 1835 (1251 AH): "He possesses a tall and commanding figure; a mild, yet striking countenance; and an address and manner courtly, affable, and dignified ... It is noticed by the Arabs, an instance of the warmth of his affections, that he daily visits his mother ... and pays in all matters implicit obedience to her wishes. In his intercourse with Europeans, he has ever displayed the warmest attention and kindness ..."

Abroad Said had considerable pretensions, ranging from the Gulf region, southern Persia and Baluchistan to the east coast of Africa and Madagascar. He claimed Bahrain, but was never able to subdue or hold it for long. But he re-

tained the hold on southern Persia, which his father Sultan had acquired with the capture of the Hormuz, Qishm, and Henjam Islands from the Bani Ma'in tribe in 1794 (1209 AH) and also the lease of Bandar Abbas and other fortified posts on the southern coast of Kerman which his father had obtained from the Shah for an annual sum of 60,000 *Tumans*. He also retained Gwadur, which remained a part of Oman until 1958, and Chahbar which his father Sultan had added to Oman's possessions. Said's motive, like his father's, was to strengthen Oman's control of trade passing through the Straits of Hormuz and Persian expulsion of his *Wali* and other officials from the coast of Kerman in 1854 was a great personal blow to him – indeed may have hastened his end. For, although the treaty with the Persians negotiated in 1856 (1273 AH) provided that Oman could appoint representatives there for a further twenty years in return for an annual rental of 16,000 *Tumans*, the Persians thereby terminated Oman's pretensions to these areas as of right. The blow may have been the greater, as Said had earlier taken one of the daughters of the Prince Governor of Shiraz as his bride. (There were no children of this marriage.)

Sayyid Said made his greatest impression on Africa where from 1829

The British Connection

In 1646 the Ya'rubi Imam Nasir ibn Murshid made a treaty with the East India Company giving "the English" the exclusive trading rights at Sohar. It was not until 1800 that there was any permanent British representation in Muscat, after the treaty made in that year providing that "an English gentleman of respectability" should always reside in the port of Muscat, and that the friendship between the two countries should "endure till the end of time or the sun and moon cease in their revolving careers". The present Embassy, built as a Consulate in 1890, is in the style of an Arab house with a central courtyard (*below*). The main gate to the courtyard (*right*) with the Royal Coat of Arms above the lintel, is set in an arch of Islamic inspiration and the great double doors contain the wicket gate which is so much a local feature. The first modern Christian missionary to Oman was Thomas Valpy French (1825–1891), formerly Bishop of Lahore, whose grave (*far right*) is in the

Christian cemetery near Muscat. This is in a cove and must be approached by boat.

(1245 AH) his heart and main interest lay. He secured Mombasa from the Mazari, who had established a local Omani dynasty, and made Zanzibar his second capital. He aimed to extend his influence by a dynastic marriage with Queen Ranavolana of Madagascar in 1833 (1249 AH) but, when she replied that she could not marry him herself and suggested a young princess, Said did not take the offer up. Five years later he offered another Queen in Madagascar, Seneekoo Nossi-be, his protection. This offer was accepted and a treaty between them provided that she should pay Said 30,000 dollars a year in return. This arrangement, however, lapsed when the Queen accepted French protection in 1840 (1256 AH).

Said was very much the "Sailor Sayyid" and travelled great distances at sea. He had about twenty ships of his own for private trade and gave his personal attention to Oman's considerable naval forces. It gave him great pleasure to command his own flagship, the *Shah Alam*, in person and it was perhaps, therefore, fitting that he should have presented the English "Sailor King" William IV with a fine ship of war, which was subsequently called the *Liverpool*. He received in return a handsome yacht, called the *Prince Regent*. He also presented a grey mare to King William IV on his coronation in 1830 and an Arab stallion to Queen Victoria on hers. But not all the presents exchanged with the British crown were so practical and acceptable. Queen Victoria sent a state carriage and harness in 1842 (1258 AH) – there being no suitable roads for such carriages in Zanzibar – and in 1844 (1260 AH) a silver gilt tea service. Said made the Kuria Muria Islands over to Queen Victoria as a gift in perpetuity on 14th July 1854 (1270 AH), a gesture which prompted an embarrassed gift of a snuff box from her Foreign Secretary, Lord Clarendon. They were returned to Oman in 1967.

Sayyid Said had thirty-six sons and daughters and one daughter, Sayyida Salma, who was obviously a woman of great character and charm, married a young German from Hamburg, Herr Ruete, and took the European name Emily. She recorded the story of her life with many fascinating details about the Royal Family and local customs in a book published in English and French, called *Memoirs of an Arab Princess*. Her son, Rudolf Said-Ruete, wrote a biography of his maternal grandfather, Sayyid Said, which was published in England in 1929.

Zanzibar

Sayyid Said Sultan gave fresh life to the age-old Omani interest in east Africa, particularly by introducing cloves as a cash crop in Zanzibar and establishing rice plantations, thus creating increasing prosperity. Many of the great European travellers in Africa have left accounts of him and his successors there and Burton, Speke, Livingstone, Grant and Stanley all had good reason to thank the Al bu Saidi rulers of Zanzibar for assistance in their African explorations. The Arabs of Oman had penetrated Africa as far as the Congo – albeit in connection with slaves as well as more legitimate forms of trade – and their knowledge and hospitality greatly assisted the European newcomers.

Omani connection with Zanzibar and the east coast of Africa probably go back into remote antiquity. The first recorded mention, however, of Omanis going to east Africa is the flight of Sulaiman and Said to the "land of the Zanj", when the Caliph's troops forced them out of Oman at the end of the seventh century AD. The first Portuguese travellers found large colonies of Omanis settled there in flourishing cities, on which ibn Batuta also commented in the fourteenth century.

However the modern dynastic connection can perhaps be dated to the Imam Sultan ibn Saif, the second Imam of the Ya'ruba dynasty. The Arabs of Mombasa appealed to him for aid after he had expelled the Portuguese from Muscat, and in 1652 (1063 AH) he attacked Zanzibar, killing a large number of Portuguese, including an Augustine priest. Eight years later, having created a more formidable navy, Sultan ibn Saif besieged Mombasa and defeated the Portuguese there, though it was left to his son, the Imam Saif ibn Sultan, to capture Mombasa, Pemba and Kilwa and to drive the Portuguese from all their coastal possessions north of Mozambique. The Imam Saif appointed Omani *Walis* in several places – a Mazrui at Mombasa, a Nabhani at Pate and a Hirth at Zanzibar – and he established military garrisons at Zanzibar and Pemba.

In 1739 (1152 AH) the Mazrui *Wali* of Mombasa threw off his allegiance to the Imamate, which by then had become much weakened by the civil war, and Pate and other states followed suit. However the Imam Ahmad ibn Said was made of sterner stuff and made very sure that Zanzibar was well garrisoned, particularly as the Mazruis of Mombasa continued not only to assert their independence but also to attack Zanzibar itself. Zanzibar thus remained subject to the ruler of Oman from the middle of the seventeenth century until the middle of the nineteenth century, though it was not until the reign of Sayyid Said ibn Sultan that very serious attention was given to developing this part of the Omani dominions.

The Sultanate Divided

When Said died in 1856 at the age of sixty-two on the sea voyage from Muscat, his body was taken and buried in the garden of his residence at Zanzibar. Two of his sons, Majid and Barghash, had been with him there, and Majid who immediately assumed authority in Zanzibar confirmed all the appointments of the officials made by his father in his African dominions. Said's son Thuwaini was *Wali* of Muscat and his son Turki *Wali* of Sohar at the time of his death.

Thuwaini, with the support of the majority of people in Oman itself, claimed the succession to the whole Sultanate, though his brother Turki asserted the same independence as many of the *Walis* of Sohar had done at various times in the past. Recognition, however, by the people of Zanzibar and the African possessions left Majid in a strong *de facto* position and he made an amicable arrangement with Thuwaini to pay him 40,000 crowns annually. Dispute subsequently arose as to whether this sum was tribute or subsidy and, when in 1860 (1277 AH) Majid refused to pay, Thuwaini resorted to arms and assembled an imposing force. Part of this had actually sailed for Zanzibar when the British Government intervened to prevent bloodshed and both parties agreed to submit their dispute to the Viceroy and Governor-General of India, Lord Canning.

Brigadier, later Sir William, Coghlan was appointed to inquire into the merits of the opposing cases and Canning's award in 1862 (1279 AH) was cordially accepted by the rival brothers. Majid was declared ruler of Zanzibar and of the African dominions, but was required to pay to the ruler of Muscat 40,000 crowns annually and the two years' arrears. This arrangement compensated the ruler of Muscat for relinquishing his claims to Zanzibar and adjusted the inequality between the two inheritances, for by this time Zanzibar was by far the richer part. With this rather odd, but empirically wise, settlement the two Sultanates went their own ways. It was at this stage that permanent British representation in Muscat was resumed as the Government of Bombay felt that Thuwaini had been at something of a disadvantage in the arbitration compared with Majid who had been advised throughout the award proceedings by Captain Hamerton, the British Resident in Zanzibar. International recognition to the creation of the two Sultanates was formally given by a joint declaration made at Paris in 1862 (1279 AH) by which the British and French undertook reciprocally to respect the independence of the two sovereign Sultans.

In the middle of the nineteenth century Oman was still described as "a first rate Asiatic maritime power". However, a very rapid decline set in after the death of Sayyid Said as a result of economic causes, the splitting of the Sultanate and instability in Oman itself. The loss of its considerable navy, which happened to be anchored at Zanzibar when Said died, added to Oman's difficulties and the introduction in 1862 of the steamer service run by the British India Steam Navigation Company between India and the Gulf put the Omanis at great disadvantage as their ships ceased to be competitive in the carrying trade. In a very few years their maritime power dwindled to virtually nothing. The gradual elimination of the slave trade, on which much of Oman's shipping was engaged, was another element in Oman's decline, particularly as the agriculture of the Interior depended heavily on slave labour.

Thuwaini's reign was not free from internal strife. In 1861 his brother Turki rose against him in Sohar and the Yal Saad of the Batina and the Bani Jabir also rebelled at the instigation of Qais ibn Azzan of Rostaq, who also allied himself at this stage with the Wahhabis. There were renewed incursions by the Wahhabis in 1864 (1281 AH) and they made insistent demands for financial contributions. With the aid of the Janaba and Bani bu Ali tribes, they raided Sur, but the British interceded to give the Omanis respite. Thuwaini's end came in 1866 (1283 AH) when he was shot with a

double-barrelled pistol by his son Salim in the fort at Sohar whilst enjoying his siesta. Salim's motive is not entirely clear, though Thuwaini was popular neither with his people nor the Al bu Said family.

Salim immediately proclaimed himself as his father's successor but such was the horror of parricide that recognition only came slowly. For a while uncertainty prevailed, trade came to a halt and Turki, basing himself at Yankul in the Dhahira, again went into opposition. The Zanzibar subsidy was temporarily withheld – the first exercise of a political tool, which was to be used on several later occasions. Omani influence at Bandar Abbas which they had held for so long was weakened. For the Persians took the opportunity on Salim's accession to terminate the lease as they were entitled to do but renewed it at an increased rent of 30,000 *Tumans* for eight years. Opposition to Salim built up rapidly and in 1868 (1285 AH) Azzan ibn Qais captured Barka, Muscat and Mutrah in quick succession, forcing Salim to leave by ship. Thus ended a short, unpopular and unhappy reign.

Azzan was proclaimed Imam by the *Mutawwain*, his religious supporters, and Muscat fell under a fundamentalist religious regime. The white flag replaced the traditional red flag, tobacco and strong drink were prohibited, and the easy-going inhabitants were made to attend the mosque. Music was banned and Mr Shore, the British Agency's accountant, was threatened "should the sound of the concertina" emanate from his house.

Azzan demonstrated ability and force of character such as Oman had not seen for a while, and, with the assistance of the influential Khalili family and Salih ibn Ali, the leading Shaikh of the Hirth of the Sharqiya, gained control of the whole country. He expelled the Wahhabis from Buraimi, which they had held intermittently since 1800 (1216 AH) and paid a subsidy to his ally the Shaikh of Abu Dhabi for protecting the Buraimi frontier of Oman. Salim's attempts to raise support against Azzan only met failure, but Turki, who also aspired to the Sultanate, was more successful. Obtaining funds from the Sultan of Zanzibar, he allied himself with the Shaikhs of Dubai, Ajman and Ras al Khaima and, landing at Khor Fakkan, went to Buraimi, winning over the Naim and Bani Qitab tribes on the

way. On 5th October 1870 (1287 AH), Azzan and Turki's forces met in battle in the Wadi Dhank and, rather surprisingly, Turki's side won.

Azzan and his brother Ibrahim, who had meantime wrested the fortress of al Hazm, which this branch of the family still possesses, from the descendants of the Ya'ruba dynasty, retired to Sohar. Turki, supported by Saif ibn Sulaiman of the Bani Riyam, won part of the Sharqiya over and advanced on the capital. Azzan and Saif ibn Sulaiman were killed in battle at Mutrah.

Turki assumed the rule but had no easy passage, for Salim, Ibrahim ibn Qais, Salih ibn Ali of the Hirth, and Abdul Aziz ibn Said, Turki's younger brother, were all in opposition, though fortunately for Turki, not united. Turki was recognised as Sultan by the British in November 1871 (1288 AH), an advantage which Azzan ibn Qais had never had, though recognition of him was about to be forthcoming just before Turki supplanted him. It was not until 1875 (1292 AH) that Ibrahim ibn Qais made submission to the Sultan and thus began paving the way, as it were, for the very long service which his son Ahmad was to give to Sultan Said ibn Taimur, up to 1970 (1390 AH), as his Minister of the Interior. However, troubles between Hinawis and Ghafiris persisted, and in 1874 (1291 AH) Salih ibn Ali sacked Mutrah and attempted to take Muscat. This humiliation, together with ill health and the influence of an unscrupulous adviser named Numaish who quickly amassed a dubious fortune, prevented Turki from fulfilling early promise. In 1875 (1292 AH) he retired to Gwadur and his brother Abdul Aziz, with whom he had become reconciled, assumed the regency in Oman. In 1873 (1290 AH) Salim again attempted to return to Oman but was captured by H.M.S. *Daphne* and sent to Hyderabad in Sind, an area with which Oman has had much contact through the ages. There he died disappointed in 1874 (1291 AH).

In 1875 (1292 AH) with health and spirits restored, Turki staged a surprising come-back, landing at Mutrah unannounced whilst his brother Abdul Aziz was away in the Wadi Samail, and resuming the rule. In 1877 (1294 AH) Salih ibn Ali and the *Mutawwain* accused Turki of "irreligiousness and laxity of morals" and launched another attack on the capital. The British responded to the Sultan's request for assistance, and H.M.S. *Teazer* shelled the rebels in the *wadi* behind the town. This was enough to give Turki strength to carry on, but in 1883 (1301 AH) Salih ibn Ali decided to make a further supreme effort to depose Turki, in alliance with Abdul Aziz ibn Said.

They informed Colonel Miles, the British Political Agent, that an attack on Muscat was impending and requested that British subjects should be removed out of harm's way. Abdul Aziz himself led a bold night attack on the walls of Muscat, the attackers clothed in black to give them extra protection, and Turki went to the ramparts to rally the defence. The attack was repulsed and Abdul Aziz' forces fell back on Sidab on the outskirts. Turki then appealed to the British Political Agent, and after British subjects had taken to boats, H.M.S. *Philomel* shelled the rebel positions. This, combined with the timely arrival of friendly shaikhs of the Hirth and Masakira, enabled Turki to win the day. Turki's second son, Faisal, pursued the rebels and brought the tribes back to allegiance. In the latter part of his reign, Turki reverted to dependence on the Ghafiri tribes, who had won the battles of Dhank and Muscat for him, rather than the Hinawi tribes on whom he depended in his middle period.

Turki used his own relations and other prominent and able men in his administration, including Said ibn Muhammad and a strong character of slave stock, Sulaiman ibn Suwailim. He had a good reputation for sound judgement and was a good ruler, enjoying the friendship and regard of the British authorities in India, who presented him with two batteries of 12-pounder guns for the Muscat forts. He made a treaty in 1873 (1290 AH) with Sir Bartle Frere for the suppression of the slave trade and made sincere efforts to enforce it.

In 1879 (1297 AH) Dhofar was re-occupied by troops from northern Oman after an interval of fifty years. At the beginning of the nineteenth century Dhofar had been ruled by Muhammad ibn Aqil Ajaibi, a former buccaneer and slave trader who governed it in a strangely enlightened manner for about twenty-five years. He was, however, assassinated in 1829 (1245 AH) and thereupon Said ibn Sultan sent a force to occupy Dhofar though, as the troops were required for service in east Africa, it did not stay long. Dhofar may earlier

have been subject to the Ya'ruba Imams, but it is not clear how firmly their writ ran. At a much earlier period in history, the Hadhramaut as well as Dhofar had formed part of the Omani Ibadhi state. Although a separate Hadhrami Ibadhi state had persisted for a while, the Ibadhis had disappeared from south Arabia by the thirteenth century AD.

After Muhammad ibn Aqil's death, an American, Abdulla Lorleyd, who had been captured as a boy of ten at sea in one of Muhammad ibn Aqil's piracies and turned Muslim, established some degree of personal autonomy by organising daring expeditions against the Qara tribes. Nonetheless, after 1829 (1245 AH), the shaikhs of Dhofar seem always to have paid homage on the succession of a new Sultan in Muscat. Despite this, there was a strange interlude between 1875 (1292 AH) and 1879 (1297 AH) when Dhofar fell into the hands of Fadhl ibn Alawi, a Mopla priest expelled from India for his part in the Mopla rising of 1852 (1269 AH). The Dhofari shaikhs had apparently met him during a pilgrimage to Mecca, been impressed with his reputation for sanctity, and invited him to Dhofar. He quickly managed to gain temporal control and with remarkable effrontery sent a letter to the Sultan, Sayyid Turki, describing himself as the governor of Dhofar on behalf of the Ottoman Porte. However, his rule lasted only a brief period and in 1879 (1297 AH) a general revolution started by the Qara tribes forced him to leave the country.

Dhofar was regained for the Sultan by a sea expedition under Sulaiman ibn Suwailim, the ex-slave. Sulaiman ibn Suwailim's rule, exercised personally and through his son Ali, was heavy handed and the Al Kathir and Qara tribes made several attempts at rebellion. Meantime, Fadhl ibn Alawi continued to intrigue with the Ottoman *Wali* of Basra – who at one time sent a Turkish flag and a commission to Salala – and with the Khedive in Egypt to stage a come-back.

A further rebellion lasted from 1895 (1313 AH) until 1897 (1315 AH) and the British Resident in the Persian Gulf accompanied the Sultan's forces in H.M.S. *Cossack* to recover control. Thereafter, Omani administration improved markedly, but Fadhl again tried, unsuccessfully, to persuade the British Government to recognise him as the ruler of Dhofar with "a national flag, green with pentagonal ventre".

In 1888 (1306 AH) Turki died and was succeeded by his son Faisal, then twenty-three, and even Salih ibn Ali who had caused so much trouble to Turki, responded loyally. Faisal had married in 1881 his cousin Aliya, the daughter of Thuwaini, and this, along with continuance of the Zanzibar subsidy, helped to consolidate his position. It was not long, however,

Formal salutes were fired from ancient muzzle-loading cannon battery on the battlements of fort Mirani until 1973.

before opposition arose. Faisal's uncle, Abdul Aziz, attempted to take Muscat and the notorious Hamad ibn Jahafi, who had caused much trouble to Turki, also joined in. Dissensions between Hinawis and Ghafiris grew in intensity and tribal fighting broke out. In 1895 (1313 AH), a serious attempt at rebellion had the support of the new Sultan of Zanzibar. Until then, relations between the two Sultanates had been cordial, but in 1893 (1311 AH) Hamad ibn Thuwaini who had spent his earlier years in Oman, where he had many friends, succeeded Ali ibn Said in Zanzibar. A stream of Omanis made their way to Zanzibar in 1894 (1312 AH) and they encouraged Hamad to take over the Sultanate in Oman.

The rebels took Muscat and held it for a while until an accommodation was reached with British help. The rebellion, however, had alarmed Faisal who strengthened the defences of Muscat and Mutrah, but his difficulties were increased by shortage of money and the treachery of his *Wazir*, who was secretly involved with Shaikh Salih ibn Ali. Nonetheless he gradually expanded his influence again.

It was not long before Oman became a bone of contention between Britain and France, after the French and Russians had determined on concerted effort to weaken British influence around the Indian Ocean. The main Franco-British disagreements were over use of the French flag to protect Omani vessels – a practice to which Faisal as well as the British objected for it enabled slave-trading to be resumed, although this was not the French intention – the French desire to open a coaling station at Muscat, and the arms trade.

At the end of the century a kind of diplomatic duel for influence was fought out between the British Consul, Major (later Sir Percy) Cox and the French Consul, M. Ottavi. The British prevailed and Sultan Faisal revoked his gift to the French of a coaling station at Bandar Jissuh near Muscat. A compromise solution, however, provided for two coaling stations, one French and one British, of equal area and identical design in Muscat Bay and the buildings erected by each country were only knocked down in 1972 when the new Oman naval base was built on the site. Further differences between Britain and France were only cleared up as the *entente cordiale* developed and after reference to the Hague Tribunal of the flag dispute.

In 1901 Muscat was brought into telegraphic communication with the world by the connection of a cable from Muscat to Jask, which linked in with the Indo-European telegraph system. Although Oman remained independent, Britain's influence grew with the visit of Lord Curzon, then Viceroy of India in 1903, and, following an outbreak of bubonic plague, with the British Agency taking over responsibility for health and quarantine in Muscat.

Faisal's administration ran into considerable debt and his financial difficulties were multiplied by closure of the Indian mint, which caused him to mint *pice* in Muscat when the scarcity of Indian *pice* caused hardship to the poorer people. However, Faisal had no serious rival to the throne and his administration improved as he grew older.

In 1913 (1332 AH) Faisal, whose reign had latterly been relatively uneventful, died and was succeeded by Sayyid

Taimur, the offspring of his union with Sayyida Aliya. In the same year the tribes of the Interior, uniting again under an elected Imam, Salim ibn Rashid al Kharusi, rebelled. Taimur, who had been groomed to succeed his father was thus immediately faced with a serious situation, particularly as Hinawis and Ghafiris were united in their opposition to him.

In 1915 (1333 AH) the tribes of the Interior, led by the Imam, attacked the capital with the aid of Isa ibn Salih of the Hirth in the Sharqiya, but were repulsed by 700 British Indian troops at Bait al Falaj. A conference at Seeb between Taimur and the Imam in the same year was abortive as the latter refused to hand back the forts in the Wadi Samail which, captured in 1913 (1332 AH), were essential to Muscat's prosperity. The Sultan's subsequent demonstration of his ability to tax produce from the Interior led to a compromise in what has erroneously been termed "The Treaty of Seeb" on 25th September 1920 (1339 AH). Under this the Sultan agreed not to interfere in "internal affairs" in central Oman; not to impose taxation in excess of 5 per cent on goods brought from the Interior; and to allow the tribes to enter Muscat and the coastal towns in freedom and

safety. The tribes on the other hand agreed to remain in a state of peace and amity with the Sultan's Government. This administrative *modus vivendi* worked satisfactorily during the Imamate of Muhammad ibn Abdulla al Khalili, who succeeded Salim al Kharusi as Imam when the latter was murdered in 1920 (1339 AH), was Imam but things went badly wrong on his death in 1954 (1374 AH). Sayyid Taimur's reign, like his father's, was characterised by financial difficulties accentuated by the trade depression of 1923 (1342 AH) and 1924 (1343 AH). He appointed Mr Bertram Thomas, the well known author and Arabist, first as Financial Adviser, and later as *Wazir*, to help him overcome these difficulties. However, Taimur, who never had much stomach for the throne, abdicated in 1932 (1351 AH) in favour of his son, Sayyid Said ibn Taimur and lived in retirement in Bombay until his death in 1965 (1385 AH).

Sayyid Said took over a country still in debt and by his own sustained and patient efforts largely restored the situation. However, his careful stewardship, which enabled him to hand over the state's finances in a flourishing condition on the succession of Sultan Qaboos in 1970 (1390 AH), eventually alienated him from the people of Oman.

The first part of Said's reign was relatively uneventful, but the death of the Imam in 1954 (1374 AH), combined with the need for oil exploration in the Interior, led to an internal crisis which was heightened by Saudi aspirations in the area. The new Imam Ghalib ibn Ali attempted to establish central Oman as a separate principality independent of the Sultan and no doubt his dream of the possibility of oil wealth was a factor. In December 1955 (1375 AH) the Sultan's forces responded by entering the main inhabited areas of the Interior without resistance and the Imam was permitted to retire to his own village. However, his brother Talib, perhaps the more forceful of the two, escaped to Saudi Arabia and thence to Cairo. In 1957 (1377 AH) he returned and gained a considerable following, including Shaikh Sulaiman ibn Himyar, the paramount Shaikh of the Bani Riyam. Although they were defeated at a battle at Firq in August 1957 (1377 AH) following British intervention, the leaders maintained themselves for a considerable time in the mountain fastnesses and it was not until January 1959 (1379 AH) that they were driven out with the help of the British Special Air Service Regiment. Even then the "Question of Oman" remained a live issue in Arab and international politics

A view of Mutrah before Sultan Qaboos's accession. The picture shows the walls of the old city, whose gates were opened

and was inscribed yearly on the agenda of the United Nations, to which Said steadfastly refused to send any representation. The matter was finally resolved in 1971 (1391 AH) when the Sultanate of Oman under Sultan Qaboos, after other countries had ceased to back the separatist movement, was admitted to the Arab League and to the United Nations.

Earlier, the need to define boundaries for the purposes of oil concessions had involved Oman in dispute with Saudi Arabia, and this to some extent conditioned Saudi Arabia's attitude towards the dissident Imam. The Wahhabi incursions into Oman in the nineteenth century had never left them with any substantial control, and they had been turned out of the Buraimi area in 1870 (1287 AH) never to return until 1950 (1370 AH). In that year a Saudi force under Turki ibn Ataishan occupied the village of Hamasa, one of the villages in the Buraimi complex of oases, of which six fell within Abu Dhabi and three in the Sultanate. Sultan Said was minded to throw them out and mustered the tribes at Sohar with the intention of

at dawn and shut at sunset even after the wall had been breached to make a motor road. The gate collapsed in 1973.

marching on Buraimi in force. He was, however, restrained by the British Government and the case was put to arbitration – a process which dragged on unsatisfactorily until October 1955 (1375 AH), when Sultanate troops and the Trucial Oman Scouts ejected the Saudis.

It was perhaps Said's tragedy that after oil revenues had begun to accrue to Oman on an increasingly generous scale in 1967 (1387 AH), he was unable to abandon the habit of economy and careful husbandry which had been imposed on him at an earlier stage by hard necessity. He did initiate some plans for development but they were too small-scale to satisfy the widespread aspirations of his people for education and for medical and other services and amenities. This, combined with the isolation he had imposed on himself by remaining in Salala and never visiting northern Oman after 1958 (1328 AH), and the rebellion which started in Dhofar in 1965 (1384 AH), made the events of 1970 (1390 AH) and the take-over by Sultan Qaboos inevitable. Said died in exile in London in 1972 (1392 AH).

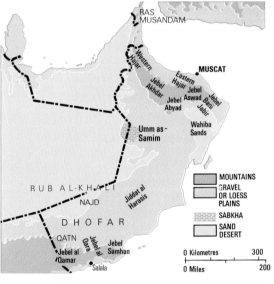

2 The Terrain

Oman possesses a rich and varied terrain. It is a land of contrasts, embracing the rocky heights of the Hajar mountains and the empty sands of the Rub' al-Khali; the Dhofar hills which turn green after the monsoon, and the flat unending plains; the majestic cliffs of the south, and neat villages set in barren wadis and girded by palm-groves; and a coastline ranging from hundreds of miles of flat beach to the rocky inlets of Musandam and Muscat.

High above his village, a farmer (far left) tends his rich crops amidst the wildness of the Jebel Akhdar. Besides its magnificent mountains and cultivated areas, Oman's terrain includes sand deserts (top left), vast plains where camels graze (above left), and a rugged coastline (left). The map shows the distribution of the types of terrain throughout the country.

Geography, Climate & Geology

OMAN is a land of contrasts. Stark mountains, high and jagged; flat un-ending plains stretching as far as the eye can see; neat villages girded by great green palm groves serenely set in barren *wadis* and strung out along the ocean shore; deserts rolling away into the Rub'al-Khali – the Empty Quarter, that great sand sea of Arabia with mighty waves and dunes rising to six hundred feet or more; a varied coastline ranging from hundreds of miles of flat beach to the rocky inlets of Musandam and Muscat; the hills of Dhofar, which catch the south-west monsoon in the summer and turn green like no other part of Arabia; and the majestic cliffs of this Southern Region. The area is 120,000 square miles, the size of the United Kingdom and Ireland, and the coastline along the Gulf of Oman runs for some 1,000 miles. It is rather a sparsely peopled country and, with perhaps 750,000 inhabitants, has a population density of only 6.1 per square mile.

The Arab names of many of the geographical features are as evocative

Above: *Seamen of the Musandam peninsula trade across the Straits of Hormuz.*

Below: *Sur's indented coastline offers shelter to the seafarer.*

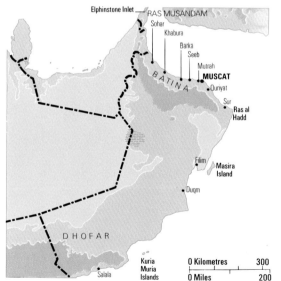

The ports which lie on Oman's coast (map above) *have contributed much to her past prosperity. Seen from the air, the coastline between Muscat and Sur* (right and opposite) *presents an inhospitable face to the stranger.*

as they are descriptive. The highest massif of the great backbone of Oman, for instance, is called the Jebel Akhdar, the "Green Mountain", even though it is green only by comparison with the arid areas surrounding it – and in places its rock is green – and does not match up to the rolling down-lands which the name suggests. Jebel Shams, the "Mountain of the Sun", is the highest point of the Hajar range and towers to 10,000 feet. Ru'us al Jibal, the "Heads of the Mountains", well describes the peaks in the Musandam peninsula which itself means "the anvil", on which the waves constantly strike their hammer blows. The great sand sea to the east is succinctly called *ar-rimal*, the sands, and few people venture there, except for the *Bedu*, who have the knowledge and endurance to cross these waterless regions.

In the extreme north of the country lies the Musandam peninsula which, known to ancient geographers as Cape Maka or Maketa, resembles a sub-tropical Norway with great fjords and inlets. The Hajar range, which stretches for four hundred miles from Cape Musandam to Ras al Hadd in a mighty sweeping curve running roughly from north-west to south-east is the main feature of northern Oman. The range rises in the Jebel Akhdar region in central Oman to 10,000 feet and gives Oman its general shape and its character. The Arabs liken it to a man's backbone, calling the area which lies on the Gulf of Oman the Batina, or "stomach", and the area to the west of the hills the Dhahira, or "back". The Batina consists of a coastal plain built up over the centuries by the outwash from the many *wadis* which descend from the mountains. This is the principal agricultural and date-growing area, and the palm gardens, watered by wells drawing on subterranean run-off from the hills, stretch northwards from Muscat for some two hundred miles with scarcely a gap. The natural vegetation of this area consists of thorny acacias of

Today a plaything, tomorrow a grim warning, this wreck teaches these sailors' children playing in Sur creek (above) the need for unceasing vigilance on the sea. Below: Masira Island, ancient landfall of seafarers, also famous for its turtles, today has strategic importance.

Oman's ships like this launch (the Omanis never use the word dhow) *have worked the coast for centuries.*

Below: *A simple wind tower may be seen along this beach at Sohar.*

various types, hardy perennial desert plants and, after rain, grass and other herbs germinating from dormant seed.

The Dhahira area on the other side of the mountains is also an outwash plain, with similar characteristics, trailing away into the desert to the west and the settlements there, such as Ibri and Dhank, depend on water led down from the hills by an ancient but sophisticated system of water channels – *falajes*.

The Hajar range is divided by a number of great *wadi* passes which run through the mountains from the desert to the sea, the Wadi Ham in the United Arab Emirates to the north, the Wadi al Qor, the Wadi Hawasina, the Wadi Jizzi and the Wadi Samail – to name the most significant. The Wadi Samail is the greatest and most striking and is regarded as the major "divide". The Omanis, therefore, call the area to the west of it the Gharbiya, or western Jebel, and the area to the east of it the Sharqiya, or eastern Jebel. To reach the

The Hajar range, stretching "in a mighty sweeping curve" from Musandam to Ras al Hadd, dominates the geography of northern Oman. The peaks rise to 10,000 feet, and man, by tenacity and ingenuity, has built for himself a life against the flanks of the mountains. The vertebrae of the range are divided by deep wadis.

settled villages of the Sharqiya area, however, the strategic Wadi Akk has to be crossed. At the southern end of the Sharqiya lies the area known as Jaalan, which includes the Bilad Bani bu Hassan, the Bilad Bani bu Ali and Sur.

The main geographical areas of northern Oman are reflected in the earlier historical division of the country into five *wilayat*, or governorates. These were Batina, based on Sohar, Sharqiya, based on Samad, Dhahira based on Ghabbi near Ibri, Sir based on Nizwa and al Jauf based on Buraimi. The Buraimi area formerly comprised several villages of palms fed by the ancient and prolific supply of *falaj* water and now lies partly in the Sultanate and partly in Abu Dhabi (United Arab Emirates). It has at various times in Omani history been called al Jau, as well as al Jauf, and Tuam, but these terms are now but little used.

South of the Sharqiya lie the Wahiba sands, a wedge-shaped sand sea about a hundred miles long and about fifty miles wide. It stretches on the seaward side from near Ras al Hadd and from Mudhairib in the Sharqiya to Filim on the coast in the Gulf of Masira with valleys running roughly north to south about half a mile wide and enclosed by dunes of a uniform two hundred feet in height. The dunes are rusty red at the base and honey-coloured higher up – blocked at periodic intervals by gradual rises of hard sand. Water is scarce but there is a well at Tawi Harian – important for those who cross this inhospitable track.

To the west of the Wahiba sands there is a broad belt, about a hundred and fifty miles wide, of gravel plain broken by *wadis* running north to south, such as the Wadi Halfain and Wadi Andam, which emanates from the Hajar range. To the west of the *wadis* and south of Yibal, which is now one of Oman's producing oilfields, lies a large area of quicksands, known as Umm as-Samim, adjoining the border with Saudi Arabia. Wilfred Thesiger, the first European

known to have seen them, described them thus: "The ground, of white gypsum powder, was covered with a sand-sprinkled crust of salt, through which protruded occasional dead twigs of *arad* salt-bush. These scattered bushes marked the firm land; farther out, only a slight darkening of the surface indicated the bog below. I took a few steps forward and Staiyun (one of Thesiger's companions) put his hand on my arm saying, 'Don't go any nearer – it is dangerous'. I wondered how dangerous it really was, but when I questioned him he assured me that several people, including an Awamir raiding party, had perished in these sands, and he told me once again how he had himself watched a flock of goats disappear beneath the surface." The extent of this phenomenon is said by the desert Arabs to be a two-days' march in every direction and only a few Duru tribesmen are aware of the safe routes across it.

South-west of Masira Island there is an enormous area of flat gravel plain called Jiddat al Harasis, where the *Bedu* of the Harasis tribe live. There are a few water holes and strange traditions surround some of them. For instance, Umm as-Shadid, which is thirty-six fathoms deep was, according to local lore, "made by a falling star and not by the sons of Adam". The Jiddat al Harasis is not lifeless – or was not until hunting parties virtually wiped out the game there in very recent years – as Thesiger witnessed in 1956: "Gazelle grazed among the flat topped acacia bushes and once we saw a distant herd of oryx looking very white against the dark gravel of the plain. There were lizards about eighteen inches in length, which scuttled across the ground. They had disc-shaped tails, and in consequence the Arabs called them 'The Father of the Dollar'".

This area of steppe merges into the steppe area to the north of the mountainous region of Dhofar called Najd, the area from which the best frankin-

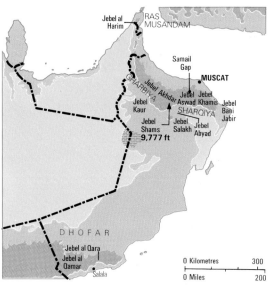

The wild grandeur of the Jebel Akhdar typifies the scenery of the highlands. In spite of the forbidding starkness settlements (right) perch on high plateaux, or cling to hillsides with their terraced fields. The map (above) shows the extent of the highlands of Oman.

The waterless faces of the Jebel Akhdar (above) *can be grim indeed but on these mountain sides, in the terraced fields irrigated by* falajes, *wheat, maize, alfalfa, peaches, apricots, figs and walnuts can be grown.*

cense, for which Dhofar is famous, comes.

There are stories of a lost city called Ubar (or Wabar) which may have lain in the sands just to the north of this frankincense-producing area and one of Bertram Thomas's companions during his desert exploration in 1930 found an undamaged pottery jar and other sherds in the sand near the Wadis Mitan and Fasad. An old camel route, across what are now almost impenetrable sands, lay from Mitan to the ancient Gerrha and Ubar may have lain on this. Arab tradition ascribes the city to the ancient Arabian tribe of Ad, who deserted it when it lost its water supply, though some say that its Ad inhabitants suffered some severe heavenly punishment for their sins. Whatever the real explanation there is evidence of sands creeping

The great ranges of Oman are known to contain copper, asbestos, manganese and salt. In the past, copper was extensively mined. A remarkable feature of Oman's geology are the geodes – hollow stones lined with crystals – which are found in the desert areas of northern Dhofar.

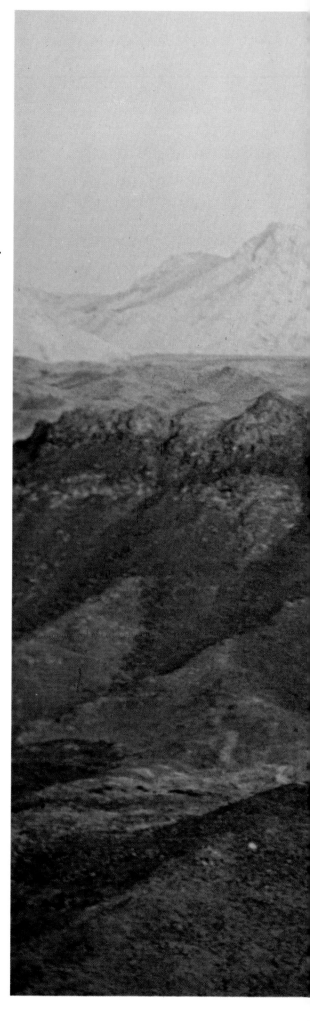

southwards and of gradually increasing desiccation.

To the south of the Najd the mountain range of Dhofar rises. It runs nearly due west opposite the Kuria Muria Islands to the border with South Yemen and the three distinctive areas of mountain form a continuous chain. The easternmost area is called Jebel Samhan, the centre Jebel al Qara, after the Qara tribe, and the western massif Jebel al Qamar or the "Mountain of the Moon". The range extends for some hundred and twenty miles and has a depth of only about twenty miles. It is one of the natural phenomena of Arabia, for these mountains catch the south-west monsoon between June and September – the only part of the south coast of Arabia to do so – and attract a heavier rainfall than any other part of Oman. In consequence the southern faces are covered with a brilliant green which for a few brief months gives them the appearance of Tuscany. The vegetation however soon turns to yellow and from November onwards Dhofar looks more like parts of Africa. These mountains of Dhofar which rise only to some 3,000 to 4,000 feet present a very curious sight from the air, with their heavily vegetated southern faces and almost entirely bald northern faces. Between the mountains and the sea there is a narrow coastal plain, about thirty miles in length and at its maximum five miles in width. Salala, the capital, and the other main towns of the southern region – Marbat, Taqa and Awkat – are situated on this plain.

Whereas the date palm is distinctive of northern Oman, the coconut palm reigns supreme in Dhofar, where the climate is not conducive to date growing. However, the fertile Salala plain, which in the past was very much more extensively cultivated than it is now, can produce a great variety of crops and vegetables. Considerable quantities were grown there for British troops in Mesopotamia in the 1914–18 war.

Salala is over six hundred miles by road from Muscat and the road lies across terrain which until recently was the haunt only of the *Bedu* and oil exploration parties. Historically the sea has, therefore, been the main means of communication between the Southern Region of Dhofar and northern Oman though air communication has become important in recent years.

The main towns of Oman are either on the coast or in the Interior and their *raison d'être* differs. The coastal towns have for countless generations provided a livelihood for fishermen, sailors and merchants involved in the import and export trade and pearling. On the other hand the main towns of the Interior are dependent on important agricultural areas and form centres for the despatch of produce to the coast and the receipt of goods for distribution in the Interior. Some towns too, such as Nizwa, Rostaq and Muscat, have acquired special significance because of their military strength – there were massive forts at all three of these places – and because they were all capitals of Oman at various periods, Muscat being the present one.

One small town which epitomises Oman is Tiwi. Ibn Batuta, who visited Oman in the fourteenth century AD, described Tiwi, which is north of Qalhat on the coast, as "one of the loveliest of villages and most striking in beauty, with flowing streams and abundant orchards". The Wadi Tiwi, which runs inland from the village, is one of the most remarkable in Oman and gives an indication of how extensively some of the other *wadis* may have been cultivated in the past. It is a *wadi* with constantly flowing water and both sides are thick with palms for many miles inland. The unique feature, however, is that the cultivated areas are on numerous small terraces which rise to a greater height above the *wadi* bed than in any other valley in the country.

The mountains of the north glow golden; their wealth includes copper.

The long tradition of agriculture has been sustained by skilled use of water. The plainlands and mountains are far from rainless – indeed flash floods can bring havoc; one Imam, in 807 AD, was drowned with seventy of his people, crossing a wadi. The challenge is to contain and distribute the water.

Climate

Oman is situated at the margin of two moisture-bearing air masses, one coming from the Mediterranean and the other from the Indian Ocean, and in consequence rainfall is irregular. The Mediterranean currents sometimes fade out, which results in lower precipitation than usual whilst the summer rain brought by the Indian Ocean air currents may not materialise if their track in any particular year does not quite reach the Oman peninsula.

Although January tends to be the month with the heaviest rainfall the pattern of precipitation is erratic. For instance in 1972 total rainfall was 108 mm of which 92.95 mm fell in February. In Muscat the average rainfall is 90.3 mm though in some years this amount is greatly exceeded, and in the Jebel Akhdar the rainfall may reach 250 mm or even 400–500 mm in an exceptional year.

Sometimes several inches fall within a few hours turning the dry *wadi* beds into rushing torrents which sweep everything before them – trees, boulders, goats and other animals, and sometimes people and cars. The boiling waters may subside after a few hours but this leaves a wake of desolation although, of course, the rain benefits the country generally by recharging the water tables. A particularly tragic example of flash flood occurred in June 1890 when a cyclonic storm hit Oman and between midnight on the 4th and midnight on the 5th, 11.24 inches (28.3 mm) of rain fell. The waters rose with such violence that seven hundred people were drowned. The Imam himself, al Warith ibn Kaab, was drowned in 807 AD (192 AH) near Nizwa with seventy of his people; all were washed away as they tried to cross the Wadi Kalbuh.

Climatically, however, Oman has enjoyed a less savoury reputation than perhaps it deserves. The Arab geographer Abdul Razak wrote of Muscat in the fourteenth century with some hyperbole: "The heat . . . was so intense that it burned the marrow in the bones, the sword in its scabbard melted into wax and the gems which adorned the handle of the dagger were reduced to coal. In the plains the chase became a matter of perfect ease for the desert was strewn with roasted gazelles." Both Alexander Hamilton and John Ovington who visited Oman in the early eighteenth century referred to people cooking fish on the dark rocks surrounding Muscat in the heat of summer while Grattan Geary, the editor of the *Times of India*, who visited Muscat in 1878, remarked that when the Shamal, the hot wind from the desert, blows, the sleepers are watered during the night like plants with a watering pot. Other devices were also used to keep people cool before air-conditioning was introduced and it was the custom in Muscat to sleep on the roof in a damp sheet. Mrs Cox, the wife of the British Political Agent at the turn of the nineteenth–twentieth century, gave herself pneumonia by an *excès de zèle* in substituting a blanket for a sheet!

These literary passages and similar ones referring to Muscat as the hottest place on earth indicate how people felt in the past about Oman's climate. The facts are that the daily average maximum temperature in Muscat reaches 41°C in the height of summer, in late June and July, whereas by contrast the highest daily average temperatures recorded in Salala in Dhofar reach only just under 30°C in the hottest month, May. The minimum average temperature for Muscat is 16.3°C and for Salalah 18.5°C. The relative humidity in Muscat ranges between 94 per cent in July and 20 per cent in May whilst in Salala it ranges between 96 per cent in August and 54 per cent in December.

Geology

The Hajar range of Oman comprises three very different forms of topography, the highly desiccated limestone country, an area of weathered igneous rocks of which serpentine is the most conspicu-

Omani agricultural enterprise and skill is displayed on the plainland fields (left). Below: *The oasis near Sur contains the fort of the* Wali, *the governor of the area.*

ous, and the area of limestone plateau. The mountains at the northern tip of Oman, the Ru'us al Jibal or Musandam peninsula, are an example of the first group, and the predominating "Musandam limestone", which, though much folded, is 5,000 feet thick, is of Jurassic or Lower Cretaceous age. This is an area of drowned valleys which stretch up to nine miles inland, where the soft Triassic shales and sandstone can be seen under the massive Musandam limestone. The most spectacular of these fjords, which have no counterpart in Arabia or Persia, is the Khor as Sham, or the Elphinstone Inlet named after a Governor of Bombay in the early nineteenth century. The country south and south-west of Muscat, behind the belt of serpentine which surrounds the town itself, bears resemblance to Ru'us al Jibal, though it is not so magnificent.

The second group is the Samail igneous series which consists of intrusive rocks – diorite, gabbro and serpentine –

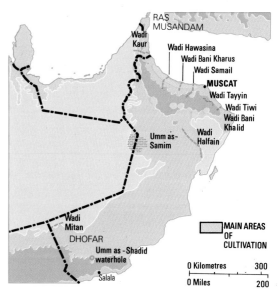

The plainlands of Oman are irrigated by falajes *and wells, using water brought from the mountains and underground aquifers. The farmers need a steady and reliable water supply for their fields; the main areas of cultivation are shown above.*

and of lava-flows such as keratophyres and basalt. It covers a larger area than other formations and a continuous belt of it stretches from the south end of the Musandam limestone to the northern end of the Jebel Akhdar. It is also found, *inter alia*, in Wadi Samail, Wadi Tayyin, Ras al Hadd and Masira Island.

The third group is most prominently represented in the great central scarp of the Jebel Akhdar itself, a towering mass of limestone with an almost vertical limestone face looking seaward over a range of low broken hills. The crest of this central range is formed by a great plateau, which falls gradually away south-westward. The summit is thus as easy of access from this side as it is difficult from the north-east.

The greater part of Oman, including the Jebel Akhdar, was submerged by the sea in Upper Cretaceous or early Tertiary times when the earlier folded rocks were covered by limestone or marlsand, and extensive dislocation and faulting

The Wadi Hawasina, swelled by welcome rainfall, is full of water.

together with up-lift in some areas and down-throw in others has resulted in marine platforms at various levels throughout the range. Odd features like the peak of Jebel Kaur which is an exotic also occur, and there are many marine fossils even at the mountain tops.

Thus Oman consists essentially of a great up-fold of metamorphic and igneous rock resting on sedimentaries, mainly Cretaceous limestone. The Oman range appears to be an extension of the great Zagros range in southern Persia, though the Oman folding movements are Cretaceous and thus earlier than those of the Pliocene Zagros. Only twenty-nine miles separate Oman from Persia at the Straits of Hormuz. Indeed the present-day marine Gulf dates only from about 9000 BC before which the area north of the Straits of Hormuz lay above sea level for several millennia – a dry lowland

A farmer of the Wadi Hawasina valley enjoys a brief rest.

with lakes and river valleys. The post-Ice Age invasion by the ocean was the last major episode in the complex geological history of the area.

It is not surprising that the great ranges of Oman contain considerable mineral deposits, though it remains to be seen how many will be exploited commercially. Copper, asbestos, magnesite, potash, phosphate, coal, chromite, manganese and salt have all been found, but copper is the only one of them to have been exploited in the past.

Geodes are a strange geological feature of Oman. These nodular stones with a cavity lined with crystals are found in the desert area of Dhofar, north of the Upper Cretaceous and Eocene limestone of the mountainous zone and were originally formed when the earth in hot ferment emitted large bubbles of gases from its surface.

Flora and Fauna

Oleander, bulrushes, sedge and fruit trees flourish in the wadis.

The flora of Oman are very much dependent on the rainfall and after plentiful rains, small plants and flowers appear in profusion including recognisable northern-type flowers such as a tiny wild pansy and cowslip. At such times the desert literally blooms. In the *wadis* oleander flourishes, together with grasses, bulrushes and sedge. In deep valleys *sawga,* a plant with a scented orange-coloured flower, is found. In the cultivated gardens along the *wadi* beds, for example in the Wadi Bani Kharus, you may see in early spring peach, apricot and almond blossom, celandine, speedwell and a form of small dandelion.

On open ground the commonest form of vegetation is the camel-thorn, *knib* or *nabag,* the leaves of which are eaten by the children as sweets. There are also several varieties of spiky acacia, such as *samra* and *sunt,* which produce a yellow mimosa-like flower. The *ashgar,* or sodom-apple with its purple flowers, flourishes in poor soil. The hillside vegetation consists largely of small trees called *surra* with a profusion of flowers in spring. On the Jebel Akhdar and other plateaux there is a steppe vegetation with low scrub, bushes and small trees. In fact the Jebel Akhdar, as its name implies, supports a relatively prolific vegetation. The thorn apple is used as a source of anaesthetic, and from the yellow flowers of *Carthamus tinctorius* comes henna which is used by Omani women as a face cosmetic. Other plants found in the Jebel Akhdar include the Oman violet, a pink and purple mountain flower (also found in Persia), cotton plants, wild potatoes, and several species which are related to Alpine plants found in the Mediterranean area and are apparently survivals from the last Ice Age; there are also northern and Indian plant species which include primula, violet, juniper and honeysuckle, and of course grasses. Poisonous plants are not uncommon, and include calatropis, whose pink flower is deceptively pretty. Among species found on the comparatively well-wooded northern face in the spring of a year of good rain are *Juniperus macropoda, Euphorbia, Euryops pinifolius, Sagaretia, Ephedra,* asparagus, *Dodonaea viscosa, Periploca aphylla,* as well as various kinds of thistle. There is also a thorny tree with black berries, known as *but,* which is one of the plants eaten for food by the *tahr.*

The Falaj System

Falaj means a system for the distribution of water amongst those who have an established right to supply. It is commonly used to describe the irrigation channel system downstream of the point where the water originates. Thus it may mean a channel tapping a flow in the upper gravels of a *wadi* (*ghayl*) or a man-made mine in which the water is brought to the surface by an underground tunnel (*qanat*).

The course of a qanat falaj *is marked by the series of access holes used in tunnelling. The access holes are left open after tunnelling as inspection vents.*

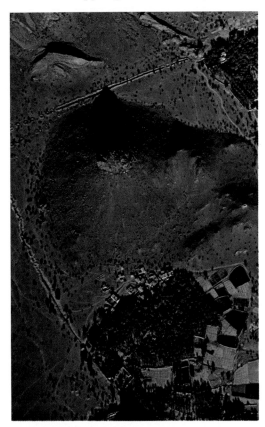

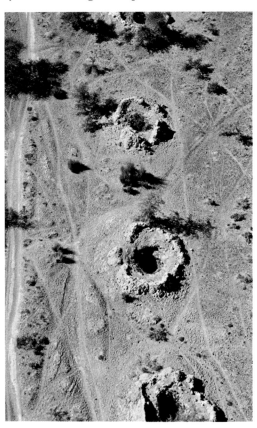

Wildlife

"A mythical and heraldic animal" is the dictionary description of the unicorn but the legend may derive from the actual Arabian oryx, whose two horns look like a single one when this timid animal is viewed from a distance – or sometimes it may grow only a single horn. The oryx was until recently found in considerable numbers in Oman, particularly in the desert area south-west of Muscat, such as the Jiddat al Harasis, but, sadly, hunting parties from Gulf states have probably rendered this graceful species of white antelope extinct in its wild state in Arabia, though fortunately there are several herds in captivity. The horns of the oryx are much prized, however mistakenly, as an aphrodisiac and are also used to effect cures, for example for snake-bite.

Oman has a number of species peculiar to it. One of these is the *tahr* or Jayakar's mountain goat (*Hemitragus jayakari*), named after Dr Jayakar, the resident surgeon in the British Agency in Muscat from 1870 to 1900. It is a shy, wary animal which generally prefers high isolated places. It stands about two feet high and is light sandy brown in colour with a very prominent black dorsal crest (more prominent in males and absent in the young) and dark markings on the face, legs and elsewhere. It has a large black muzzle with a distinct pale streak leading from the front of the eye towards the corner of the mouth. Both sexes have horns, rarely more than sixteen inches long, curving backwards behind the ear like an ibex; the animal is in fact similar to the ibex and both species are called *wa'al* in Arabic. It used to be much more prolific but is now in danger of extinction as it is shot for meat which is regarded as particularly excellent in the female. However, conservation measures are being taken; in Jebel Aswad, where the *tahr* is found, game wardens have been organised to protect the species.

The gazelle, *dhabi*, which used to abound, has now also been reduced to very small numbers by hunting parties and the same applies to the Marica gazelle, *rhim* (*Gazella subguttorosa marica*), which used to inhabit the edge of the Rub' al-Khali. Other species which are indigenous, but as far back as 1968 were in danger of extinction due to excessive hunting, are the Goitred gazelle, of which the Marica gazelle is a race, and the Dorcas gazelle.

Foxes abound and leopard, wild cat and panther still survive. Wolves howl in the mountains of the Jebel Akhdar and in Dhofar, where the striped hyena and the porcupine are still also to be found. There are also hyrax, the coneys of the Bible, the Arabian hare, and the black hedgehog (*Paraechinus hypomelas*) – a relict species found only in Oman, South Yemen, Iran and Russian Turkestan – in the Jebel Akhdar, though the Ethiopian hedgehog is more widely distributed. Among the smaller creatures, there are jerboa, Cheesman's gerbil, the spiny mouse, the common mouse and rat, and several kinds of bat including the Egyptian fruit bat, the Oman mouse-tailed bat and the large naked-bellied tomb bat. Lizards, some of which are aggressive and reach two feet in length and others which may be eaten when necessary by the *Bedu*, are found in varying guise all over the country. The Jebel Akhdar is the natural habitat of a number of these rarer animals and, with the approval of the Sultan, it was chosen as the site for the establishment of a national park where they could be protected, with the co-operation of local tribesmen, who would be materially compensated for the loss of their hunting ground. Besides being the home of the black hedgehog and the spiny mouse, it also harbours toads, whose camouflage markings make them hard to see, the Egyptian vulture, which has distinctive black and yellow colouring, a large species of dragonfly and a number of rare butterflies.

The arrival of a swarm of locusts is welcomed by the *Bedu*, who catch and eat them and, in years when they come in such numbers as to devastate the crops, they can in compensation be seen for sale in mounds in the market places of the towns.

Among the less attractive creatures there is the horned viper (*Cerastes cornutus*) found in many parts of Oman, and a diminutive boa is found in the sands. The harmless colubrid snake is found in wet *wadis*, and there are puff adders and other vipers, including a relict species with horns (*Pseudocerastes persicus*) found in the Jebel Akhdar. Great spiders some three or four inches in length with hairy legs, pendulous bodies and a nasty bite, are also common as are centipedes up to six inches long, black beetles, many varieties of fly, mosquitoes near pools, biting ants and termites which make conical mounds on

The ghayl falaj *does not involve as much labour in construction as the underground* falaj. *Although the channel may run for several miles, the* water is drawn directly from a wadi source. A falaj *in the Wadi Samail* (above) *is divided and runs both east and west of the hills.*

67

In the sands that nomads now inhabit, just beyond the region that provided incense for the world, it is said there lies a lost city.

the Salala plain similar to those in Africa. Small fish, which eat debris and nibble the toes of bathers help to keep the *falajes* clean, and are also common in *wadi* pools, in which they mysteriously reappear even when a pool has been dried up for some years. There are molluscs such as freshwater snails, and toads are numerous. Butterflies of great beauty flit round the gardens and cultivations and are specially plentiful around the Jebel Akhdar and the Qara mountains of Dhofar: *charaxes, danaidae, nymphalidae, pieridae, lycaenidae, hesperidae* and other varieties.

Although there is so much varied wild life, if often takes a long time to discover it and the visitor is not likely to meet too many of the less attractive species.

Birds
Oman has birds of many varieties, rare and common, migratory and domestic. Magpies and crows in large numbers fly along the Batina coast and amongst

the palm groves there is always a constant clamour of bird song. Along the coast there are flamingoes, herons and gulls, duck, geese, waders and tern. Inland there are Francolin partridge, sand grouse, bulbul and the beautiful bee-eater. The eagle soars high over the mountains and kites and Egyptian vultures are to be seen everywhere. There are also Upchers warblers, the brown babbler, the yellow vented bulbul, Hume's chat and the wheatear of Arabia.

Falconry is the great sport of Arabia but it is not practised much in Oman except by the tribes of the Dhahira. Two types of hawk, the peregrine and gyre-falcon, are flown against the quarry – usually McQueen's bustard, a winter visitor – and rabbits, hares (*Lepus capensis omanensis*) or small gazelle.

Domestic Animals
The domestic animals of this part of Arabia are goat, sheep, cattle – in small numbers except in Dhofar – chickens

The grazing and water rights of the Bedu are defined by traditional usage.

and of course dogs, including the graceful saluki, and cats. The country is more suitable generally for goats than for sheep. Omani camels are some of the finest, fleetest and most graceful in Arabia. The donkeys of the Jebel Akhdar are some of the sturdiest and fleet of foot, with greater powers of endurance than the hardworking and patient donkeys of the plains and lowlands.

Horses
For many generations horses were exported from Oman to India on a considerable scale. Ibn Batuta, writing in the fourteenth century, mentions the export of thoroughbred horses from Dhofar, and Marco Polo, writing earlier, in the thirteenth century, refers to the export of fine Arabian horses – not only from Dhofar, but also from Qalhat.

Albuquerque in the sixteenth century

comments on the export of horses from Qalhat, Muscat and Khor Fakkan, and horse and cattle breeding in the Sohar region. The trade statistics show that Oman was still exporting horses to India – many were required as mounts for the Army – in the first half of the nineteenth century, though some of these may have originated in Persia.

The Bani Battash tribe, who live in the Wadi Tayyin area inland from Quriyat, were amongst the most famous horse breeders. The Bani Jabir, the largest tribe in Oman – tracing their descent from the ancient Arab tribe of Dhubyan, famous in Arab poetry – were also renowned as horse breeders.

Omani tradition holds that the Ya'rubi Imam, Saif ibn Sultan, had no less than 90,000 horses in his Regular Army, quite apart from those owned by individuals, and even if one allows for some exaggeration, this is still an enormous number in a country where there are now so few. Other records refer to thousands of horses being used in various campaigns in Oman in past centuries.

It is thus clear that Oman was, until relatively recently, an important horse breeding and exporting country, which gives yet another indication that the area under cultivation in previous generations must have been considerably larger than that to which it had sunk by 1970, for feed, grazing and hay must have come largely from irrigated areas.

Horse breeding has frequently been an absorbing interest for Oman's rulers. Wellsted, who visited Oman in 1835, described Sayyid Said ibn Sultan's stud: "Several of the Imam's horses are of the noblest breed in Najd, some of his mares being valued at from 1,500 to 2,000 dollars; and one horse, the most perfect and beautiful creature I ever saw, was considered to be worth an equal sum. He maintains a portion of his stud at Muscat; but the greater number is at Barka and Suweik, where they pay great attention to the breed and rearing of these noble animals." The present Sultan's interest in horses is, therefore, based on a very long Omani tradition.

Marine Life

The long sandy beach of the Batina is alive with crabs emerging from their burrows and scurrying into the sea like visitors, with their protruding antennae, from another planet. Their cousins, the hermit crabs, gather in huddles and exchange shells on the beach making a curious clacking noise as shells rub against each other. The myriads of crabs display the richness of the coasts of Oman in marine life great and small.

The water in Muscat seems to boil with fish, the sea is so full of them. There are whales, whale sharks, and sharks, though it is extremely rare for one of these to attack a man in Omani waters. There are swordfish, sailfish, tuna, King Mackerel, barracuda, garruppa and rays; flying fish and richly coloured tropical fish of all sizes, like the parrot and the angel fish; snappers and sardines.

Dolphins gambol in their schools in the harbour at Muscat and often play round the bows of the wooden ships. Sometimes, too, the great whales are equally playful and Bertram Thomas describes how: "A playful whale helped to beguile the moments – a ponderous dark green monster that came and lay alongside us like a submarine beside its parent ship, proud to prove itself not much smaller than the *Fath as Salam* [the local craft on which Thomas was travelling]. It seemed to me perilously friendly as it dived just under us, to rise but a few feet away and break surface with a snort, before sinking heavily again, with a little wash and multitude of bubbles to mark its going. Nor were our sailors unconcerned. With an eye on our dinghy, which lapped about astern of us, they kept up a frightening din by drumming empty kerosene tins. The wind freshened to deliver us, and by noon we came close hauled to Risut where I landed."

Multi-coloured crayfish and crabs abound among the rocks which are alive with coral, red and green, yellow and purple. Moray eels with their vicious barbed teeth and jellyfish of various types are also found, with sea anemones, sea slugs and sea urchins. In some years in early summer the sea is alive with jellyfish – blue Portuguese men-of-war and long "snakes" of purple jelly strung together. There are also molluscs of many kinds in abundance, cowries, volutes, cones, bivalves and clams, and at certain seasons the sea is stained with the orange of plankton which becomes phosphorescent at night.

The author of the *Periplus of the Erythraean Sea* writing in the first century AD noted that Masira Island produced a considerable amount of tortoise shell of fine quality for export. The island is still notable for the turtles which frequent its shores and several of

Some plants can be put to practical use. This bush (below) *exudes a poisonous white glue-like substance.*

Acacia flourishes in the wadis. *Much of the desert is covered in camel-thorn and scrub which bursts into flower after rain.*

the world's known species have been identified there.

Pearls

Oysters are found off the coast of Oman, but pearling has never been as important along the coast of Oman as within the Gulf, where the waters are shallower and do not plunge swiftly to the ocean depths. Nonetheless a certain amount of diving for pearls was done until the 1960s, and Muscat has at various times been an important market both for pearls and mother of pearl.

Oman's Fauna

Oman has a rich and varied wildlife, with many species being peculiar to the country. One of these is the shy, wary *tahr*, or Jayakar's mountain goat. The *tahr* prefers high, isolated places; once prolific, it is now in danger of extinction as it is shot for its meat, which is particularly excellent in the female. But effective measures are being taken to protect the wildlife of Oman, and the gradual diminution of the animal population may be reversed.

The legendary unicorn – "a mythical and heraldic animal" according to the dictionary – may be the Arabian oryx, whose two long horns look like a single one when viewed from a distance. Indeed, sometimes the oryx may grow only one horn. Although the oryx is declining in the wild, there are several herds in captivity.

Foxes abound, and leopard, wildcat and genets still survive. In the mountains of the Jebel Akhdar and in Dhofar, wolves, striped hyena and porcupines are found. There are also hydrax, the coneys of the Bible, the Arabian hare, and the black hedgehog – found only in Oman, although the Ethiopian hedgehog is more common.

Jerboa, the spiny mouse, the common mouse and rat, and several kinds of bat, including the Egyptian fruit bat, are some of the country's smaller creatures, as is the gruesomely-named naked-bellied tomb bat. Lizards are found throughout the land, some of which are eaten by the *Bedu*, who also eat the locusts which occasionally swarm over Oman, devastating the crops.

Among the less attractive creatures there is the horned viper, and in many parts of Oman a diminutive boa is found in the sands. Other snakes include the harmless colubrid, and puff adders and various vipers. Scorpions and stinging spiders up to four inches long are plentiful. The conical mounds of termites are common on the Salala plain, and six-inch-long centipedes, black beetles, flies, mosquitoes and biting ants are populous.

The butterflies are of great beauty. The flowers which attract them are dependent on the rainfall, and after the rains appear in profusion. Oleander, grasses, bulrushes and sedge flourish in the *wadis*, whilst the *knib* (camel-thorn) and other acacias cover much open ground. Small trees called *surra* flourish on the hillsides, and on the plateaux there is a steppe vegetation with low scrub, bushes and small trees.

The waters of Muscat are full of fish – kingfish, swordfish, sailfish, tuna, flying fish and many others. Crabs scuttle along the beaches, whilst crayfish and molluscs abound. Several of the world's species of turtle have been found on the shores of Masira Island.

Magpies and crows fly over the coast, with flamingoes, herons, gulls, geese, waders and tern. Inland there are Francolin partridge, sand grouse, bulbul, bee-eaters, eagles and falcons.

The rock-thrush (above) *and coastal hooded crow* (below).

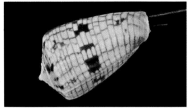

The many molluscs of Oman's waters provide not only food, but also interest for collectors. They can make charming jewellery.

The timid and beautiful bee-eater of inland Oman (above).

Effective measures are being taken to preserve rare species, such as the delicate, fast-moving desert gazelle (above).

This graceful oryx (above) is part of the captive herd belonging to Shaikh Qasim ibn Hamad al Thani of Qatar. Private herds guarantee survival for the oryx, now nearly extinct in the wild. The Ethiopian desert hedgehog (top) is a common sight; less often seen is the desert-dwelling Omani wildcat (below right).

The wildlife in Oman is now being preserved.

The ibex is believed to be the progenitor of the domestic goat.

The milkweed butterfly (above).

The lizards of Oman (above) grow up to two feet long.

The presence of leopards in Musandam has been confirmed.

Hyenas are found in the Jebel Akhdar and Dhofar.

71

3 The People

The people of Oman – the hardy mariners of the coast, the farmers, irrigating the land with complex falajes *or cultivating the high mountainsides, the* Bedu, *the merchants and traders of the cities have throughout the ages exploited the resources of their country. The discovery of oil has brought new jobs, whether in the petroleum industry itself or in the other spheres which the resulting expansion has made possible. But the best of the old ways survive. And underlying all else the deep-rooted faith of Islam remains.*

The Wali, *the governor of the area, is the local representative of the central Government and problems and disputes from all the region are brought to him for settlement. He must be intimately acquainted both with local and central government affairs. Left: a former* Wali *of Nizwa (later a government Minister), seated on the right of the doorway, studies a written appeal.*

Racial & Tribal Origins

From the simple cotton dresses worn by these Ibra girls (left), to the ornate gown worn by a young Salala beauty (above), the dress of Omani children is colourful and varied.

THE nineteenth-century traveller, James Silk Buckingham, described Omanis as "the cleanest, neatest, best dressed and most gentlemanly of all the Arabs" who inspired a feeling of confidence, goodwill and respect. Though his comments referred to the people of Muscat, many visitors to Oman would consider it true of the Omanis as a whole. However, the Omanis are a people spread over a large country the size of the United Kingdom and Ireland and are diverse in ethnic type, in culture and pursuits and even in language.

Racial Origins

Much remains obscure about the origins of the Omanis and how they became settled in their present areas. The people who reached such a high degree of civilisation in the fourth and third millennia BC may have been indigenous and the sprouting of civilisation in Oman may have been as rapid a phenomenon as it was in Iraq. Alternatively there may have been immigration of people with a higher culture. In the earliest days of human settlement, there may have been a veddoid belt crossing the ancient world from Africa to Melanesia, occupying all the intermediate lands, including Arabia, Baluchistan and India. The middle parts of this belt later perhaps became transformed, giving rise to the Hamitic people of Africa and their cousins in the Indian sub-continent.

Thus the original inhabitants of the Arabian peninsula may have been the people known as the Cushites, a Hamitic people who may have laid the foundations of the caravan roads and seafaring from the coastal ports. At an uncertain date – probably in late Pleistocene times – a Western Asian stock broke southwards into the Arabian peninsula and the lands linking Mesopotamia with the Punjab – Persia, Baluchistan and Afghanistan. At this time Arabia was a well-watered and fertile land such as to tempt a race of adventurous hunters. People with Armenoid features then settled in northern Oman introducing brachycephalic features, and to some extent these features were also transmitted to the peoples of the south in Dhofar through migration and miscegenation. The peoples of the south nonetheless also retained something of their original features, which makes many of them akin in looks to the Somalis, Danakil, Hadendowa and Egyptians, their brachicephaly being unique.

The Phoenicians

The origin of the Phoenicians, that great seafaring race of the Mediterranean, could possibly lie in Oman. The Greek historian, Herodotus of Halicarnassus, in the sixth century BC quotes the opinion of learned Persians that the Phoenicians emigrated from the Erythraean Sea to the Mediterranean where they settled and immediately started to make voyages. Disputes rage about what was meant by the Erythraean Sea of the ancients which was named after Erythras, a King whose tomb is supposedly on the island of Hormuz on the north side of the entrance to the Gulf. However, the term Erythraean, or Red Sea, seemingly applied to the western part of the Indian Ocean together with the Persian Gulf and the Red Sea.

Similarity of place names in the Levant on the one hand and Oman and the Gulf on the other – for example Sur and Sha'm – and the physical similarity in situation and appearance between Sur in Oman and Sur (Tyre) in the Mediterranean has been thought by some to indicate a common Phoenician origin. The time scale could fit as well, for the Phoenicians first made a significant appearance in the Levant in the second millennium, a millennium on which there is strangely

The white robe, with the ornately embroidered cap worn by coastal people (below left) or enlivened with a blaze of the orange cashmere shawl (below) is chosen for its practicality in the heat.

Feminine flair causes the girl from Sur (below) to complement her golden skin with glowing russet.

little archaeological evidence in Oman, suggesting that there might have been some collapse of civilisation in the area, leading to migrations. It is not entirely impossible, therefore, that shipwrights of Oman fathered those who built and sailed the "ships of Tarshish".

The Tribes

Oman is a country of tribes and, despite the essential homogeneity of its various components, the tribes have played a very prominent role in the country's history, which from early Islamic times has been well recorded. Tribal rivalries and alliances have dominated internal politics until very recently, and even now the large tribes still have importance.

The main strands of internal Omani history in the last two and a half centuries have centred round the Bani Hina and Bani Ghafir tribes who gave their names to the two great Hinawi and Ghafiri factions which divided Oman and dominated politics during this period. The present inhabitants are, according to the Arab genealogists, descended from two main Arab stocks: the Yemeni or Qahtan tribes originating in south Arabia, and the Adnan or Nizar tribes who emigrated from north-west Arabia. The Hinawi faction traditionally represent the Yemeni tribes and the Ghafiri the Adnan, though centuries of feuding, and coalescence and splitting of alliances, have increasingly blurred earlier distinctions. Nonetheless this factionalism, which at times was as bitter as that between the Guelphs and Ghibellines in mediaeval Florence, affected not only the politics of inner Oman but also the southern region of Dhofar and the present Union of Arab Emirates.

The main groups of tribes in northern Oman may be divided into the *Hadhr* and the *Bedu* – the classical Arab division between town and desert dwelling people. Apart from the Bani Ghafir and Bani Hina, there are several important sedentary tribes in central Oman. The Bani Ruwaha whose senior shaikhs are the Khalili family, from which the Imam Muhammad ibn Abdulla al Khalili (1920–1954: 1338–1373 AH) came, live in the Wadi Samail. The Bani Riyam control the Jebel Akhdar and the approaches to it from the south through Tanuf and Birkat al Moz, and the Abriyin of Hamra live on the south side of the Jebel. Another significant tribe

which dominates one of the strategic *wadis* of the central massif is the Bani Kharus who control the northern approach to the Jebel Akhdar and who have also played an important part in east African history. The Maawil live in the prosperous Wadi Maawil, and provided the Julanda kings of Oman before and immediately after the advent of Islam. The Hawasina control the Wadi Hawasina which leads through the mountains roughly from north to south and have traditionally provided guards for the ruling family and many of the *Walis*. The other great gap through the mountains, the Wadi Jizzi, is inhabited by the Bani Kaab.

The Sharqiya area to the south of the Wadi Samail is the home of the Hirth who have not only played a dominant part in internal Oman politics but also in the colonisation and settlement of Oman's colonies in east Africa. The Awamir, who have a particular reputation for the making and maintenance of *falajes*, also live in this area, though this tribe also has sections in Buraimi and on the Batina. South of the main Hirth area is the tract known as the

Jaalan, with the settlements of the Bilad Bani bu Hassan and Bilad Bani bu Ali, against whom British expeditions in aid of Said ibn Sultan were sent in 1820 and 1821. The Bani Khalid live in a remote valley – one of the best watered in Oman – to the north of Kamil and Sur in the Sharqiya.

The tribes of the Dhahira area to the east of the Hajar range north of the Jebel Akhdar itself include the Bani Kaab who have provided a number of eminent Omanis, with their tribal centre at Mahadha. Other sedentary tribes include the Bani Battash who inhabit the area south of Muscat and were formerly famous for horse breeding and the Bani Jabir, at times the paramount tribe in the country and now living mainly in the Wadi Samail and along the Batina coast.

The desert tribes include the Duru who inhabit the area to the south and the east of Ibri, and the Naim, together with their sub-sections the Al bu Shamis and the Al bu Kharaiban, the only tribes in Oman who practise the Arabian sport of falconry.

To the south of the Sharqiya there are other *Bedu*, the Wahiba, Harsusi and the Janaba tribes, the last of whom formerly owned towns on the desert fringe such as Adam, the home of the Al

Every tribe in Oman, whether numbering thousands, or only one or two families, has preserved its own proud traditions.

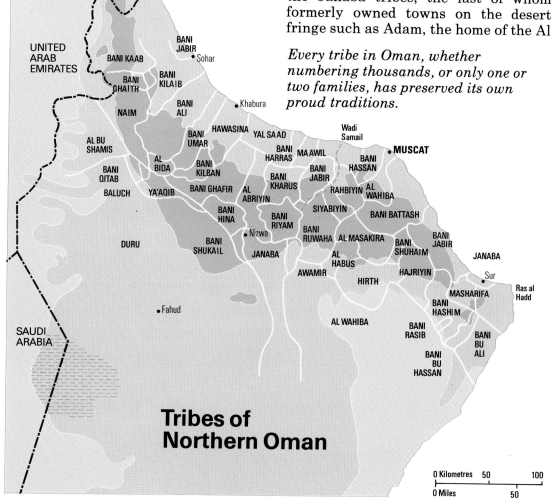

Tribes of Northern Oman

0 Kilometres 50 100

0 Miles 50

bu Said. The Harsusi, though probably not Mahra in origin, nonetheless speak a dialect of Mahri.

In Dhofar the main tribes are the Mahra, who live both in the eastern and western part, the Al Kathir who inhabit the mountains and the plains to the north, and the Qaras, who live in the central area. Several distinct languages are spoken apart from Arabic: Mahri, Jibali and a Mahri dialect, Bathari. In the extreme north of the country live the Shihuh who speak an Iranian dialect and may have produced a notable figure of ancient times mentioned in the Bible, Bildad the Shuhite, one of Job's Comforters.

Omani tribes have played a significant role in Gulf politics as well as at home. Omanis were amongst the most important troops when al Muhallab led the Arab tribes in the conquest of Khorasan and Kerman, and later they provided the ruling dynasties in Siraf, Qais and Hormuz, the great trading *entrepôts* of the Gulf before the advent of the Europeans. There has in fact throughout history been so much coming and going between the northern and southern shores of the Gulf that Omani and Arab influence has traditionally been as much felt in southern Persia as Persian influence on the Arabian shore.

The Division of the People

The Omani people may be divided into six main categories: first the inhabitants of Muscat, Mutrah, Sohar and Sur, and other coastal places where the people have for generations lived by seafaring, trading and fishing; secondly the people of the Batina coast where agriculture depends on wells; thirdly the cultivators, the classical *Hadhr*, living in towns like Nizwa and Rostaq and settled villages of the Interior who depend on the *falaj* system of water conduits resembling the *qanats* of Persia for their livelihood; fourthly the *Bedu* of the plains to the south and west; fifthly the Shihuh, the mountain people of the Musandam peninsula and sixthly the people of Dhofar, some of whom are Hamites and have much in common ethnically and linguistically with the people of south Arabia and parts of east Africa.

Headdress can indicate a man's origin or home area such as Dhofar (above) *and Sur* (right).

People of the Coast and of the Interior

A silver carpet of sardines (left) *dries in the sun at Salala. Sardine-fishing is an important industry in the area.*

Coastal People

The pattern of navigation in the Indian Ocean was determined in the days of sail by the north-east and south-west monsoons. Every December the north-east monsoon blows with remarkable steadiness until February. On this Arab vessels sailed down to Zanzibar and the coast of east Africa with cargoes of dates, sailing back again with the south-westerly monsoon, which blows from April until September, with cargoes of ivory, beeswax, tortoiseshell – actually of course the shell of the turtle – and, until the trade was suppressed, slaves. Indeed Muscat was over a long period the chief port of Arabia for the reception, sale and onward transit of African slaves. Although the trade was infamous, once in Oman or Arabia slaves' treatment was remarkably good, as the Arab institution of slavery was never so harsh as that in the Americas and West Indies. Lt. Colonel John Johnson, who visited Muscat in 1817, for example, remarked,

Oman's waters are known to be exceedingly rich in fish. Modern methods of refrigeration could soon improve the diet of a population which is already fond of fish. Surplus sardines become cattle fodder and fertiliser.

The effort of launching the boat (above left) is amply rewarded by a glittering catch at the end of the day (above right).

After sorting, the day's catch is spread out to dry naturally in the sunlight chequered by the shade of the coconut palms (below).

Modern methods of processing will augment, but perhaps never supplant, the traditional sardine, dried on the beach.

"The status of a slave in the family of a Muhammadan very commonly resembles that of an adopted child, entitling the individual to some share in the property of his master at his decease and frequently before that event. The adopted slaves interest themselves strongly in the welfare of their masters and are ready even to lay down their lives in their defence; they are perfectly trustworthy and instances are not wanting in which they have been left sole heirs of the property which their care had helped to accumulate."

Nonetheless, the Sultans of Oman and of Zanzibar co-operated with the British in the gradual suppression of the slave trade. Indeed close friendship and association with the British made it inevitable that Oman would be affected by British attitudes. The slave trade was greatly exercising reformists in Britain during the first half of the nineteenth century and their ardour and influence grew after Britain's own abolition of

While the merchandise bringing ships to Oman has ranged from concrete to ivory, petroleum to ostrich feathers, the fishermen have plied the same ancient trade.

domestic slavery in 1833. By a strange coincidence, one of the leading lights in the reformist movement was a Member of Parliament, General T. Perronet Thompson, who, as a Captain in the Army and the first British Political Agent in Arabia between 1819 and 1827, was close to Said and led the British expedition against the Bani bu Ali in 1820.

The people of Muscat have for many generations, as they do now, provided food, water and cargoes for visiting ships, though in the late nineteenth and early twentieth centuries this activity diminished as agriculture in Oman went into temporary decline. Indeed it would until very recently have been difficult to recognise descriptions of Muscat given by earlier travellers. Grattan Geary, the Editor of the *Times of India*, who visited Muscat in 1878, for instance, confirmed Albuquerque's impressions of the abundance of food in Muscat, remarking "Dates are seen at every store, fruit and vegetables from the cultivated spots in the interior are abundant." This abundance of produce suffered an eclipse for some decades but agriculture is now being revitalised. Muscatis, however, including a number of Indian traders settled for many generations, have grown rich on *entrepôt* trade as well as direct exports and imports, though *entrepôt* traffic is now not as important as it was in the eighteenth and early nineteenth centuries.

In their heyday the ships of Muscat varied in size from 300 to 600 tons, the finest being the *baghalas* with high poops beautifully carved like a galleon. These ships brought muslin and piece goods from Bengal, drugs and spices from the Far East, timber, rice and paper from Malabar, and European imports such as lead, iron and tin from Bombay. They were also involved in the rich coffee trade from Mocha on the Red Sea and Mauritius. From Zanzibar they brought gold dust, ostrich feathers, tamarind and ivory.

The market areas of Muscat and Mutrah are a happy combination of

traditional and modern. In the narrow streets there are people of every colour mingling with one another. Omanis with pale, grave, dignified faces, and beards, wearing traditional Omani dress; brown Indians and Pakistanis in their own distinctive white dress and caps, though many nowadays wear European clothes; people of blacker colour denoting their African ancestry or origin. The women glide by in dark robes or in the rage of colour which some of them wear. The men are there to shop, visit the barber or visit friends and chat. The women cluster round the cloth stalls with their rich display of gaily coloured materials looking for stuffs of their choice, for even the lady in black is likely to be wearing gay clothes underneath her dark camouflage and veil. Women also flock round the silversmiths' and goldsmiths' shops looking for a piece which pleases, enquiring the price, fingering, inspecting and moving on to another shop to repeat the process. The atmosphere of the market is polite, and lengthy bargaining not customary. In fact Muscat and Mutrah tend to be fixed price markets rather than the place for bargaining

For Omanis, the sea is the natural highway. Several types of traditional craft are still built in Oman.

which so many oriental markets are – not that a bargain may not sometimes be struck!

There are few animals except for the occasional donkey in the wider streets, and near the vegetable market. Camels were never brought into Muscat and Mutrah and visitors with produce from the Interior or the Batina seeking consumer goods in return left their mounts in the camel park outside the town. Now, however, the sight of a camel has become a comparative rarity in the towns, so fast has been the onslaught of the internal combustion engine.

It has through many ages been customary amongst the merchants in the *entrepôts* of the Oman and the Gulf region to have an area of gardens to which they can resort in the summer months and Seeb has always fulfilled this need for the merchants of Muscat and Mutrah. No one can say when the custom started but it may be significant that this was the custom in the Kingdom

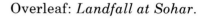

A day's fishing begins at dawn and continues while the light lasts, but there is also much night fishing.

Overleaf: *Landfall at Sohar.*

Apart from sardines and King Mackerel (kanad) *many varieties of fish, ranging from small tropical fish to great sharks, are found locally.*

of Hormuz, which for so long was *suzerain* of the coast of Oman until the Portuguese came. The habit was remarked by Marco Polo who wrote: "The residents avoid living in the cities, for the heat in summer is so great that it would kill them. Hence they go out (to sleep) at their gardens in the country, where there are streams and plenty of water." Duarte Barbosa, the Portuguese who visited Hormuz in 1518 (924 AH) remarked: "The merchants of this isle and city are Persians and Arabs . . . These noblemen . . . and principal merchants . . . have country houses on the mainland whither they go to divert themselves in summer." The residences in Sib have grown more elaborate with time but the old custom is still continued.

If the trading importance of Muscat has fluctuated from time to time, the importance of fishing along the Batina coast has never diminished. Fish has always been an important part of the

people's diet, not only on the coast but also in the Interior and the traditional pattern of internal trade involved the exchange of fish for the agricultural produce of the farmers living inland. The boats and techniques with the net used by local fishermen have changed little through the ages, though in the last few years the long, graceful fishing canoes of hollowed-out tree trunks called *huris* have all been fitted with modern outboard engines giving them greater range. It is a familiar sight in Muscat to see scores of fishing boats scattered widely over the still sea, and at night fires, which they all carry, stab the darkness. The catch is not only sold for local consumption, but sharksfin and dried fish remain significant exports.

Batina Cultivators
Along the shore of the Batina coast there are rich plantations of dates, which continue almost uninterrupted for some 200 miles from Muscat to Khor Fakkan, where the rocky massif again breaks out into the sea. The people of this area are of mixed blood and over the centuries there has been a consider-

able influx both from India and the African continents. Though there are traces of ancient canals on the Batina plain, which have long since fallen into disuse, water is nowadays raised by mechanical pump. In the past it was done by a system whereby the bucket from the well was attached to a rope, which was drawn over a wooden pulley and pulled up by a bull, donkey or camel walking down a man-made incline. The gardens here are lush and the varieties of date different from those grown inland. Certain fruits such as peaches and apricots which flourish in the mountains cannot be grown, but other varieties such as Indian almonds and figs do well. Between the cultivated area on the Batina and the mountains there is a wide plain providing good grazing for camels, goats and donkeys. Bertram Thomas in *Alarms and Excursions in Arabia* has described the nature of the Batina coast: "My journey with the Sultan was to take us through this populous province: now along the golden beaches, past little Arab ports ever associated with Sindbad the Sailor, and little fishing villages whose men go forth to grope under the

The Northern Coast

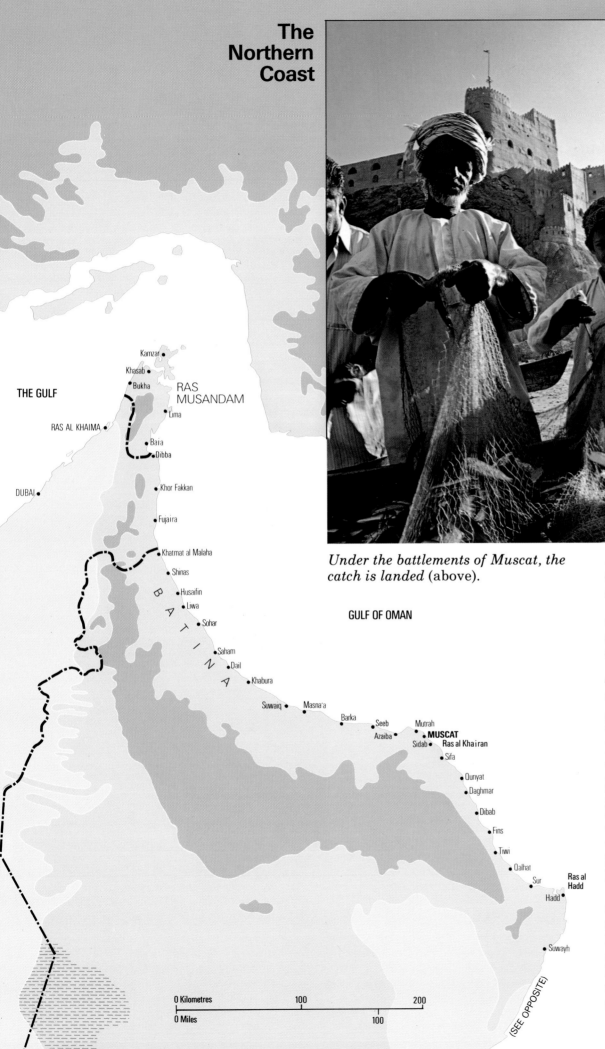

Under the battlements of Muscat, the catch is landed (above).

A packet-boat plies nightly between Sur and Muscat and vice versa (above right) carrying passengers and cargo.

sea for precious pearls; now through the shady date-grove; and now along the hot dazzling plains beyond".

The People of the Interior

The heartland of Oman is the great central massif called the Jebel Akhdar or "Green Mountain" and its main towns, Nizwa, Rostaq, Izki and Bahla, have at various times in the past, before the present Al bu Said dynasty brought it to Muscat in the later eighteenth century, been the capital of Oman. Ibadhism, on which the centuries old Omani Imamate was based and which is strangely confined to Oman and north-west Africa, has its deepest roots here.

In the markets of the Interior, the splendidly dignified Omani merchants sit outside their shops on stools or cross-legged on the floor, as their forebears always have. In the silversmiths' shops blowlamps glow and there is a confusion of purposeful activity on the floor of each square shop. *Khanjars*, decorated guns

THE GULF

RAS MUSANDAM

Kamzar

Khasab

Bukha

Lima

RAS AL KHAIMA

Baia

Dibba

DUBAI

Khor Fakkan

Fujaira

Khatmat al Malaha

Shinas

B A T I N A

Husaifin

Liwa

Sohar

Saham

Dail

Khabura

Suwaiq

Masna'a

GULF OF OMAN

Barka

Seeb

Mutrah

Azaiba

MUSCAT

Sidab

Ras al Khairan

Sifa

Quriyat

Daghmar

Dibab

Fins

Tiwi

Qalhat

Sur

Ras al Hadd

Hadd

Suwayh

| 0 Kilometres | 100 | 200 |
| 0 Miles | 100 | |

(SEE OPPOSITE)

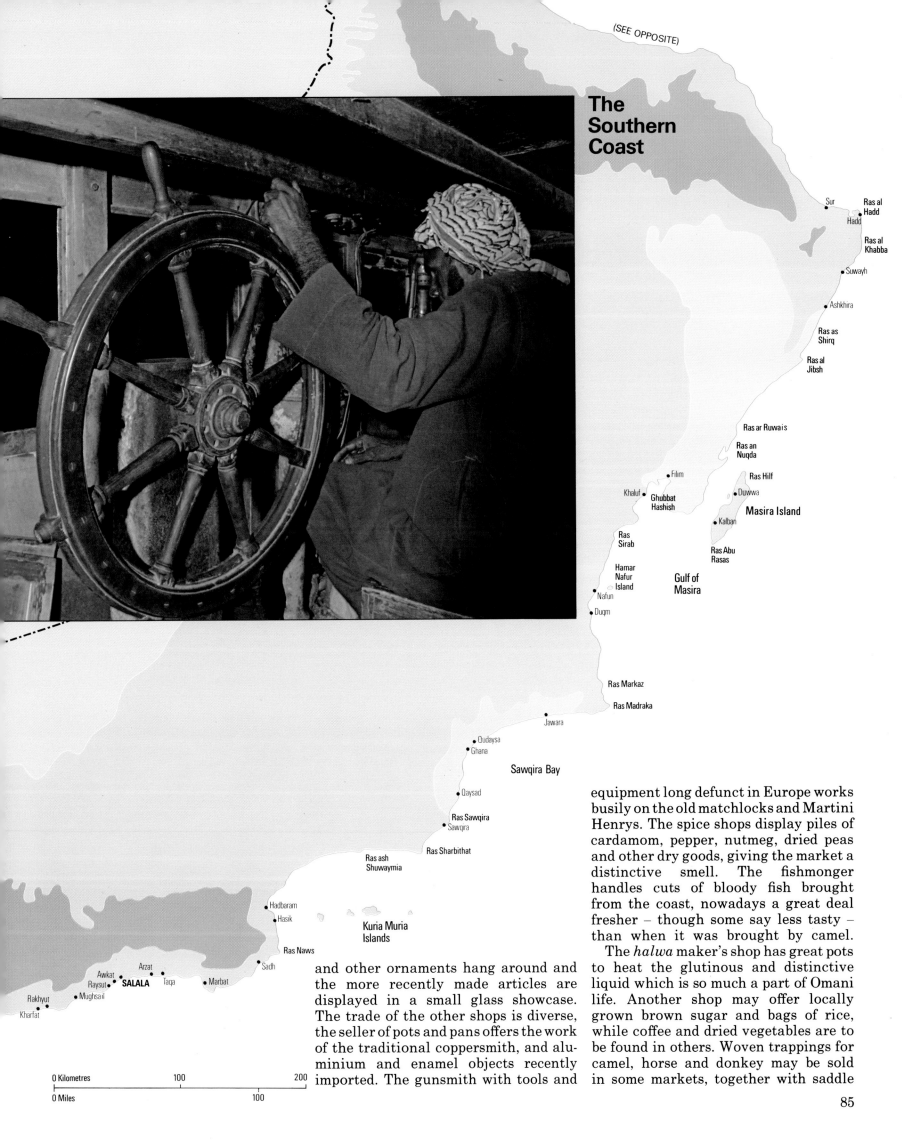

(SEE OPPOSITE)

The Southern Coast

Sur
Ras al Hadd
Hadd
Ras al Khabba
Suwayh
Ashkhira
Ras as Shirq
Ras al Jibsh
Ras ar Ruwais
Ras an Nuqda
Filim
Ras Hilf
Khaluf
Ghubbat Hashish
Duwwa
Masira Island
Kalban
Ras Sirab
Ras Abu Rasas
Hamar Nafur Island
Gulf of Masira
Nafun
Duqm
Ras Markaz
Ras Madraka
Jawara
Qudaysa
Ghana
Sawqira Bay
Qaysad
Ras Sawqira
Sawqira
Ras Sharbithat
Ras ash Shuwaymia
Hadbaram
Hasik
Kuria Muria Islands
Ras Naws
Sadh
Arzat
Awkat
Raysut
SALALA
Taqa
Marbat
Rakhyut
Mughsail
Kharfat

and other ornaments hang around and the more recently made articles are displayed in a small glass showcase. The trade of the other shops is diverse, the seller of pots and pans offers the work of the traditional coppersmith, and aluminium and enamel objects recently imported. The gunsmith with tools and equipment long defunct in Europe works busily on the old matchlocks and Martini Henrys. The spice shops display piles of cardamom, pepper, nutmeg, dried peas and other dry goods, giving the market a distinctive smell. The fishmonger handles cuts of bloody fish brought from the coast, nowadays a great deal fresher – though some say less tasty – than when it was brought by camel.

The *halwa* maker's shop has great pots to heat the glutinous and distinctive liquid which is so much a part of Omani life. Another shop may offer locally grown brown sugar and bags of rice, while coffee and dried vegetables are to be found in others. Woven trappings for camel, horse and donkey may be sold in some markets, together with saddle

0 Kilometres   100   200
0 Miles   100

Haggling in the market places is not the usual Omani practice as elsewhere in the East. Traders tend to hold to prices they have quoted.

bags, rugs and other woollen articles for the tent or house. The fruit sellers display their oranges, limes, dates, bananas, and, in the season, apricots and peaches. The brilliant green alfalfa is always on sale close by for animal feed. In Nizwa an auction of animals is held under a great tree adjoining the market and the cattle, goats and sheep are driven round and round a ring of potential buyers, whilst the auctioneer calls the odds. Nearby is the area where the camels and donkeys are tethered whilst the owners visit the market and all the while there are people coming and going on animals, though car and lorry have been fast replacing more traditional means of transport.

Manufactures of this area include cloth, pottery, and *halwa*. The people of the Interior make their living from agriculture and their gardens of palms and fruit trees. The gardens are irrigated by tapping a water table and leading the water through channels to the land. Huge areas are still cultivated in this manner, although observation of Oman from an aircraft immediately reveals that the area under cultivation was at one time much larger. Oman was rightly once described as a land abounding in fields and groves with pastures and unfailing springs. The groves mainly consist of date palms, of which there are reputed to be more than one hundred varieties. Mangoes, pomegranates, peaches, apricots, grapes, citrus, lucerne, wheat and tobacco are also grown.

Each town of the Interior has its own individual character and yet the market area in each bears striking fundamental resemblance to the others. There is a characteristic Omani style of market akin to the Yemeni. In most places the market area is enclosed within walls which can be secured and guarded by night, and it is usually situated close to the fort, the local centre of defence and authority. The streets are narrow and the shops are in rows; they are square in design, giving immediately on to the street, and usually on a raised platform. At night the shop can be shut up completely – there is no glass front and

In the market-place (above) *a group of men sit in a sociable circle and make kebabs. The pieces of lamb are cut up, threaded on sharp skewers and grilled over the fire.*

The shade of a tree provides a pleasant schoolroom for these children (below). *The open-air "one-tree" Qur'anic schools have now mostly been replaced by state schools in modern buildings.*

Women form their own little circle for an exchange of views and a cup of coffee.

Woman's role includes cooking, sewing, washing clothes and linen, drawing water, and weaving.

thus each owner can secure his own with a simple lock. Some markets are completely covered and others have wide verandahs protruding from the shops themselves but construction varies from place to place. Frequently the shops are built of mud brick and faced with a rough mud mortar.

The flavour of the smaller Omani towns of the Interior is well captured by Ian Skeet. In his book *Muscat and Oman*, he describes how "Ghafat is in a crook of the mountains where Jebel Kaur sticks out almost at right angles from the main range, a monstrous landmark ... the largest 'exotic' in the world, and the geologists love to wrangle over whether it appeared one primaeval day from the guts of the earth, or was tossed over from the sea. Ghafat is the capital of the Bani Hina; it is an extensive series of date gardens with full *falajes* flowing through them, and in the centre a collection of neat two and three storey mud houses emanating an air of strength and wealth."

He labels Hamra of the Abriyin, which is close to Ghafat on the south side of the Jebel, as the most attractive of all the towns in Oman: "there is a road encircling the gardens and beside it the *falaj*, and all the gardens at a slightly lower level – you walk down a couple of steps and then along well-ordered paths with neatly arranged gardens on either side, all very geometrical and systematised; walls, and lime trees spilling over them; sprays of dates like a skyful of fireworks; the bright green of the ubiquitous lucerne, the universal Omani animal fodder ... the town centre with its tall elegant mud houses with wooden windows casting strong Italianate shadows, and a wide flight of steps leading from a sort of piazza to an upper level of the town. In the main *majlis* of the *shaikh*, which is a long narrow room (with texts from the Qur'an painted on walls and ceilings), the many windows open straight out on to a grove of lime trees, and what with the burble of water from a *falaj* beneath and the chirping of birds in the trees, you begin to lose grasp of desert realities; until you re-focus on a room full of

bearded Omanis clutching their rifles and their camel sticks, and your Umbrian dreams are dissipated ... Behind Hamra the mountains slope almost from the roofs of the houses up at the peculiar tilted angle of the range towards its highest peak at about 10,000 feet."

In such communities as these the labour is divided between men, women and children. The male role includes participation in the business of the family and the community, attending the mosque, supervising the date plantations or working in them or in the fields, ploughing with a humped bull, keeping a shop, taking produce to market, visiting neighbouring places for trade or shopping, mustering with the other males if the Shaikh summons them, building houses, digging wells, making or repairing a *falaj*, shooting birds and game and practising shooting – for many are excellent shots – weaving and cloth making, grooming, riding and using the family donkey.

The female role is to cook for the family and prepare all the meals, coffee and tea for family and visitors, to sew, make and mend such clothes as are not bought from a local shop or brought from further afield, wash clothes and linen, draw water, wash up after meals in the *falaj*, weave, in some areas, and do embroidery.

The small children, both boys and girls, herd goats, sheep and poultry, though women too participate in this, which is more a female than a male role. The small boys stay with the mother and participate in activities on her side of the house until they are about eight, after which they gradually become more involved with the male activities.

Amongst the *Bedu* the division of labour may be somewhat different. For instance, the men often herd the camels and other animals and make the coffee, particularly when on the move. Indeed, even in the settled areas there are often goatherds for larger herds of goats and their cries and peculiar sounds as they communicate with the goats to keep them moving can be heard echoing strangely round the hills.

87

Use of water provided by the falaj *system is strictly regulated – not only, of course, for agriculture, but drinking, washing and ablutions.*

Life in the Interior

A description of the Wadi Bani Khalid gives some impression of life in the Interior of Oman. Names persist in Oman for very long periods and it may be that, as suggested by Bertram Thomas in *Alarms and Excursions in Arabia*, the name of the *wadi* implies an ancient connection with the Chaldeans. It is one of the best watered valleys in Oman and at least in its upper reaches there is a constant stream emanating from an underground river. So strong is its flow that the local people say it comes from Basra in Iraq! In its lower reaches it flows underground to Kamil, Wafi and other Jaalan settlements at Bilad Bani bu Hassan and Bilad Bani bu Ali.

How green this valley is. Mountains rise up above it bare, stark and magnificent in their brown and purple contour. In the *wadi* bed itself there are large pools and wide expanses of green water meadow with great clumps of oleander in pink flower, tall trees of various kinds – willows, acacia with yellow, mimosa-like flowers, and other thorny trees of Arabia as well as palms in the well-tended gardens.

The people have the attributes of mountain people the world over and during the Id holidays when they are in festive mood come down from the villages higher up the valley, men and women dressed in their holiday clothes, for the traditional Id dancing. Some come on foot and others on donkeys with bells jingling cheerfully. The men in brilliant white wear silver *khanjars* and belts with other silver ornamentation. They carry rifles – mainly old Martini Henrys – and on the head wear cashmere shawls of bright orange, red and purple, which show up strikingly against the tawny background of rock. The women and girls wear clothes of many bright colours edged with silver thread and embroidery, their heads covered by cloth in the manner almost universal in the East, but unveiled. The men are warm in their Id greetings – "Peace be upon you", "A blessed feast", "We are celebrating the feast", "May your feast be blessed" and so on, with the traditional "May you be in God's keeping" on departure. People can be heard playing drums for the dance and singing melodiously at the tops of their voices; this makes a wonderful harmony of mountain sounds, drums, human voices and bells all mingling. The ancient guns too have their role to play over the holiday in *feux de joie*.

Durability of Custom

The world seems to be moving at an ever-quickening pace and change in modern Oman is now accelerating. However, many traditional Omani customs are preserved, more especially in village life. The women have a special role to play in the family and for a village woman the day starts at about 5 a.m. when her first duty is to heat water collected from the well or *falaj* on the previous day. She next makes *laban* (yoghourt), washes, and says her prayers before making coffee and waking her husband and the children. After breakfast she and the children perform the chores of the household, which may include care of animals – camels, goats and hens – cleaning the house, and preparing lunch. The next phase is the siesta in the heat of the afternoon, after which follows a time for social intercourse, visiting and chatting, accompanied by coffee and dates.

Wheat and maize are sometimes grown under the palms which produce not only dates but fronds for housebuilding and making shasha *boats.*

Women do much of the labour in the fields. Here, they are harvesting the wheat crops.

Manners and Hospitality

Good manners and humanity are a distinctive feature of Oman, on which many travellers throughout the ages have commented. For example, Alexander Hamilton, who visited the town of Muscat in 1721, wrote: "The Muscati Arabs are remarkable for their humility and urbanity" and he recounts that he was walking one day in the streets when by chance he met the Governor of the city. "According to my duty," he says, "I went into the door of a shop to let him and his guards have the street, which are generally narrow, but he, observing by my complexion and garb that I was a stranger, made his guards go on one side and beckoned me to come forward and stood until I passed him." Hamilton goes on to contrast the treatment of prisoners of war taken by the Omanis and Portuguese in 1650. "The Portuguese use their captives with great severity, making them labour hard and inure them to the discipline of the whip. But the Arabs use theirs with very much humanity, only making them prisoners at large without putting them to hard labour and allow them as much diet

money as their own soldiers receive."

These innate good manners of the Omanis are clearly demonstrated by the natural ease, dignity and politeness of small boys in their fathers' *majlises* or homes. Hospitality is one aspect of manners and any Omani would feel it incumbent on him to invite a stranger at least to take coffee with him. Hospitality is indeed a sacred duty and even the most impoverished *Bedu* must share his frugal meal with a stranger. For instance, Thesiger in *Arabian Sands* describes how, when passing some tents in the desert, a man came running out shouting " 'Stop! Stop! . . . Why do you pass my tent? Come, I will give you fat and meat' . . . He took my camel's rein and led her towards the tents. . . . The tents were very small, less than three yards long and four feet high, and were half-filled with saddles and other gear. An old woman, a younger woman and three children . . . watched us as we unloaded. . . . They slaughtered a young camel behind the tents."

Another striking example of Omani hospitality was the conduct of an elderly man when a small body of troops arrived

at his village to arrest him. He would not submit to arrest until he had served coffee to his captors, but, this done, he gave himself up willingly.

The traditional courtesies which Omanis exchange are deeply rooted in their Islamic traditions and nearly all the phrases used mention the Almighty, just as they did in earlier European tradition. Any phrase importing action in the future for example is prefaced by "If God wills". "Praise be to God" is similarly used in relation to all present conditions or past mercies.

It is usual, particularly away from the larger towns, to greet strangers and frequently people hail one another over considerable distances of desert or mountain. Greetings are more demonstrative and often more dignified than in the West and courtesies elaborate and repetitive. Indeed a degree of repetition is almost essential to ordinary politeness, and two people may spend a considerable time insisting gently – by using the word "tafaddal", be so good – that the other will precede him in taking coffee or beginning a meal, or walking through a door.

The main meal of the day, at noon, includes rice, with fish, meat, or chicken stew.

The ox is still used for cultivating, and threads its way through the palms as it pulls the plough.

The bidar *reaches the dates to fertilise them by climbing the palm with a rope looped round the rough bark.*

Food

The main items of diet are dates, rice, fish, meat, wheat cakes and fruits such as bananas, citrus and mangoes. The family usually start the day with dates and coffee and breakfast may consist of bread with sour milk or yoghourt (*laban*), or possibly a vegetable stew. Wafer thin bread made from wheat is eaten with butter and honey and sometimes eggs are put into the thicker round or flat bread. The main meal of the day, taken about noon, is rice with a fish, meat or chicken stew and the evening meal is usually light and similar to breakfast. Coffee, frequently flavoured with cardamom, and dates, are taken at any time of day, and *halwa*, the characteristic Omani sweetmeat – made traditionally in the very early morning of ghee, starch, brown sugar, cardamom and honey – may also be served to guests.

If a visitor calls on an Omani household, the men will be shown to the *majlis*, the preserve of the men, and the women taken to the *harim* quarters, the preserve of the women. The host will always offer *qahwa* or "coffee" – which is a very elastic word meaning in practice anything from a cup or two of coffee to a comparatively large meal. This may include tea, fruit of various sorts, fizzy drinks, wheat bread, a light meat dish, biscuits and *halwa*. A dinner or lunch offered to a guest could well be much more elaborate with a *khuzi* – a goat or sheep piled on a mound of rice – with side dishes of stews, meat and vegetable, and possibly mutton or goat baked in an earth oven and kebabs.

It is still usually *de rigueur* to drink about three cupfuls of coffee before leaving and the host or his servant will go on filling the tiny cups until the cup is shaken – a sign that the guest has had sufficient. Although the custom is now dying, it used to be invariable for rosewater to be sprinkled over a guest's hands and head and for incense to be taken round in a smoking censer of silver or clay. This was the signal that the entertainment was at an end and the Omani proverb runs, "After the incense, there should be no sitting on."

Sweet dates are eaten at eventide.

Above: *After winnowing, the straw is dried in the sun to be used for fodder and bedding.*

Dress

James Silk Buckingham, the celebrated journalist and traveller who visited Muscat in 1816, spoke with approbation of the simplicity of the people's dress and the "equality of value between the dress of the wealthiest and the lowest classes of the people".

The typical Omani man of the old school in the Interior has a long beard and wears a turban of dazzling white cloth, and a white robe or *dishdasha* with a distinctive little tie at the neck. Around his waist he wears a belt, very often of silver thread, to carry the *khanjar*, the typical carved Omani dagger, the sheath of which is frequently richly decorated in silver. He may well also carry a small silver container for *kohl*, which men as well as women apply, much to the detriment of their eyes, and another silver tube-shaped container for tweezers – a sensible precaution in a land where thorns fallen from the trees are so prevalent! The usual undergarment is a *wazara* or *lunghi*, often brightly coloured, which is wrapped round the body and serves as the only day-time garment of people labouring in the hot sun.

Over his white robe the Omani man will often wear a *bisht*, a cloak which

"Marrying a strange woman is like drinking water from an earthenware bottle," runs a local proverb.

may be black, fawn or light coffee-coloured or even off white, edged with gold thread. Sandals of leather are worn on the feet. The men's headdress varies and, whereas the people of the Interior usually wear the turban of white cloth, the people of the coast wear an elaborately crotcheted cap most of the time. Some, however, both in the Interior and on the coast, wear turbans of cashmere wool of various qualities according to rank and means. The *Bedu* too often wear cashmere turbans of bright colours, orange, purple, yellow and green, which contrast brilliantly with the landscape.

Omani women's clothes vary somewhat from place to place. All the women, however, cover their heads with cloth in some manner. In the towns it was the custom, at least until recently, for the better off to wear a veil and a black *abaya* or cloak of fine material. There are areas, for instance in parts of the Batina and Dhofar and amongst some *Bedu* tribes, where the women wear a mask, *birqa*, which sometimes takes quite an elaborate form and covers their noses, giving them a bird-like appearance. Some *Bedu* women wear a long black dress with a stiff black veil and only tiny slits for the eyes. In central Oman the women are frequently not veiled, but wherever in the country a mask or a veil is worn veiling begins at puberty. The coquettish effect of the veil is often enhanced by the woman gathering the head-veil, *lahaf*, with the teeth and revealing one eye only.

Women's dress in Oman is generally far more colourful than anywhere else in eastern Arabia until Kurdistan is reached to the north. In fact they are often dressed in a riot of colour. The usual pattern is a long straight dress with long sleeves, which is worn over trousers gathered tight around the ankles. The Batina women also wear the thin head-veil, *lahaf*, which trails behind them. Purples and blacks are popular colours there and the dress is made of the same material.

The women in the Interior, in such places as Nizwa, Samail and Izki, wear

This little girl from Sur (above) *with her toy trumpet is dressed for the Id.*

similar clothes, though the colours may be brighter than on the coast, with oranges, yellows and greens predominating. An additional outer garment, consisting of two large pieces of cotton sewn together, called a *laisu*, is worn in these regions. In the Sharqiya and Sur areas a garment called a *shatha* is also worn – a shawl consisting of two pieces of cloth joined together with lace.

Marriage

Marriage and the family lie at the heart of Islam; even though marriage is regarded in Sharia law as a civil contract, the fact that it is legal and possible for a Muslim marriage to be terminated by the husband saying "I divorce you" three times to his wife, has created an impression that divorce is easy and frequent in Islam. In practice it is not particularly common, and many Omani marriages are essentially monogamous, although a man may legally have up to four wives at any one time. This, however, has usually been the prerogative of

the rich and even then a man has a difficult task if he is to obey the Prophet Muhammad's injunction that all wives should be treated in every way equally. The sanctions of divorce are in themselves a deterrent, for the man who divorces his wife has to pay her alimony and there can be difficulties about custody of the children. Moreover, divorce is not to be enterprised lightly by Muslims and the oath on the divorce is the most binding of vows. For a divorce is regarded as an act of finality on which there can be no going back – at least without a devious legal process.

Though custom has been changing rapidly, it was common for a girl to be betrothed and married at the age of eleven or twelve. Such marriages were always arranged, and a man normally married his first cousin by his father's brother as his first wife. "Marrying a strange woman is like drinking water from an earthenware bottle; marriage with a cousin is like a drink from a dish – you are aware of what you drink." If the man and the girl came from the same village they would normally have seen each other, but, if they came from

Traditionally celebrated with jewellery, song, music and dance, the Omani wedding is an occasion of splendour.

separate villages they might well never have met until the arranged marriage took place.

In the case of marriage to a virgin girl, the arrangement is made between relatives of the two parties, though the girl herself has to give her consent to a proposal. A man may himself propose marriage to a widow or divorcee by raising the matter with a male relation of his intended wife. For the contraction of any valid marriage, bride price, *mahr*, has to be paid and the customary amount used to vary from area to area, being as high as 1,500 Omani Riyals in some places. However, one of the measures taken by Sultan Qaboos after his accession, was to fix bride price universally at 300 Omani Riyals. *Mahr* is a bridal gift from the husband to the wife and becomes the property of the wife. She has full right to dispose of it exactly as she wishes and it remains hers even in the event of divorce. *Mahr* may take various forms. It may be in the form of a money payment, but more usually it comprises a series of gifts, including jewellery, clothes, and even a wedding bed or bed linen. However, part of it

may also be in kind and such items – for instance materials and food – may be draped round the reception room at the wedding celebrations. There may be sacks of flour and rice, sugar, coffee beans, onions, dresses and fancy sandals. Often about half the bride price is paid in gold which it is easy for the bride to keep in the event of a divorce.

The formal arrangements for marriage are clear and well-recognised. The first stage, as we have seen, is the "asking". Then follows the commitment, *milha*, which stipulates the amount of *mahr* and the trousseau which the bridegroom and his family are to provide. It may also settle the date of the wedding. The legal completion of the ceremony comes with the signing of the marriage contract – or oral affirmation of it – in front of a religious judge (*Qadhi*). The *Qadhi* asks the bridegroom in the presence of witnesses if he will take the girl and when the agreement of the girl's father, or other representative, has also been given, the civil contract is duly signed.

The legal ceremony over, there are usually wedding festivities, with separate parties for the men and for the

women. The celebrations consist of eating and drinking – naturally with no alcohol – with dancing, and in some areas, singing. Sometimes there are a series of celebrations on different days. The girl is specially made up for the occasion, and in the Interior her hands, feet and face are painted with henna, which is used by men and women in all sorts of celebrations. It is, however, in Oman, used only on the body and not to dye the hair. Some wear a yellow paste ground from the orange flowers of a small shrub called *shooran*, and a floral design is sometimes painted on the hands. For the first night a bride will often wear green clothes – green being a sign of fertility. The culmination of the marriage ceremony is when the newly weds are escorted to their home, be it house or tent; this is the first occasion on which the two will ever have been on their own together, unless they knew each other as children before the age when small girls are veiled and put into *purdah*.

In the event of divorce a woman has to wait a certain period, *'idda*, before she may remarry. This provision of Islamic

Though the woman's first place is in the home, attitudes towards women are gentler, and opportunities for them are greater, than elsewhere in Arabia.

Education for girls is an important step in the modernisation of Oman. The girl (above) attends an Ibri school.

law is to ensure that there is no doubt about the paternity of any child which she may subsequently bear. The wife returns to her own family and usually takes with her any children under five. After this age the father is entitled to, and usually does, take the children. The divorce rate is in fact much higher in the towns of the coast than in the Interior.

The Omani attitude towards women is gentler than in many other parts of Arabia. The women are not so closely ·confined to the *harim*, are frequently not veiled and wear outer garments more colourful and indeed gorgeous than elsewhere. In Oman too, unlike most parts of Arabia, the male allows the woman to ride the donkey and walks himself. This aspect of Oman was re- marked on by the nineteenth-century British traveller William Giffard Pal- grave, who noted that "In Oman . . . the harem is scarcely less open to visitors than the rest of the house; while in daily life the women of the family come freely forward, show themselves, and talk like reasonable beings, very differ- ent from the silent and muffled status . . . elsewhere."

The market, as at Izki, is a rendezvous and news forum, as well as a place of trade.

Birth, Puberty and Death

Although there is greater joy when a male child is born, rather than a girl, there is not the shock and even anger which greets the birth of a girl elsewhere. (This attitude may possibly have its origin in the practice of infanticide of girl children before Islam in parts of Arabia – a practice of which the Prophet Muhammad deeply disapproved.) Nowadays an increasing number of births happily take place in hospital but until recently the average Omani child was brought into the world by a local midwife, usually an elderly woman. After the child was born it would be anointed, dressed with *kohl*, ash, or a mixture of the two. Salt was used for healing the woman and preventing infection, though it often produced unpleasant side effects. Boys may be circumcised either at about fifteen days or at about six years. There are no puberty rites in the north, but there is usually a celebration to mark the occasion and there may be dancing.

In the mountains of the Southern Region of Dhofar, however, in contrast to the north, elaborate ceremonies attending male circumcision at the age of fifteen were graphically described by Bertram Thomas in *Arabia Deserta*. "Large numbers of men and women assemble round a large open space. On a rock in the centre sits the boy of fifteen, a sword in hand. This sword, which has been blunted for the occasion, he throws into the air to catch it again in its descent, his palm clasping the naked blade. Before him sits the circumciser (usually a shaikh or man of good family), an old man; behind him stands an unveiled virgin, usually a cousin or a sister, also sword in hand.

She raises and lowers her sword vertically, and at the bottom of the stroke strikes it quiveringly with the palm of her left hand. The stage is now set. The boy sits, his left hand outstretched palm upwards, in suppliant manner, waiting for the actual operation. This done, he has promptly to rise, bleeding, and walk round the assembly, raising and lowering his sword as if oblivious to the pain. The rite is terminated by songs and running, and the firing of rifles, the women opening their upper garments as a gesture of baring their breasts . . . . Both male and female circumcision as practised in Dhofar bear resemblance to ancient Egyptian practices."

Hair fashions too may have an ancient sexual connotation, for Dhofari boys wore a central lock like the Egyptian Horus, with the hair shaved on either side. After the circumcision, the hair was permitted to grow normally.

When death comes, the body is washed carefully – washing is a very important part of the religious ritual both for the living and the dead. Certain spices, such as *riha* which has a smell somewhat like lilac and *kafour*, a dry white powder of great fragrance, are sprinkled over the body and between the fingers and toes. Orifices are blocked with cotton wool and the body is then put into a new piece of white muslin. The time between death and burial is very short, and burial takes place on the same day, unless death occurred at night. Burials only take place during the day time and the bier on which the body is laid is carried to the grave by close male members of the family.

After a man has died, his wife goes into mourning for a period of four

Old men still go to the market at Mintirib (below). They will rise to prod the livestock with their camelsticks and talk of prices. Animals are led round in circles during the auction at Nizwa (below right); the men will make their bids from the seated circle. On their visit to market they may well also buy freshly-made halwa *from the confectioner (right).*

months and ten days, and during this time she is not allowed to see another man; thus any doubt about paternity or succession is removed. During her period of mourning the woman stays indoors seeing only the immediate members of the family. She wears old clothes, not necessarily black ones, and only does her essential toilet, neither styling her hair nor painting her face, nor wearing jewellery. The night before a widow comes out of mourning she goes through a ritual bathing ceremony, and after this she is allowed to receive visitors.

The Wali *of Sur* (far right) *displays the traditional dignity of his office. Like the donkey rider at Wadi Muaidhin* (right)*, he wears both a traditional* khanjar *and modern wristwatch.*

Local Authority

In all the major centres there is a *Wali*, or Governor, appointed by the central Government and a *Qadhi* or judge who performs the judicial functions. This simple structure has provided the bones of the administration for centuries and the *Walis* and *Qadhis* come from families who have traditionally given service to the state for generations. Such families have moved from post to post within the country, and sometimes in former days have been posted to Gwadur and other posts on the southern coast of Iran and the east coast of Africa. In some areas

Local authority is invested in the Wali, *the governor, and judicial functions entrusted to the* Qadhi, *who interprets the law.*

tribal shaikhs have always carried great influence and government has traditionally been conducted partly directly through the *Walis* and partly indirectly through the most influential of these tribal shaikhs.

Ibn Batuta has left a description of how government was conducted in Oman when he visited Nizwa in the fourteenth century AD (eighth century AH). The inner part of Oman was then governed by the Bani Nabhan, who belonged to the Arik branch of the great south Arabian tribe of Azd. He writes: "Its Sultan is an Arab of the tribe of Azd b.al Ghawth and is called Abu Muhammad ibn Nabhan. Abu Muhammad is among them an appellation given to every Sultan who governs Oman, just like the appellation 'Atabek' among the kings of the Lurs. It is his custom to sit outside the gate of his residence in a place of audience there. He has no chamberlain nor vizier, and no one is hindered from appearing before him, whether stranger or any other. He receives a guest honourably, after the custom of the Arabs, assigns him hospitality, and makes gifts to him according to his standing."

This scene describes the way in which business has traditionally been done in Oman over the centuries and, until very recently, it was the custom of some *Walis* in the Interior to hold audience outside the gates of their forts in exactly the same manner as in ibn Batuta's day.

Dhofaris

Some six hundred miles of desert separate the northern and the southern regions of Oman and consequently it is not surprising that the people in Dhofar differ considerably from northern Omanis. Connections between the Dhofaris and some of the people of South Yemen have existed throughout history particularly, as excavations at Samhuram near Salala show, on account of the trade in frankincense, of which Dhofar was the primary producer. However, there have also been deep-rooted tribal and governmental connections

This typical Omani (above) *is equipped for any emergency, with rifle,* khanjar, *belt of cartridges, thorn-tweezers,* kohl *and an Ibri rug for good measure.*

The local scribe will no doubt become redundant as literacy increases. Below: In Rostaq market place, he writes a formal letter for the grocer.

A common heritage binds the several components of the nation, embracing merchants and seafarers, traders and farmers, southern Dhofaris, Bedu *tribesmen, Shihuh from the northern tip.*

The rifle, symbol of manhood, will accompany a man everywhere (above). *Here, the stock is bound with silver wire as decoration, in typical fashion.*

Henna, as elsewhere in Arabia, is employed as a dye for the hands and feet in Oman (below). *The nose rings are a typical ornament of Sur.*

with northern Oman and Dhofar's present relationship with the north goes back well over a hundred years. The tie is particularly close now as the present Sultan of Oman, Qaboos ibn Said, is half Dhofari.

The Dhofaris consist of people of the mountains and people of the plains. The mountain dwellers are divided into the Qara, who are traditionally the masters, the Shhero (sometimes incorrectly called Shahra) who were formerly a serf class, and the Arabs of Al Kathir, whilst in the lower valleys the Mahra predominate. There are also minor divisions. All have by long custom looked to one of the coastal towns for their trade and supplies. The mountain people are intimately bound up with their animals, for which they have the same sort of affection as some of the African tribes. They pasture their sleek little cattle and their camels, goats and sheep on the grass which grows in great profusion following the monsoon, when for a while the stern bare valleys are turned into green rolling country. It is the dependable and heavy rainfall that endows Dhofari country with its special character.

The Dhofaris probably do not exceed 25,000 or 30,000 in number overall but they are endowed with great natural intelligence. There are numerous tribes and sub-tribes in Dhofar but the people mainly speak, besides Arabic, Mahri, Jibali, (Shheri) and Bathari. Many, too, speak a dialect of Arabic. Some tribes are divided between mountain people and *Bedu* of the northern desert or Najd. The frankincense tree, the olibanum, still thrives in parts of Dhofar, but the gum is no longer harvested on a big scale and is mainly used for local consumption, for the great trade in frankincense which flourished for so many centuries has virtually dried up.

In Salala, the capital of Dhofar, there are considerable numbers of people whose original home was in Africa and African influence is seen when on religious holidays they dance in the streets, the women wearing the brightest colours, to rhythms brought from the African shore.

The two frontiers are the sea and the desert. The remarkable Shihuh face both ocean and Gulf; the far-ranging Bedu *patrol the sands.*

The Shihuh

The Shihuh tribe of the Musandam peninsula is small in number but of peculiar interest. Some people consider they are the remainder of the original population of the Arabian peninsula, who were driven into their mountain fastnesses in much the same way as the ancient Britons were driven into Wales and Cornwall. They carry a small axe of distinctive shape which is the peculiar badge of the Shihuh tribe. Their houses are usually simple mud structures although some may be of stone. Some live in the hills which are so barren that the hill dwellers' standard of living is lower than in other parts of Oman where the rainfall is higher; rainwater in these hills is so precious that it is stored in tanks. The people manage to grow some wheat or barley in cultivated patches; however they are still poor, despite the increasing efforts made by the Omani Government on their behalf. Those who live on the coast have a staple diet of fish and shellfish, and fishing is now their main means of support, although diving for pearls formerly helped them to gain a livelihood.

There are two tribal divisions within the Shihuh – not necessarily related to their habitat – the Bani Hadiya and the Bani Shatair. A Shihhi form of Arabic is generally spoken, but the Kumzar section of the Bani Shatair speak a language of their own akin to Persian. The latter's headquarters are in the small town of Kumzar, a place with some curious aspects. It is situated in a narrow cleft in the rocks and there is barely any flat land around it. Perhaps because of this or because of traditional customs, the dead in Kumzar are buried under the family houses in a manner similar to the custom in parts of Cairo.

Bedu

The *Bedu* live in the deserts to the west and south of Muscat, some of them being true desert dwellers and others living on the fringe of the cultivated areas. Tribes such as the Duru have palm gardens which they care for in the summer months and there is a gradual tendency towards permanent settlement. Indeed this is a process which has probably been going on since time immemorial. They may be "two house families" with a *Bedu* tent for most of the year and a house of mud or palm fronds for the summer. The *Bedu* tent may vary from something large and well equipped, though this is unusual, to a simple and primitive shelter. In either case, woven rugs of camel and goat hair are used, alternate red and black stripes being typical of western Oman, which when sold in the markets are known as *Ibri* or *Nizwa* rugs. The women weave the fabrics used for tent building, rugs, and the accoutrements of camels and horses. This area does not have the black tents of Najd but the cloth is usually hung over thorn trees to provide shade. Wilfred Thesiger, in *Arabian Sands*, describes the virtues of the desert life: "All that is best in the Arabs has come to them from the desert; their deep religious instinct, which has found expression in Islam; their sense of fellowship, which binds them as members of one faith; their pride of race; their generosity and sense of hospitality; their dignity and the regard which they have for the dignity of others as fellow human beings; their humour, their courage and patience, the language which they speak and their passionate love of poetry."

The Omani claim to descent from the main stocks – the Qahtan tribes of south Arabia and the Nizar from the north – pre-supposes a period of desert migration before their arrival in Oman, a fact which tends to confirm the age-long nature of the settling process. The *Bedu* own herds of goats and camels and sometimes range over great distances. Their life is simple and hard, but the pattern is changing as large numbers of *Bedu* are being employed in the oil companies and the ever increasing contracting work. The total population of Oman is reckoned at between 750,000 and a million but of these perhaps only 25,000 to 30,000 are *Bedu*.

Wilfred Thesiger in *Arabian Sands* gives a fascinating description of the

A way of life "demanding the bare necessities, producing nobility".

Bedu mode of life:

"In the sharp cold of the winter morning we rode to the Saar camp, passing herds of fat milch camels, which the herdsboys had just driven out to pasture. Small, black, goat-hair tents were scattered about over the valley . . . and dark-clad women sat churning butter or moved about getting sticks or herding goats . . . The small children were seated in camel litters.

. . . We spent the following day at Ali's tent. This was only about twelve feet long, woven of black goat's hair and pitched like a wind break under a small tree. Among these Bedu tribes there is no contrast between rich and poor, since everyone lives in a similar manner, dressing in the same way and eating the same sort of food.

. . . Most of them demanded only the bare necessities of life, enough food and drink to keep them alive, clothes to cover their nakedness, some form of shelter from the sun and wind, weapons, a few pots, rugs, water skins and their saddlery. It was a life which produced much that was noble, nothing that was gracious."

The drawing of water is entrusted to the modestly veiled Bedu *womenfolk.*

101

They are garrulous and while away the long marching hours with chatter as they move over the barren terrain. Despite the great austerity of their life, they are merciless critics of anyone who lacks patience, good humour, generosity, courtesy, loyalty or courage. One of their greatest compliments is to tell someone that he "has not fallen short" of their ideal – which is a most exacting one – in matters of human behaviour. *Bedu* tribesmen are brought up from birth to endure the physical hardships of the desert, to drink the brackish water of the desert wells, to eat gritty unleavened bread, to suffer the maddening driven sand and blinding glare in a land without shade or cloud, and to put up with extremes of cold and heat.

The *Bedu* are always awake and moving about as soon as it is light. When on the move they have little to cover them apart from the clothes they stand up in, however cold it may be, and even if there is a frost on the ground. Early in the morning they rouse their camels from sleeping places and the strange, ungainly beasts rise to their feet, roaring and gurgling at being disturbed. The

What looks like an impossible riding position is simple to the Bedu.

men shout to each other in harsh, far-carrying voices, and the hobbled camels shuffle past with their forelegs tied to prevent them from straying too far, their breath appearing substantial in the cold air. Someone gives the call to prayer. Amongst some *Bedu* tribes the men pray singly, but in others they pray together in line, facing towards Mecca. Every act connected with prayer has, as Thesiger described, to be performed exactly and in order: "He washed his face, hands and feet; sucked water into his nostrils, put wet fingers into his ears, and passed wet hands over the top of his head. [He] swept the ground before him, placed his rifle in front of him and then prayed towards Mecca. He stood upright, bent forward with his hands on his knees, knelt, and then bowed down till his forehead touched the ground. Several times, he performed these ritual movements, slowly and impressively, while he recited the formal prayer."

Bell-like sounds ring out as coffee is pounded in a brass mortar, the stroke

varying and producing the semblance of a tune. If there is no hurry, bread is baked for breakfast – by the men if they are travelling alone; otherwise by the women when the family are all together in their encampments. Tea is drunk, sweet and black, and then coffee, bitter, black and very strong. Coffee drinking is a formal affair even in the middle of the desert when a few men are on the move together. The server stands to pour a few drops into the small round china cups which he then hands ceremoniously to the others with a little bow – and he will go on serving until the recipient shakes his cup to indicate that he does not want any more. Not more than three cups are usually taken.

The tents of the *Bedu* are often very temporary and flimsy affairs, and may be as small as three yards long and four feet high. They are not usually large like the tents in the northern part of Arabia. They will contain the saddles and other gear needed for their Spartan life. The family utensils may consist of a kettle and coffee pot, blackened with soot from the wood fires, sundry cooking pots of various sizes, a large round tray or

Simple but effective straw stoppers protect the precious water from the desert dust.

two, and a few plates and cups. Such ephemeral dwellings leave but few traces, and H. St John Philby described "the characteristic odds and ends of old Badawin camps – horns of the Rim gazelle, cartridge cases, fragments of leather and the like", which he found on deserted *Bedu* sites.

Omanis ride a camel in a manner totally different from the style of north Arabia and most of the Arab world, where the rider sits on a heavy wooden saddle placed over the hump. Thesiger describes how his camel was saddled with the small Omani saddle: "Sultan picked up my saddle, which was shaped like a small double wooden vice, fitted over palm-fibre pads and girthed it tightly over Umbraisha's withers, just in front of the hump. This wooden vice was really the tree on which he now built the saddle. He next took a crescent-shaped fibre pad which rose in a peak at the back, and after fitting it round the back and sides of the camel's hump, attached it with a loop of string to this tree. He then put a blanket over the pad, and folded my rug over this, placed my saddle bags over the rug, and finally

put a black sheepskin on top of the saddle bags. He had already looped a woollen cord under the camel's stomach so that it passed over the rear pad, and he now took one end of this cord past the tree and back along the other side of the saddle to the original loop. When he drew the cord tight it held everything firmly in place. He had now built a platform over the camel's hump and the fibre pad which was behind it. Sitting on this, the rider was much farther back on the camel than he would have been if riding on the northern saddle.

"A Bedu who is going to mount a crouched camel stands behind her tail. He then leans forward and catches the wooden tree with his left hand as he places his left knee in the saddle. Immediately the camel feels his weight she starts to rise – for it is usually she-camels which are ridden in this part of Arabia – lifting her hindquarters off the ground, and he swings his right leg over the saddle. The camel then rises to her

knees, and with another jerk, is on her feet. The Bedu either sit with a leg on either side of the hump and a little behind it, or kneel in the saddle, sitting on the upturned soles of their feet, in which case they are sitting entirely by balance." They prefer to ride kneeling, especially if they mean to gallop.

The nobility of *Bedu* life does not lie in material things, but is well epitomised in the greetings they exchange with one another. As Philby says: "Very beautiful is the meeting of Arabs in the desert, with their greetings of each other – very formal, very long-drawn-out and repetitive, for every member of each party exchanges the same friendly enquiries and assurances with each member of the other, until all have greeted all, and they part or proceed to any business that may be in hand. Peace be upon you! And on you be peace! How is your state, oh Salih? In peace; how are you, oh 'Ali? In peace! May God give you health! May God improve your condition! How are you? In peace! And then follows the abrupt transition to business with: What is your news?..." This courteousness is characteristic of the Bedu.

103

The haughty camel (below) *will kneel for unloading at a word of command from its owner.*

"*Very beautiful," wrote Philby, "is the meeting in the desert, with their greetings – formal, long drawn-out, and repetitive . . ." Then abruptly: "What is your news?"*

Islanders

The mode of life in other peripheral areas such as Masira and the Kuria Muria Islands also differs from that in most of northern Oman. Masira Island has most of the features of the Omani mainland – *jebel*, plain, coast, scrub and palm – in miniature. However, the people were not in recent decades, until the reign of Sultan Qaboos, permitted to erect buildings in any permanent material – a punishment for the massacre of the crew of the *Baron Inverdale* in 1904. Work at the R.A.F. Station brought people from various parts of the island who had previously lived in palm-frond dwellings into a growing town on the edge of the camp and they built their houses out of oil drums which, though effective as shelter, grew increasingly hideous as rust set in. The improvement in standards of building has been very marked since the accession of Sultan Qaboos.

The history of the Kuria Muria Islands has been even stranger. These five small islands off the coast of Dhofar are called Hallaniya, Jibliya, Suda, Haskiya and Gharzaut. They were ceded to the British Crown by Sayyid Said ibn Sultan on 14th July 1854 without payment, although Lord Clarendon, the Foreign Secretary, did send Sayyid Said a snuff box in recognition of his generosity. A concession to extract guano from the island was then given to Captain Ord, a British merchant captain, and the company which he formed. The company extracted 26,191 tons in 1857–58 (1274–75 AH) and 14,250 tons in 1858–59 (1275–76 AH), but their licence was terminated in 1861 when they fell down on royalty

Still keeping the shape of the goat (above), *this waterskin is light, flexible and unbreakable.*

payments. This flash in the pan interest in guano was of sufficient importance at the time to engage the attention of not only the Foreign Secretary but also the India Office, the Colonial Office, the Admiralty and the Bombay Government. But the islands did not feature in history again until the middle of the present century.

Indeed the islands have been inhabited only by a small number of fishermen, who, latterly at least, have dwelt on Hallaniya alone. British sovereignty was largely nominal and when the islands were visited by Sir William Luce, then Governor of Aden, and Sir George Middleton, then Political Resident in the Persian Gulf, in 1960, the headman of the village asked them if they had a permit from the Sultan, even though Sayyid Said's gift to the British Government had been made over a hundred years previously! The islands were returned to Oman in 1967 (1387 AH).

Bedu men and their camels relax after a day's journey. At dawn or before they will set off again.

Festivities

Though the swords are sharp, injuries in this Id dance (above) – originally a form of military exercise – are rare, thanks to the formal movements and the performers' skill.

Camel-racing is a favourite pastime in Oman (above). A thrilling chase across dusty sands, this one is being run near Sur.

A gathering of men in a barasti *house (above). Each man holds his rifle, symbol of virility and protection.*

The instruments at this Mutrah wedding ceremony (above) *are traditional; the pipe seen on the left of the picture is a relative of the western oboe.*

The main occasions for festivities are the two Id festivals, weddings, National Day, and the birthday of Sultan Qaboos. The Id al Fitr falls at the end of the month of fasting, Ramadan. Although it is technically the lesser of the two Id festivals, it is an occasion for rejoicing and celebration, with visits to family and friends, and music and dancing. The men perform elaborate sword dances, whilst all around them is singing and general celebration, with much firing of guns into the air. The music of the coastal regions shows strong African influences.

In some parts of Arabia, the Id al Fitr is known as the Id al Kiswa, since it is the occasion for Muslims to wear new clothes.

On the tenth of Dhu al Hijja falls the Id al Adha, sixty-nine or seventy days after the Id al Fitr. On this occasion, all Muslims make a sacrifice, and the pilgrimages to the holy places of Islam (*Hajj*) reach their climax.

Weddings, too, are celebrated with much feasting, dancing and finery. The bride is often decked out in gold jewellery worn for that occasion only.

National Day is notable for military parades in honour of the Sultan and everyone joins in the public festivities.

Omani weddings are dignified yet joyful affairs. Above: *The men perform a stately and traditional dance, in which elaborate movements with the rifle play an important part.*

4 The Habitat

The great majority of Omanis are not desert wanderers but townsmen and villagers living where men have dwelt since ancient times. The foundations of some houses which are still inhabited go back for centuries. While new development is springing up, old buildings hold their own, with their trellised plasterwork, woodwork and subtle architectural devices for making the most of the lightest breeze in the hot weather. Styles of home differ between north and south, between coastal plain and mountain areas, and of course between richer and poorer.

Muscat is unique, locked between steep hillsides and the sea at the head of a deep and beautiful bay, latterly graced by the glittering façade of the new palace between the sixteenth-century forts of Mirani (left), and Jalali (right).

"THE rich man in his castle, the poor man at his gate." These words might have been written to describe almost any Omani town or village for they were all in the past dominated by a great turreted fort – *qal'a* – the residence of the Sultan's Governor – *Wali* – or sometimes an important shaikh.

The fort is the traditional seat of authority, however impoverished the occupant may have been, and all the houses and market buildings pale into insignificance before its battlements and fortified walls, its massive gates, and gatehouses manned by *askars*, guards armed with rifles and bandoliers. Control of these fortresses, often strategically situated on great rocks, has always been the aim of anyone wishing to dominate the politics and government of Oman or of particular areas. Until recently, therefore, all the most important, such as Sohar, Rostaq, Nizwa and Muscat, have witnessed the sort of Omani warfare which was common for many decades if not centuries, conducted with ancient muzzle-loading cannon, matchlocks, flintlocks, and Martini Henrys.

Towers and forts on the jagged hills around the areas of green cultivation typify the Omani landscape, defending the approaches to the towns and some-times standing sentinel even over different parts of one place where tribes or groups have been in feud. However, the great forts in Muscat are Portuguese, both built by that same Philip of Spain who launched the great Armada against England after conquering Portugal in 1580 (988 AH). The western fort, Mirani, perhaps derives its name from the Portuguese *Almirante* (meaning "Admiral") and was completed in 1587 (996 AH). It was originally known by the Portuguese as fort Capitan, because it was the residence of their Commander. The eastern fort was finished in 1588 (997 AH), and is now called Jalali, probably after one of its notable commanders although it was originally known as San Jao. An inscription in fort Mirani reads in translation: "In the reign of the very high and mighty Philip, first of this name, our sacred king, in the eighth year of his reign in the crown of Portugal, he ordered through Dom Duarte de Menezes his viceroy in India that this fortress should be built, which Belchior Alvares built, the first captain and founder 1588."

Belchior Alvares' fort was not the first on the site of Mirani. In 1522

Above and right: *Bait Fransa, as it is locally known, is one of the six finest eighteenth-century houses in Muscat.*

110

(929 AH) Dom Joao da Lisboa began a new fort, but his work was almost immediately destroyed by the Captain-General of the Turkish fleet, Admiral Piri Rais, who captured Muscat briefly in the same year. Muscat was again sacked by the Turks in 1582 (990 AH), and the Portuguese then directed their Viceroy in India to build up the two great forts and strengthen the defences.

In the early seventeenth century the Portuguese extended the fortifications. In 1610 (1019 AH), a sea level bastion was built at fort Mirani to prevent small boats running in close beneath the arc

of fire of cannon emplacements in the fort itself, and an inscription commemorating this event reads in translation: "Experience, zeal and truth built for me the defence of the cross which defends me, on the order of the Very High and Powerful King Don Philip, third of this name in the year 1610." In 1617 (1027 AH), Don Garcia da Silva, the Spanish Ambassador to Persia, visited Muscat, staying in the Augustinian Convent on the site of which Bait Graiza (a corruption of the Portuguese *igreja* meaning church) was later built, and a detailed account of his programme in the town survives. Between 1623 (1033 AH), and 1626 (1036 AH), the wall of the city was rebuilt substantially in the same form as it stands today and the outlying watch towers, the fortifications of Muscat Island north of Jalali, and a new customs house date from this period. The original chapel in fort Mirani still survives, although its roof has been subsequently repaired and a massive column erected to support it. There is a cup for holy water in the wall with a Latin inscription: "Ave Maria gratia sancta plena Dominus tecum."

Fort Mirani has never been taken by storm in its 350 odd years. When it fell to the Ya'rubi Imam Sultan ibn Saif in

December 1649 (1059 AH), it was taken, according to Omani tradition, by a stratagem in which an Indian merchant of Muscat called Narutem played a key role. There was at the time an impasse between the Imam's troops and the defending Portuguese, but an affair of the heart brought matters to a head. Narutem had a very beautiful daughter whom the Portuguese commander Pereira wished to marry, but, despite the offer of a temptingly high bride price, Narutem refused his consent on religious grounds. He did not think it right for a Christian to marry a Hindu. Narutem was accountant to the Portuguese Treasury and contractor to the shops in Mirani and Jalali, and Pereira retaliated by threatening to deprive him of this profitable office. Narutem then asked Pereira for a year's grace to prepare wedding clothes and ornaments. At the same time, he advised that, if Muscat were to withstand a long siege, the foul water in the forts' cisterns should be replaced, the gunpowder removed and pounded and the old wheat discarded for new supplies. Pereira gave Narutem the year's grace and also authority to proceed with the replenishments he suggested.

Narutem then saw a way out of his dilemma and after depleting the forts'

Once Bait Fransa was the home of the French Consul in Muscat. The elegance and finish of its airy inner court (above) *are typical of the homes of Muscat's leading citizens in recent centuries.*

111

supplies as instructed, but not replenishing them, he wrote to the Imam Sultan ibn Saif recommending an attack on Muscat on the following Sunday, when, he said, the Portuguese would be drinking wine and playing musical instruments. The Imam took his advice and attacked successfully, thus paving the way for the final expulsion of the Portuguese from Oman.

Representatives of foreign powers have been resident in Muscat since the eighteenth century, towards the end of which a representative of the Great Mogul occupied a house known as the "Nabob's House". In the same period a local resident acted as "Consul for the English", but it was not until 1800 (1215 AH) that a formal treaty with Britain provided that an "English gentleman of respectability should always reside at the port of Muscat". Since then there has been continuous British representation, although the succession of British resident representatives was interrupted between 1810 and 1861 as the climate of Muscat was considered too unhealthy. Between 1800 and 1810 (1215 and 1225 AH) the first four representatives all died *en poste*. No permanent representative was again appointed until 1861. Since then there has always been a British Consul who was also known at various times as Political Agent or Political Resident, being an appointee of the British Government in India until 1958. Thereafter appointments were made by the Foreign Office, and the first British Ambassador was accredited in 1971.

It was always the custom of the early representatives to live in local houses and even the greatly expanded British Consulate building built in 1890 (1308 AH), was built in the Arab style with a central courtyard. This was a building deliberately designed to impress and was a far cry from the "miserable hovel" in which the first four representatives had lived. An earlier building on the present British Embassy site dated back roughly to the 1820s, but where the original representatives lived is not known. From the 1860s the seat of representation seems to have been on the present site, though this was not actually purchased until 1878 when the house previously leased from Bibi Zeinab bint Muhammad Amir was acquired.

The Sultan of Oman entered into commercial and consular treaties with the United States in 1833 (1249 AH), and

Architectural Styles

The Bait Zawawi, now the United States Embassy, overlooks a little bay known as Chinaman's Cove.

The graceful window screen (below) – mashribiya – *is typical of Omani houses.*

Mashribiya *window styles are used in modern buildings* (below).

There are three main types of architecture in Muscat: first the traditional Arab, then the Portuguese, and finally the modern. Traditional Arab architecture is represented by the beautifully proportioned Bait Graiza which is situated under Fort Mirani on the site of the Augustinian convent built by the Portuguese. There are also five houses built in the same style towards the end of the eighteenth century. All of these are being preserved, though much of Muscat's old market area, with its picturesque, narrow streets but unsubstantial buildings, has been swept away to make room for modern development. The Portuguese monuments are the two great forts of Mirani and Jalali, which perch on the rocks on the opposite sides of the Muscat harbour. These still give Muscat much of its unique character. The two Portuguese churches which stood in Muscat at least until the early eighteenth century, have been built over, though a small chapel remains in Fort Mirani.

In the summer heat of Muscat, free flow of air through many windows is essential (above).

Bait Nadir in Muscat (above), another eighteenth-century home, is earmarked as a museum. Below: Another fine house tells of the luxury enjoyed by past families of Omani merchants of the time when Muscat was the entrepôt of the whole Indian Ocean.

In neighbouring Mutrah, the port's market (suq) is overlooked by the fine Arab building (above).

Modern mashribiya *work (below) was chosen by a leading member of the ruling family for his Muscat home.*

Grace, in Islamic style, is a feature of many Muscat windows (centre left).

Muscat

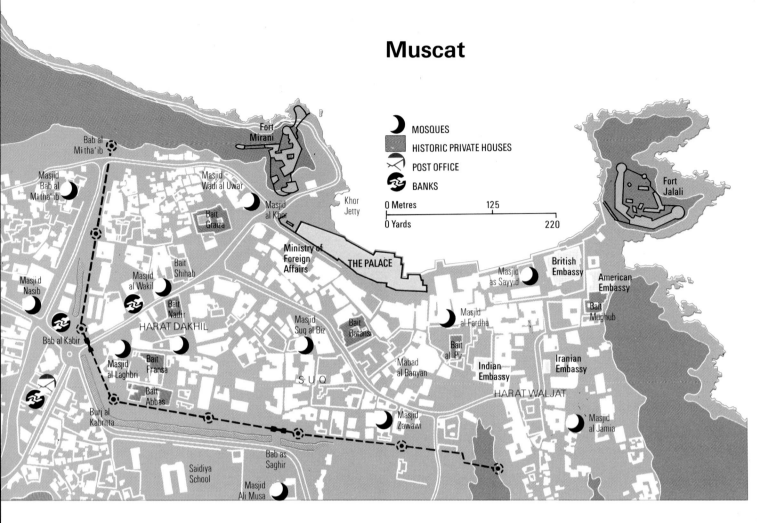

Legend:
- MOSQUES
- HISTORIC PRIVATE HOUSES
- POST OFFICE
- BANKS

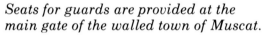

0 Metres — 125
0 Yards — 220

Map labels:
Fort Mirani, Bab al Mitha'ib, Masjid Bab al Mitha'ib, Masjid Wadi al Uwar, Bait Graiza, Masjid al Khor, Khor Jetty, Fort Jalali, Masjid Nasib, Masjid al Wakil, Bait Shihab, Ministry of Foreign Affairs, THE PALACE, British Embassy, American Embassy, Masjid as Sayyid, Bab al Kabir, Bait Nadir, HARAT DAKHIL, Masjid Suq al Biz, Bait Batansi, Masjid al Fardha, Bait Mughub, Masjid al Laghbri, Bait Fransa, Bait al Pir, Bait Abbas, SUQ, Mabad al Banyan, Indian Embassy, Iranian Embassy, HARAT WALJAT, Burj al Kabrita, Masjid Zawawi, Masjid al Jamia, Bab as Saghir, Saidiya School, Masjid Ali Musa

Over one of the little gates to Muscat's suq rises an elegant arch.

Seats for guards are provided at the main gate of the walled town of Muscat.

The main entrance to the British Embassy courtyard (above), *is barred by a studded teak door. Visitors crouch to enter by the inset wicket gate* (left). *Mogul influences are illustrated by the door* (below).

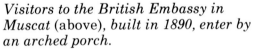

Visitors to the British Embassy in Muscat (above), *built in 1890, enter by an arched porch.*

The new but traditional town gate (below) *harmonises with older work such as the two little gates* (above).

The main gate (below) *in Muscat's walls was restored by Sultan Said.*

Muscat & environs

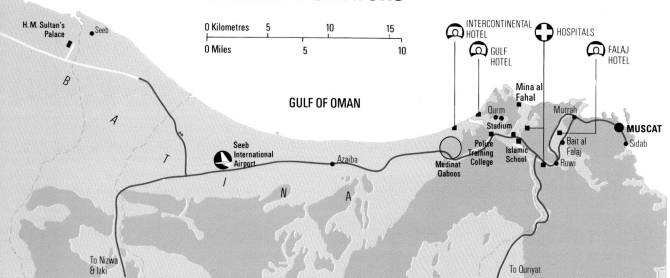

The "capital area" of today embraces Muscat and Mutrah, and the coastline from Seeb to Sidab.

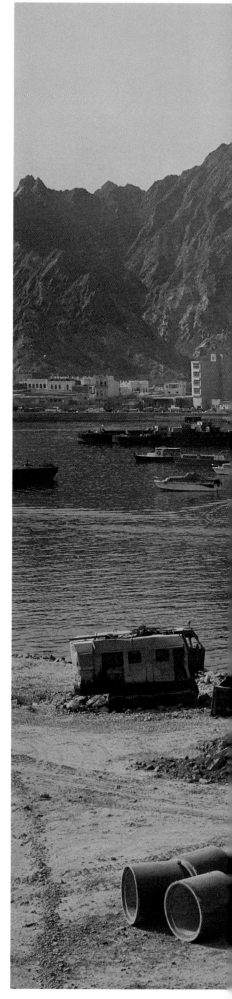

with the Government of France in 1844 (1260 AH). The treaties with Britain were more numerous and spread over a long period, 1798 (1213 AH), 1800 (1215 AH), 1837 (1253 AH), the first treaty of Friendship and Commerce, 1891 (1309 AH), 1892 (1310 AH), and a series of treaties in 1822 (1238 AH), 1845 (1261 AH), and 1873 (1290 AH) against the slave trade. A commercial declaration was made in 1877 (1294 AH) with the Dutch Government, but apart from the British only the French and the Americans had resident consuls. The British Agent, whose duties were prescribed by the Government of India, also held a consular warrant from the Foreign Office in London after 1863 (1280 AH).

The French Consul lived from 1894 (1312 AH) to 1914 (1333 AH), when the post was closed, in a house belonging to the Sultan – one of the complex built in the late eighteenth century, which Sultan Qaboos has preserved as part of Oman's cultural heritage. This house was known during the period of French occupation and just afterwards as "Bait Fransa".

The United States Consulate was situated, from 1880 (1298 AH) when it was established until 1917 (1336 AH) when it was closed, in an elegant house behind the British Embassy. It was built in local Arab style with a central courtyard somewhat similar to the British and French consulates. The United States and France had no further permanent representation on the spot after the closure of their consulates, until diplomatic relations were established with the Sultanate in 1971 (1391 AH) after the

accession of Sultan Qaboos.

The premises of the British Embassy evoke many historical associations. A tombstone of a Portuguese soldier is to be seen in the courtyard. A gate on the east side, carved in authentic Omani style but decorated also with the British consular crown, was used for visits of ceremony between the British representatives and the Sultan, whose palace was situated beyond the customs area, on the other side of the Muscat Bay. The faces of the portraits on the walls bear testimony to the variety of the characters who have had the opportunity of observing, and playing a part in Omani history – such men as Sir Percy Cox, Colonel Jayakar, a surgeon and naturalist, who gave his name to a unique species of goat, and Colonel Miles, whose book *The Countries and Tribes of the Persian Gulf* is still a classic. In the courtyard between the two main blocks of buildings stands the stump of an enormous flagpole, which was dismantled in 1972 (1392 AH) when its superstructure became dangerous. This was the flagpole which was clasped, as in other British establishments in the area, by slaves claiming their freedom. Up to 1965 (1385 AH) or so, the British Government issued manumission certificates to any slaves seeking to establish their free status in the following terms: "Be it known to all who may see this that the bearer . . . has been manumitted and no one has a right to

The "corniche" at Mutrah sweeps round the rim of the fine natural harbour.

"Prosperity brought by sea trade has made Oman a country of gracious houses as well as castles."

Merchants' homes (above) *skirt the waterfront at Mutrah.*

A whitened exterior (above) *reflects the sun and diminishes the heat within.*

This window (above) *opens in four sections to control ventilation and the access of sunlight.*

The Arab arch finds a place even within a square doorway (above).

Some of Mutrah's older houses display oriental flamboyance.

Colours enhance the simple beauty of many of Mutrah's windows.

The picture shows typical structural techniques in Omani homes (right).

interfere with his/her liberty."

Admiral Boyle Somerville, who visited Muscat in the early years of the present century, has left an entertaining description of the British Embassy during the Cox's time. "The Residency was a house . . . to be approached with some circumspection, in spite of the hospitality of its inhabitants. It is built around four sides of a central courtyard. You come into it through an archway at the back, and find a broad flight of stairs on the right hand, leading to the cool verandah and living rooms on the first floor, which thus are well raised above the heat of the ground, and look widely forth on the harbour. Mrs Resident was a lady whose kindness of heart extended itself far past the plane of humanity, and reached down even to our distant and nasty little relatives, the apes. She kept, in the courtyard of the Residency, a collection of the more highly-coloured of these creatures. No Thames barge brilliant in red, blue and yellow can display more startlingly effective bows, or a more originally conceived stern decoration than could these simian guardians of the stairs; and no bargee ever had such a command of the language of execration as they. They gnashed their teeth, yearningly, on the unfortunate visitor;

they leapt and danced at the full extent of their straining waist chains, clucking and gibbering at him, or hideously shrieking battle, murder and sudden death; they seized the handrail – mercifully a stout one, and they could only just reach it – and shook it in impotent fury. In brief, they put the wind up you. By closely hugging the wall on the starboard hand, and not hauling to the wind again until well past these dangers, it was, however, just possible to circumnavigate them; and the delightful welcome that greeted the visitor on the top landing was quite well worth the perilous passage below."

At the same time, Sultan Faisal ibn Turki kept the King of Beasts in the adjoining palace, as Theodore Bent describes: "The palace is entered by a formidable-looking door, decorated with large spiked bosses of brass. This opens into a small court which contained the most imposing sight of the place, namely the lion in his cage."

The prosperity brought by sea trade has made Oman a country of gracious houses as well as of castles and towers. In Muscat itself there are six splendid houses built during the latter half of the eighteenth century and belonging to the Al bu Said family. The Bait Graiza

("House of the Church") is the largest and finest, and is named after the Augustinian Convent which formerly stood near the site. All these houses, which are of lofty appearance and well proportioned, have courtyards in the middle and the buildings which surround the square are surmounted by crenellations of a similar shape to those of Mogul architecture. The siting of the windows is absolutely harmonious, the doors and windows are finely carved, and simple stone stairways give access to the first floor. There is a mosque with a beautifully carved door of the same date on the eastern side of Muscat within the walls. In Ibra, in the Sharqiya region, there is also an area of well-built houses of roughly the same date. Now virtually a ghost town, it is approached through an arched gateway – a little walled town with its own fortifications running up the barren hills nearby. A tunnel leads from one house to the main fort of Ibra on the other side of the *wadi*. These substantial houses of stone may have been commissioned and lived in by very wealthy people in their heyday, which can be approximately dated by a beautiful carved doorway bearing the date 1192 – that is, corresponding to 1778 AD. The houses contain elaborate arches of Mogul design and the craftsmen who built them probably came from India or Persia. One house contains a curious feature – a tower, round externally, but with a square room inside.

There has always been a close connection between the Sharqiya and the Omani settlements in east Africa, and wealth gained from the east African trade enabled merchants who had prospered to build these substantial houses – which perhaps explains why rough pictures of ships are so often depicted on walls in Oman at great distances from the sea. Such large houses required plentiful labour to build and maintain and with the suppression of the slave trade they gradually fell into decay, sad reminders of a more prosperous past, though one is still used to house looms and carding gins for weaving loin cloths – *wazaras*.

The Omanis lived well in east Africa for many generations and when the Portuguese, under Vasco da Gama, arrived there in 1498 (904 AH), they were astonished at the prosperity of the Arab possessions. Vasco da Gama remarked that Malindi, near Mombasa, was a

"Noble City" and the "King" received the Portuguese envoy in a palace strewn with carpets – oriental rugs at this date were so costly that they were used in Europe to cover tables rather than floors – and furnished with stools inlaid with ivory and gold.

In the southern region of Dhofar the homes of the people differ markedly from those of the north. In Salala itself there are a number of square set elegant houses of a design more distinctive of Dhofar itself and Hadhramaut than of the north. Built of mud brick covered in stucco, they are sometimes several storeys high and the arched windows are covered with wooden screens of the *mashribiya* type. Sometimes there are distinctive devices round the flat roofs, and there is a large cluster of such houses in the coconut groves to the north of Salala – for the coconut is as distinctive of Dhofar as the date palm is of the north. In the coastal towns of Taqa and Marbat there are similar houses and the forts occupied by the shaikhs and *Walis* are modified versions of these. The palace of the Sultan in Salala was originally built by Sultan Turki ibn Said but has been added to subsequently by several Sultans and now it forms an interesting turreted labyrinth on the sea shore.

The coastal plain of Dhofar has been important since time immemorial and the ruins of the town of Samhuram, a city which depended for its prosperity on the incense trade, stands on the Khor Rori near Taqa. Other ruins associated with the incense trade are the fort in the Wadi Andhur and the fort and houses at Hanun on the desert road north from the Jebel. All these old buildings are of stone, some of which is finely dressed.

Near Salala itself – a garden city surrounded not only by groves of coconuts but also fields of lucerne and vegetables with clusters of paw-paws and other fruit trees – stands the ruined town of Balid, covering an extensive area. This mediaeval town was occupied until the sixteenth century and was visited by ibn Batuta and earlier by Marco Polo, who described it as a "beautiful large and noble city". Ibn Batuta remarks that "The city of Dhofar lay in an isolated desert region." The Habudi ruler Ahmad ibn Abdulla had removed the town from inland to the coast in 1223 (620 AH) to protect it from attack. The new city, built on the ruins of an ancient Sabaean city which boasted a citadel one hundred feet high, was named al Mansura. The *suq*, in which the majority of sellers were female slaves, was outside the city to the west in a pleasant area called al-Harja, but its smells did not please ibn Batuta on account of the quantity of fruit and fish sold there.

There are other ruins on the plain nearby at Robat and local tradition holds that this was once Eryot, the proud city of the Shhero (or Shahra), who are by common consent locally the most ancient tribe of the area deriving their descent

Many Salala homes (above) *have a classic simplicity to their design.*

The homes of humbler citizens of Salala are neatly ranged within sight and sound of the sea which provides their livelihood.

Evidence of Dhofar's monsoon rainfall is seen in the rooftop waterspouts. Many such houses are built of packed clay bonded by straw.

Dhofar Windows

Until quite recently Oman's Indian Ocean possessions stretched from the Makran coast of what is today Pakistan to the African islands of Zanzibar and Pemba. In Dhofar, architectural and decorative styles display these varied influences, and both Mogul and African ideas blend with those of the Arab.

The carpenter's design complements the plasterer's in this Dhofar window.

A touch of African brilliance decorates some of the shutters of Dhofar's homes.

Functional – but exquisite – trellis-work decorates this window.

No window is precisely like another. Yet all are graceful.

from Shaddad, son of Ad.

The coastline to the west of Salala is magnificent, with great cliffs and little sandy beaches. When the sea is rough the great waves break with cascades of white foam over the dark rocks and the headland of Raysut is especially dramatic. On this headland there is an old castle or fort of indeterminate date, attributed by some to the Portuguese, but probably dating from a much earlier period. It stands in marked contrast to the new harbour at Raysut commissioned

The limestone cutter's craft is greatly skilled: along a certain line, one blow suffices.

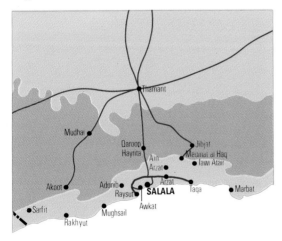

Salala & environs

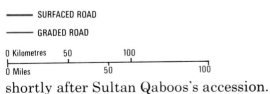

——— SURFACED ROAD

——— GRADED ROAD

shortly after Sultan Qaboos's accession.

On the mountains of Dhofar there are many enclosures made of stone walls which, from the air, form an apparently unrelated series of circular and oval patterns. These are in fact the walled areas inside which the people of the Qara mountains cultivate small fields of barley and maize protected from cattle, goats and camels. Sometimes enclosures of the same type, but smaller in size, are pens for the people's animals. The houses are round in shape and sometimes of considerable size, perhaps fifteen feet or more in diameter. The roofs are thatched with the long grass which grows on the mountain during the rainy monsoon period though black plastic is sometimes now used as well. The house serves as the focal point for each family and the sparsely furnished interior is made dim with smoke from the cooking fires which they kindle inside. Theirs is a hard life, revolving very much round the small sleek cattle which thrive on the Jebel, though they also keep goats and camels.

Bertram Thomas who toured the area in 1930 (1349 AH) relates that it was the inviolable rule that one half of a man's cows should be slaughtered as a sacrifice after his death, in the manner of some of the ancient peoples. He also well described the setting of a settlement in the hills of Dhofar.

". . . we left the wadi by the pass of Sa'arin, to climb 500 feet into steep stony country. Then followed rolling yellow meadows where hay stood to a man's middle, and occasional clumps of giant trees crowned the hills or nestled in the hollows. Behind and below us in the distance, was the faint blue sea, and round us, undulating down country with the wooded cliffs above Nihaz occasionally edging the western skyline. Here at 1,500 feet the bird life so plentiful in the valleys below dwindled to a few sparrow-hawks and many large storks, but butterflies, grasshoppers and locusts were many and various.

And now we looked down upon a pleasant vale that was our immediate destination, Al 'Ain, a Shahari settlement of Had bi Dhomari, where a spring comes bubbling out of the ground in the belly of a wooded trough. Two wild fig trees, as big and shady as good English walnuts, and bursting with apple-like fruit, made inviting bivouacs, and there I halted. A three hour's climb had made me thirsty, but it is impossible to obtain milk during the noonday, and the curds that were brought me arrived belatedly after I had dealt with the milk of a brimming fresh coconut.

From over the brow of the hill appeared a party of Qara tribesmen of Sheikh Hasan, in extended order, singing their peculiar danadon chant of the mountains. Their fellow-tribesmen of Ain mustered to meet them, one drawing his sword to dance in honourable welcome."

Dhofar Doors

Doors in Dhofar, as in other parts of Oman, tend to give a house its personality and distinction. Dhofaris share with other Arabs a lively sense of privacy, and family life goes on within the walled confines of the home. Dhofari doors are notable for their bright colouring, and carving is not such a feature as it is in northern Oman. The doors are fitted with large individual locks as protection, but this does not diminish the traditional hospitality offered when a visitor goes to a house in Dhofar.

Delight in strong colours (right) *perhaps derives from Dhofar's long association with Zanzibar, and other parts of the east African coast, where bright cloth was for long a major item of trade between the Omani Arab and African worlds.*

Above and below: *The locksmith's art has developed along its own lines in Dhofar.*

On hot summer nights every shutter will be flung wide open.

Sur

The principal coastal town between Salala and Muscat is Sur, an administrative centre governed locally by a *Wali*. Sur, too, has its distinctive style of architecture and exterior decoration – forms which reflect the ease and serenity of the town.

Prosperous citizens of Sur made their fortunes from trade. Sur's new source of wealth could be coal and manganese found inland.

Crenellations (below) decorate the exterior of one of Sur's many elegant houses.

In Oman, a great trading country, many oriental styles are amalgamated, as in this door at Sur.

The eyes peeping out upon the world beyond from this window are reflected in the craftsman's design above.

The Inland Forts

Many Europeans make the mistake of attributing all the forts in Oman and the Gulf to the Portuguese. Several Omani forts, however, are of great antiquity, and those at Bahla and Rostaq date from the period before Islam and were probably originally Persian in construction. Rostaq, the Arabised form of a Persian word signifying an outlying or border district, probably traces its name to the Sassanid period when it came under the Persian capital at Dastajird or Sohar. The great fort at Sohar also pre-dates the Portuguese who themselves carried out modifications and additions. Albuquerque found there in 1507 (916 AH) "a fortress of square shape, with six towers round it, having also over the gate two very large towers". The fort was so large that it then required more than a thousand men for its defence. It has subsequently had a very turbulent history and most of the towers have consequently been rebuilt many times, only the north-western one retaining its original shape.

The great fort at Nizwa was built by Sultan ibn Saif (1649–1688: 1059–1079 AH), one of the great Imams of the Ya'ruba dynasty who finally drove the Portuguese out of Muscat. This took twelve years to build, and was reputedly financed from the spoils of the sack of Ras al Khaima. Its enormous round tower has a diameter of approximately 120 feet and contains not only impressively strong fortifications but also dungeons and oubliettes.

The Ya'ruba dynasty is responsible for two other notable architectural achievements and the early Al bu Saids made some fine architectural additions to several forts and built some splendid large houses. The fort at Jabrin was commissioned by Bil'arub ibn Saif in about 1670 (1081 AH) largely as a country home or retreat, though for a while it was regarded as the capital of Oman. Massive and impressively strong, it is also decorated with ornately carved doorways, painted ceilings of rare beauty and graceful arches in the Mogul style. The square windows are latticed and stone mullioned, and the fine plaster work includes adornment of the entrance to the tomb where Bil'arub himself is buried and Qur'anic inscriptions. The Imam's private *majlis* at the top is a light, airy room, with a delicately painted ceiling and fine views over the plain towards the towering heights of the Jebel Akhdar. Learning flourished in Bil'arub's day and he founded a famous school in the shadow of the new "palace".

The fort at al Hazm, which stands on the approaches to Rostaq from the coast, is another great Ya'ruba monument. It was built in 1708 (1126 AH) and was for a while the capital of Oman when the Imam Sultan ibn Saif II moved from Rostaq. Its gun turrets, containing five huge Portuguese and Spanish cannon probably brought from Muscat in the nineteenth century in the time of the Imam Azzan ibn Qais (1868–1871: 1285–1288 AH), are magnificently decorated with fine plaster work, which is also a feature of the vaulted ceilings around the courtyard. A strong *falaj* stream, which also feeds the neighbouring plantation, flows through the fort, just as at Jabrin, and there is also a small school on the upper storey. The tall and splendidly carved entrance doors are oddly masked by subsequent mud construction and above them there is a slit in the ceiling and a water tank close by so that if attackers fired the wooden door the fire could be easily extinguished. There are also slits for pouring boiling honey – such was the custom – or oil on

Behind the women drawing their daily supply of water stands Sohar's fort.

The entrance to Sohar's castle is protected by pointed "elephant studs" (below).

Below: *Traditional* Askars *guard the great castle of Bahla.*

attackers, and the inevitable dungeons. Al Hazm curiously remained in the hands of the Ya'ruba family – long after the Al bu Said had supplanted them as a dynasty in 1747 (1160 AH). It was taken from them finally in about 1870 (1287 AH) by Ibrahim ibn Qais, the son of the Imam Azzan ibn Qais, and father of Sayyid Ahmad ibn Ibrahim, who for many years was Minister of the Interior to the late Sultan Said ibn Taimur.

One of the forts built by the Al bu Said dynasty, in the eighteenth century, was at Bait al Falaj, which, as its name implies, was a house depending on a *falaj* water supply from the nearby mountains. Ever since Oman has had a modern army, the fort there has been its headquarters, and Bait al Falaj has consequently acquired a special fame amongst soldiers. In some ways, therefore, Bait al Falaj corresponds to the Horse Guards at Whitehall – a military headquarters where old and new military traditions meet.

In the past it was only the most wealthy and influential part of the population who lived in fine houses. Along the whole of the Batina coast and even in Muscat itself, the usual dwelling was – and often still is – made of palm fronds and called a *barasti*. They are

sometimes quite complicated in design and, though normally a single room of varying size, they may even have two storeys. These light structures, which are kept together by cords of palm fibre, have obvious disadvantages in wet or cold weather, but for the greater part of the year, when it is hot or very hot, they provide shade and are cool, as the breeze can easily penetrate the walls. Many *barastis* are rectangular in shape with a stout upright pole at either end, and pitched roofs – in fact model "Robinson Crusoe" houses.

Omani men like to have sitting-out places where they can chat with their neighbours, drink coffee, and offer hospitality to visitors, for offering hospitality is here, as elsewhere in Arabia, a sacred

A bird's eye view shows the relationship of Bahla's castle to the town (above).

duty and pleasure at one and the same time. These sitting-out places, which are usually mere palm-frond shelters against the sun, are open to the breezes and may be found by the sea, in the pleasant palm gardens of the Batina or in the Interior, or even high in the Jebel Akhdar, with magnificent views over mountain and plain.

The pointed arch is a feature of Omani architecture and is found in the interior of the great castles (for example Bahla, above), *the old market in Muscat or in the colonnade of an old Muscat house which is also adorned with the more ornate serrated version of the arch.*

Interior Woodwork

Unlike most of the rest of Arabia, hardwood trees have in the past grown in parts of Oman. This source of wood, supplemented from India and Africa, has helped to keep alive in Oman a remarkable tradition of woodcarving over hundreds of years.

The doorway screen (above) *declares the home-owner's taste.*

Every window screen tests the designer's ingenuity.

The rose inspires the woodcarver's handiwork (above).

Arab design is based on deep studies of geometry.

In many places the houses are built of mud and some elegant dwellings are constructed in this material, though some structures are a combination of stone and mud. In Nizwa, for example, there are narrow, winding streets of grey mud-built houses, where planning shows innate sophistication, far exceeding that of many conscious modern designs in environmental wisdom, and where winding streets are so aligned as to give shade to man and beast in the hot weather. The streets lead out beyond the city's defensive walls and gatehouses to the gardens beyond, and there too are numerous well-proportioned houses among the groves, little country estates where the humped bull can be seen ploughing among the trees. Some of these houses have gracious external staircases and mud walls enclosing the paths which wind through the groves from one small settlement to another.

Bertram Thomas described a typical Omani house which he visited in the Interior in the 1920s: ". . . Arab country houses are very much alike, being entirely without amenities or decoration . . . Glass windows are unknown, as is reasonable in so hot a climate, and interior decoration, where plain, sun-made brick does not wholly forbid it, takes the form of a simple plaster stucco . . . The upper chamber . . . was typical. Low, square-shuttered, iron-barred windows level with the floor surround the four sides, and each is carried up to a blind, pointed arch, a shelf flush with the upper window-sashing making a sort of alcove wherein gay coffee-cups, water-ewer, and incense-burner are the usual furnishings. The exposed rafters are black with smoke stain, for the chimney is unknown in tropical Oman, but the whole floor is covered with gay coloured carpets . . . Ornate wooden pegs punctuate the walls at man's height, and from them depends an armoury of rifles slung barrel downwards, common double-edged swords, cartridge belts, powder flasks and daggers . . ." It is, however, a feature of many of the houses in the Interior, even those built of mud brick, to have ceilings painted in gay colours and sometimes with illuminated texts from the Qur'an.

Sometimes great and important structures too are built of mud, such as the old fort of the Shaikh of the Bani Riyam at Birkat al Moz, with its courtyards, doors and elegant rooms with painted ceilings. The great walls surrounding

Barasti *homes at Sohar are built of woven palm-fronds. The houses are strong, and allow the free passage of air-currents in the heat.*

Coastal villagers use traditional materials for house-building.

Right: *Mountain villages "grow" out of the cliffs on which they are built.*

Bahla in a seven mile ring are also constructed of mud – parapets, steps, battlements, guard houses and all.

Houses in the mountain villages in the Jebel Akhdar are rectangular in shape and, built on the rocky sloping hillside, resemble those of Kurdistan. Their flat roofs are turned yellow in autumn by

steep terraces watered by a bubbling *falaj* stream.

In the mountains of northern Oman and Dhofar there are many caves to which people have traditionally resorted in time of trouble and where nomadic families and their animals still sometimes take shelter from the elements.

the biblical book of Genesis, "And unto Eber were born two sons; the name of one was Peleg, for in his day was the earth divided."

The word *falaj* is commonly used to mean the whole of the irrigation channel system downstream of where the water originates. Thus it may mean a water

In the Jebel Akhdar villages are cut into the cliffside.

the maize cobs put out to dry and ripen and the arches of stone stairways evoke a feeling of antiquity and timelessness. The animals are often kept downstairs whilst the family live above and have their reception rooms there.

Large villages like Shuraija, which earlier travellers such as Lieutenant Wellsted in the 1830s called Shirauzi, suggesting a connection with Shiraz in Persia – there is similarity in that vines and roses grow in both places – are approached by mountain paths, made fit by the labour of man for the sturdy and sure-footed mountain donkeys to traverse. In places, steps have been cut into the rock or constructed laboriously of stone against precarious rock faces. Shuraija itself, where, at this altitude, the deciduous trees such as the walnut turn to gold in autumn, is surrounded by

The Falaj System

The origins of the widespread and sophisticated water-system in Oman are very ancient. Omani legend attributes them to Sulaiman ibn Daud – Solomon the son of David – who visited Oman on a magic carpet and caused his *djinns* to construct the 10,000 water channels in ten days. *Falajes* which never dry up, however dry the season may be – the majority of which are in the Dhahira and Buraimi areas – are still called *Daudis*.

It is estimated that 90 per cent of the rain precipitation in Oman enters aquifers, which are tapped in three different but complementary ways – wells, and *falajes* of two sorts (*ghayl* and *qanat*).

Falaj means a system for the distribution of water amongst those who have established rights to a source of supply. The word derives from a Semitic root of great antiquity which finds mention in

Where there is water, there is human life. So men combine their skills to catch and channel the mountain's water for cultivation.

channel which has tapped a flow in the upper gravels of a *wadi* (*ghayl*) and been constructed alongside or carved into the rocky walls of a *wadi* for several miles. Alternatively it may mean a "man-made water mine in which the water stored in an aquifer is brought to the surface by means of a tunnelled conduit" in exactly the same way as the *qanat* in Persia. Sixty-five feet is the average depth of the mother well, though it may be as much as 200 feet. From the mother well – *Umm al Falaj* – until the tunnel debouches, there are shafts sunk at regular intervals of some fifty to sixty feet, which are used both for the initial construction and for subsequent inspection. The tunnel may run between two to six miles underground.

A very large number of the *falajes* of the *qanat* type were built in pre-Islamic times and those of al Jauf region, which was colonised and developed in Achaemenid times, date from some 2,500 years ago. During another major period of construction in Sassanid times there was extensive development in eastern Oman based on Mazun – Sohar. With the coming of Islam and the expulsion of the Persians the villages and cultivated areas were organised and regulated by the Ibadhi religious authorities (*Ulema*) and their legal rulings can be traced back to the very first Imamate in the ninth century AD (third century AH).

In central Oman, which has a relatively high population and reliable *falajes*, land tenure is mainly freehold held in smallish lots by tribesmen, and large scale landholding by landlords has never been a feature of this region throughout history. However, in the northern part of the country which did not remain so

firmly within the Ibadhi fold there is a different system of land organisation – a form of share-cropping. At the very root of village life is the need to preserve water rights. The distribution of water is, therefore, carefully controlled and recorded in *falaj* books and there may be no less than two hundred owners of permanent water rights in a single *falaj* to say nothing of the owners of temporary rights.

Each community dependent on a single *falaj* in a settlement represents a self-sufficient hydrological society, whose members must co-operate, despite deeply rooted differences and tribal enmities which have caused separate fortified quarters with towers and battlements to be built. In Izki, for example, there are two adjoining quarters, called Yaman and Nizar – which represent the basic tribal difference in Oman like the divisions between Hinawi and Ghafiri. The inhabitants of each quarter are historically opposed to one another but, as they are dependent on the same *falaj* system, are compelled to co-operate. Civil wars – particularly the disastrous wars of the ninth century AD (third century AH) – were responsible for destroying much of the country's *falaj* system and there is no doubt that much

larger areas were under cultivation even in comparatively recent times. But even this larger area would only have been a part of what was cultivated in the sixth century AD. The very art of *falaj* making has to a large extent been lost, though the skill is preserved by the Awamir tribe, who also have a near-monopoly on repair work.

A reasonable sized *falaj* of the *qanat* type may support about 1,000 people and produce a flow of about nine gallons per second to irrigate an area of some forty hectares of permanently cultivated land. A *falaj* with a really good flow may support larger settlements of up to 2,500, and if a number of *falajes* are concentrated in one area they may thus sustain a population of about 8,000.

Virtually all the perennial water from a *falaj* is used for date palms, although citrus, bananas, pomegranates and mangoes may also be irrigated. Lucerne – alfalfa – is planted in basins outside the palm groves, and grain and leguminous crops are grown from the winter surplus discharge of the *falaj*.

A strict system of priorities for the use of water is followed. At the top of the *falaj* where it comes to the surface, there is an opening where drinking water may be drawn and all have free

access to this. In the residential area the water is also communal and the order of domestic usage is: drinking water, bathing facilities with the men's bath area upstream of the women's – each in little enclosures – and then the place where the dead are washed. Mosques often have their own direct access for ritual ablutions. After all this the water is divided for irrigation and there are usually a number of bifurcations from the main channel. Underground channels need to be cleaned and channels kept in good repair by cementing, and upkeep of the main network of primary channels is the responsibility of the communal *falaj* organisation. Individual owners are responsible for channels in their gardens.

The principles of shareholding in the water are complicated. Distribution to the garden is, however, usually arranged in a set order and each plot of land has a prescribed period of time allocated to it. This is known as the cycle, and in many towns and villages there is a sundial in a central place, by which the periods due to each garden are measured. Thus, though land, water rights and crop may be owned separately, land usually changes hand in practice with a set allocation of water based on a previously

Water flowing from the mountains, or tapped from the underground water-table, comes tumbling into the village after its long journey.

The skill of the falaj-builder has been passed from father to son for more than two thousand years.

Aqueducts are built to span depressions along the water's route to the villages.

existing distribution system.

On small *falajes* with only a few owners, arrangements for upkeep can easily be made on an *ad hoc* basis and in areas where there is a capitalist system, the landowner or a landlord will carry out maintenance and repairs. However, on *falajes* with a large number of shareholders in central Oman an agent is usually appointed for the administration of groups of primary shares so that reference to each of the owners does not have to be made every time money has to be spent. The group of primary shares – the *qa'ada* share – is registered as a trust, *wakf*, and administered by the agent, who sells shares in the available *falaj* water to people who require it but are without permanent shares. This may be done by auction. Those interested in buying a particular lot may hold out their camel sticks and touch the auctioneer and withdraw them as they retire from the bidding until the highest bidder is left.

The creation of a *qa'ada* share requires the general agreement of the shareholders in the main *falaj*, but if there are objections these are heard by the *Qadhi*, the religious judge. The amount of water due to a particular plot is based on a time scale; the periods of time sold vary

but in much of central Oman an *athar* share is the equivalent of half an hour's watering. Prices also vary but they were all until recently computed in *qirsh* – the Maria Theresa dollar, which was formerly used as currency. The general rule is that a man draws his water for a fixed period from a fixed point, but in some places, for instance in Izki, he holds a share above the point where the main channel first divides and may in consequence draw his water where it suits him from the main network of *falaj* channels.

Agricultural work is still largely done on a strictly traditional basis, and the *bidar* who has a key role carries out duties which have been prescribed since before Islam. Historically always a freeman, he receives payment in kind for his labour, which includes watering, cutting the ripe dates, fertilising the female flowers and tying up the date bunches. He does no weeding and is answerable in his task of distributing water within the village gardens to the supervisor of the irrigation channels of the *falaj* – the *aarif* – and not to individual owners. Weeding is done by another man called the *haris*.

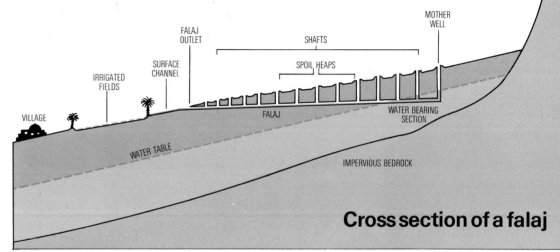

Cross section of a falaj

Care and upkeep of the falajes *are community responsibilities and necessitate harmony in village life.*

A secrecy pervades the steps and passageways of the villages of the Interior, as here, at Muaidin, among the hills.

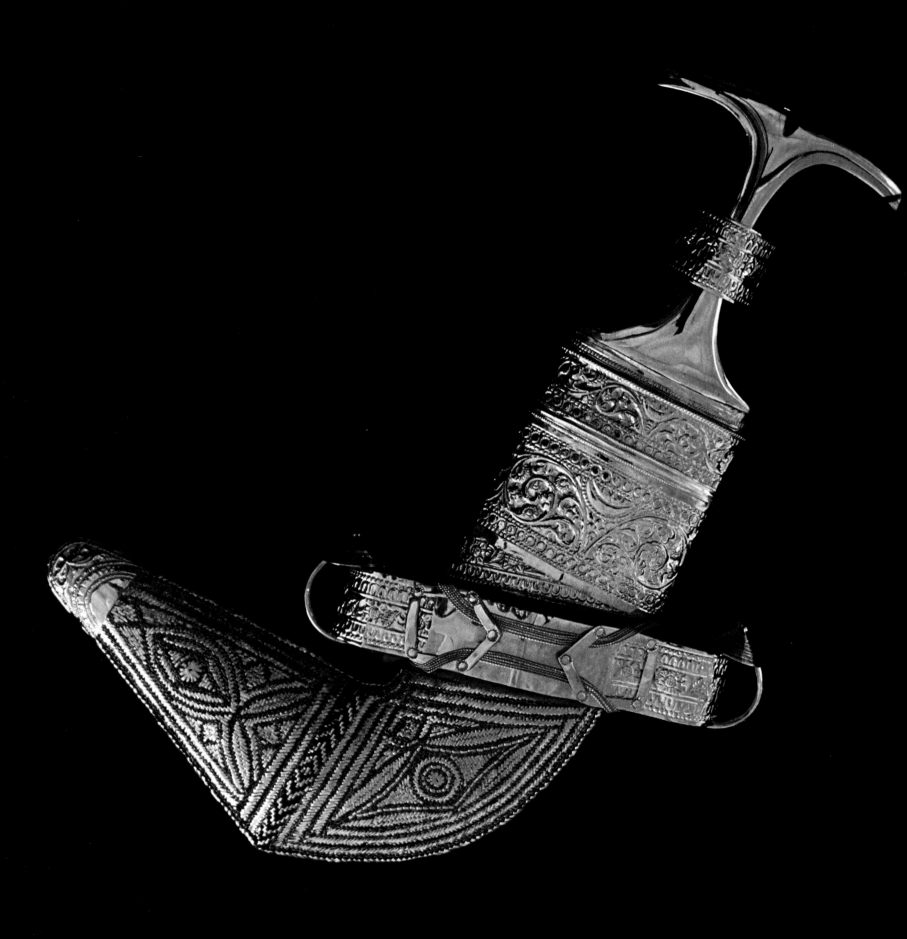

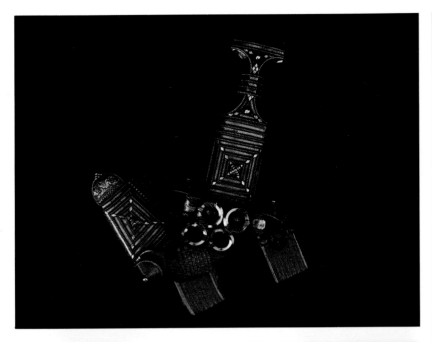

5
The Cultural Heritage

Omanis are instinctive designers. There is no single type of handiwork that they do not render in some way graceful and peculiarly their own. In wood, in silver, in gold, in plaster or clay, in cloth, in beadwork or gold or silver thread, in housebuilding or shipbuilding, in tool-making, jewellery and weaponry, the story is the same: the sense of design triumphs. Omanis have married hand and eye.

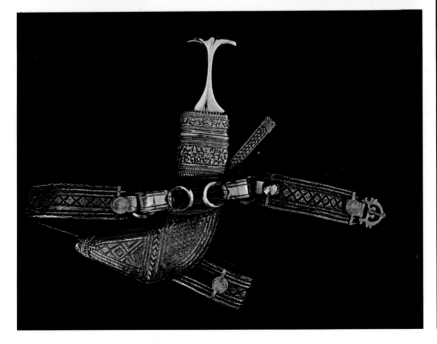

Far left: *The Omani ceremonial dagger, the* khanjar, *is sometimes provided with a hilt and scabbard of gold, when presented as a gift. Notice the five rings of the* Sharqiya khanjar (top), *used for securing the belt. The fine* khanjar (centre) *is worn by the* Wali of Sur. *The delicately chased silverwork of the* khanjar (left) *is typical of the Nizwa area. The handle is made of horn and silver and, tucked in behind the sheath, is a sharp knife with a fine handle.*

Each passing generation makes its contribution. But man's true culture is what carries through from the past.

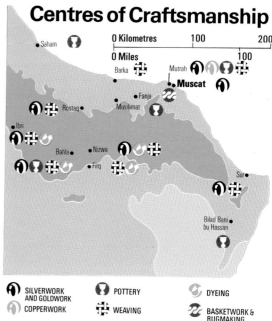

Centres of Craftsmanship

SILVERWORK AND GOLDWORK
POTTERY
DYEING
COPPERWORK
WEAVING
BASKETWORK & RUGMAKING

The map shows the principal centres of craft manufacture in the northern part of Oman.

OMANIS may be numbered amongst the innovators in the field of human culture. In the third millennium BC they were already building round structures of fine masonry and, one of the world's first recorded shipbuilding people, they later helped to pioneer the sea route to China and to develop the science of navigation. In the agricultural sphere they increased the efficiency of the *falaj* systems by the use of inverted siphons – a sophisticated way of leading water across a *wadi* bed below the surface – and their mining techniques were notable when, as so often in the distant past, copper was the basis of their economy.

Latterly, however, Oman can lay little claim either to innovation or experiment and its material culture has been geared to actual local needs. The country is fortunate, however, to preserve a still continuous tradition of craftsmanship going back hundreds of years, though new methods are now being introduced alongside the old. Traditional culture is displayed in the work of silversmiths, goldsmiths and coppersmiths; shipbuilders and carvers; potters, weavers and builders, and in the people's dress.

Mysticism surrounds the ancient art of metal smithing, and gold has been associated for thousands of years with the sun and silver with the moon. The

This Nizwa khanjar-*maker uses a beak anvil, various pliers, and a blowlamp and bellows.*

silverwork of Oman exemplifies the variety and beauty of local craftmanship and, as in other Eastern countries, a considerable proportion of a family's wealth is invested in the gold and silver jewellery worn by the women and silver objects used by the men. Silver vessels and utensils, such as coffee pots, incense burners and rose-water sprinklers used for formal entertainment are also often of great beauty and value.

The curve of the Omani *khanjar*, the most typical badge of the Omani man, distinguishes it from daggers worn elsewhere in Arabia; its sheath has a near right-angle bend. The most exotic sheaths are made of gold and gold thread or a combination of gold and silver, but at the other end of the scale the simplest are of plain leather, though even these usually have some little silver decoration. *Khanjars* are worn on formal occasions and at feasts and holidays, and almost all Omani men boast one. The finely chased silver varies in design from place to place. The best handles are made of bone and silver and it is the mark of a good *khanjar* sheath to have seven silver rings, two to hold the belt and five through which strands of

decorative thread are woven as ornamentation. The top of the handle of the most usual *khanjar* is flat but the "Saidi" type worn only by members of the Ruling Family has an ornate cross-shaped top. The design is attributed to the wife of Sayyid Said ibn Sultan in the early nineteenth century, a Princess of Shiraz, who is also credited with introducing the distinctive many-coloured turban worn by the family.

Khanjars are supported on belts of locally-made webbing, sometimes interwoven with silver thread or belts of leather covered by finely woven silver wire with handsome silver buckles, and a knife with an ornate handle of silver thread is often stuck into a simple leather pouch behind the sheath. The handle and scabbard of Omani swords are also frequently ornamented with silver and silver thread in the same style as the *khanjars*.

The weapons carved by Omani men are usually decorated with beautifully executed silver rings round the barrel and stock, the amount and the quality of the ornament varying according to the owner's pocket. Crescent-shaped powder horns, a feature of the Sur and Sharqiya areas are often made of silver and sometimes also decorated with gold. Other silver objects sometimes used by men include small pipes for smoking a

Khanjars

Khanjars in Oman are of various designs. But all are composed of many parts. Even a Minister in his office will wear his khanjar *on formal occasions.*

Below: *Only the Al bu Said family uses the design of this Saidi* khanjar *hilt.*

This detail (below) *shows the trunk of a* khanjar *and its silver rings.*

The tip of the scabbard (below) *is said to be thus designed for "balance".*

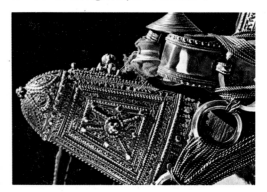

The most distinctive "badge" of the Omani man is the curved dagger called the *khanjar*, traditionally worn at the waist. The shape of the *khanjar* is always the same and is characterised by the curve of the blade and by the angle of the bend of the sheath. Sheaths may vary from simple covers of plain leather to ornate silver- or gold-decorated pieces of great beauty and delicacy.

Jewellery

The silver pendants of such earrings are said to represent the hand of Fatima. The lower pair are from Dhofar.

Sometimes the heavy pendants are hung from decorative chains. The triangular sils *is worn in Dhofari headdresses.*

Most women wear anklets from their marriage onwards. They jingle as the girl walks.

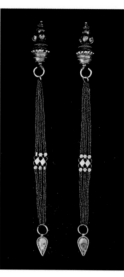
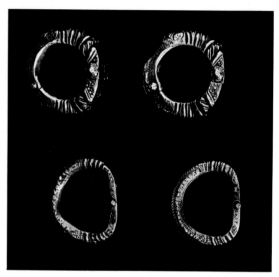

Bottom: *Anklets and bracelets from northern Oman which are hinged.*

Such a beautiful knife (below) would be used for very practical purposes.

Bottom: *The* manjad *necklace, from Dhofar, is worn over and under opposite shoulders.*

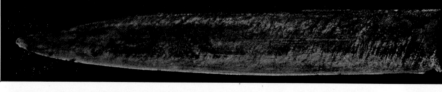

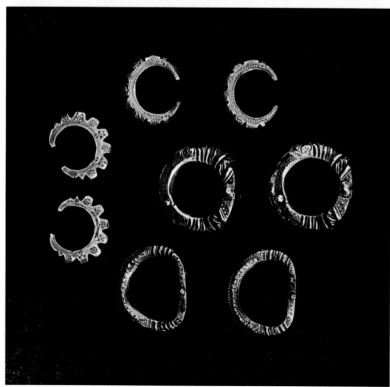
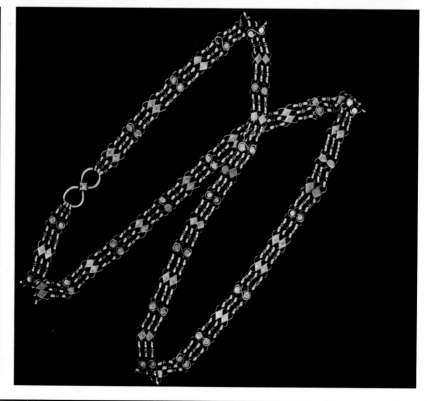

Left: *Thorn picks and tweezers are essential for men. The* hirz (above) *on its three-strand chain comes from Nizwa.*

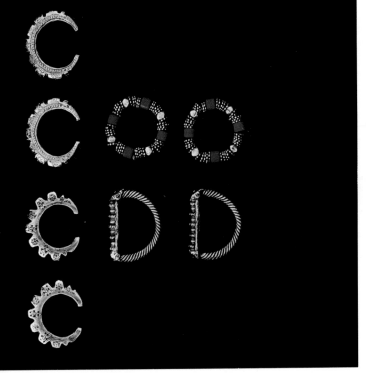

Left: *The bracelets on the left are from the north, while the others are from Dhofar.*
Above: *Inside the* hirz *is often a verse from the Qur'an*

The Omani woman, like so many of her counterparts in Eastern countries, tends to wear much of her wealth in the form of jewellery and gold and silver ornamentation. These objects are often of greaty beauty and represent the acme of the art of Omani silversmiths and goldsmiths. Nowadays jewellery is frequently of gold, but until relatively recently was more often of silver. The main objects are rings, earrings, nose rings, headpieces, bracelets, armlets, anklets, necklaces, chains and amulets. Rings are worn on feet as well as hands and a complete set of hand rings consists of one for all five fingers of each hand. Each ring has a distinctive name.

Headpieces are of two main types. Those worn hanging down from the locks at the back of the head are usually of round or semi-circular design with small bell-like danglers and are sometimes mounted with stones. Another type worn hanging down on either side of the head give the impression of earrings and indeed may sometimes be worn alternatively as headpieces held in position by a silver chain or as actual earrings.

Coins or round pieces are used extensively. They are often worn in the centre of the forehead hanging down from the headpiece. Special wedding jewellery of gold is now made with small ornamental objects hanging down from a chain attached to the head scarf.

Anklets are usually of heavy silver. They open up so that they can easily be put on and are secured by a heavy silver pin. Bracelets and armlets differ in design from region to region, but both anklets and armlets often jingle attractively as the woman moves around.

Jewellery for the neck consists of ornate pieces on beautifully wrought chains or sometimes a number of silver pieces mounted on a thick cord. Such necklaces often include amulets, consisting of verses from the Qur'an inserted in an oblong silver box as protection, particularly against the Evil Eye. The beauty of gold and silver work is achieved by hammering, fusing and filigree techniques.

The little chain attached to the nose ring leads either to headdress or earring.

whiff of the locally grown tobacco, and toilet sets, consisting of tooth pick and ear spoon.

The women and children wear a heavy weight of silver: necklaces, anklets and bracelets, earrings, head-pieces and rings. A charm necklace with an oblong box delicately embossed or chased, called a *hirz*, is the most commonly worn object. It is worn on a silver chain and contains verses from the Qur'an as protection against the evil eye. Small silver shapes and tinkling bells which are attached to the *hirz* are an ancient device, used as long ago as the Achaemenid dynasty in Persia (c 550–330 BC). Large silver medallions on chains, sometimes with inscriptions in Arabic, are common and Maria Theresa dollars, mounted on barrel-shaped loops identical in design with those found in Iraq, Iran and in an Etruscan tomb are frequently used on necklaces.

Silver bracelets, *banjari*, are often worn and many women's legs are heavy with thick silver anklets which jingle as they move – perhaps originally designed to monitor their movements as well as to sound attractive. Earrings are sometimes of enormous size and, while the women cover their heads with soft cloth, young girls are bareheaded but instead wear elaborate pieces of silver jewellery secured by wool thread in their plaited hair, often with jingling danglers. Large coins hanging over small girls' foreheads are a charming feature and women often wear paired rings on the fingers and thumbs of each hand and foot. Magic or talisman rings help to give a sense of security.

Dhofar jewellery differs in design and style from that of Northern Oman. The *manjad*, a heavy silver chain of elaborate linkage worn over one shoulder and under the other arm, is typical of the Southern Region which is also notable for the *sils*, a triangle of very finely decorated silver and little dangling chains with tinkling bells on the end, worn on the headscarf.

Bahla, Rostaq, Nizwa, Ibri, Sur, Muscat and Mutrah all have their silversmiths and each place has its own distinctive design. Nizwa's is appliqué geometric, Rostaq's a rose and stem pattern and Ibri's a lozenge shape though patterns have latterly become interchangeable.

The techniques used resemble those in many other parts of the East. Sheet silver is heated and beaten into dies and then the two halves of the moulded shape are soldered together. Anklets and bracelets are sometimes made by forging pure silver, filling it with a mixture of hot pitch and resin, or wax,

Such a gold necklace might only be worn on a girl's wedding day.

and, when this has cooled, embellishing the surface by embossing. Chisels are used for this and for chasing whilst round-edged punches are employed for decorative work involving no cutting. For engraving a beaked anvil, flat and narrow pliers, round-nosed pliers, a wooden filing block and a simple blow lamp and bellows are required. The silversmiths in Oman usually use melted down Maria Theresa dollars, which were until recently used as local currency, as the very high silver content engenders confidence in the customer that he or she is receiving value for money.

Gold is now, with increasing wealth, tending to replace silver jewellery and goldsmiths flourish in Muscat, Mutrah and other market centres. The techniques are those used in other parts of Arabia, Iran and the Indian subcontinent and the small square jewellery shops savour of an age-old tradition. A favourite device on a piece of jewellery is the English gold sovereign which is frequently used for embellishment. Weddings and festivals often give rise to commissions for special headpieces and gold rings for fingers, nose and ears, and bracelets, often follow traditional silver designs. Salala is noted for distinctive necklaces of gold beads interspersed with coral.

A Mutrah girl's bridal headdress is hung with gold coins.

A Mutrah goldsmith keeps his flame hot by constant blowing (above right).

Traditional coppersmithing is carried on at Nizwa.

Household Utensils

Though copper is no longer mined in Oman, copper and brass household utensils are made in Nizwa, Mutrah and one or two other places. The Nizwa coffee pot has a distinctive waisted shape and is often made of copper and decorated with brass bands around the stem and on spout and lid. A peculiar feature is a series of little diamond-shaped danglers hanging near the handle. It was common practice to insert small stones into the hollow of the lid which was supposedly a precaution against poisoning, as the clatter of the stones would betray the presence of a sinister hand if the lid were opened by some unauthorised person. Copper trays, incense burners and long-handled spoons are examples of the coppersmith's art.

The average Omani eats well but household utensils are relatively simple, consisting of coffee pots of various sizes, pans for cooking – formerly of copper but now usually of aluminium – kettles, bowls and round trays of various sizes, around which the traditional meal is eaten. Enormous coffee pots of copper or brass are used for tribal and large family gatherings but the brew made in them is generally then transferred to smaller pots, or nowadays thermos flasks, before being served. It is customary to grind the coffee for each occasion.

Traditional chests decorated with brass nails are found in many houses,

Metal Vessels

In such an incense burner (above), *sandalwood will usually be burnt.*

Vessels of copper, brass and silver are much used in household ceremonial in Oman as well as for ordinary domestic use. A formal meal of any sort will entail the use of several different sorts of vessel.

An Omani host will offer coffee to any caller and this is poured from a metal coffee pot into small round coffee cups. Traditionally coffee pots are made of copper or brass, or a combination of the two metals – or even of silver – and the usual shape in Oman is the waisted pot distinctive of Nizwa with a large beak and a round top ornamented with a spike or "coxcomb". At great tribal or family gatherings coffee is usually made in a coffee pot of enormous size, from which the usual sized pots are filled and the coffee served by servants.

The traditional Omani meal of mounded rice and meat, with garnishes of many kinds in separate bowls, is

Delicate silverwork distinguishes the beak of this coffee pot.

served on a large round brass tray. After a meal or after eating anything sticky, water to rinse the hands is offered in a beaked, round copper bowl, decorated with fine chased patterns.

After a formal meal it is usual, at least in wealthy households, to offer rose-water to the guests and this is sprinkled on the hands or over the head from a round silver bottle. The rose-water

A rose-water sprinkler.

Left: *Two typical Nizwa coffee pots flank a larger Bedu coffee pot, used at tribal gatherings. Decorations on sea chests were done by seamen on their long voyages.*

A brass pot for halwa.

Smoke from the incense burner (above) *is wafted into the beard and under the armpits after formal meals. Below: Rose-water sprinklers give fragrance to a household.*

A finely chased coffee pot.

Floral designs are popular for the waists of coffee pots.

comes from the Jebel Akhdar where roses are specially grown. After the rose-water smoking incense may be served from a graceful silver vessel and carried round from guest to guest. Incense is the sign for departure as the Omani proverb shows: "After the incense, there is no sitting on."

Nizwa smiths combine brass and copper.

Oman is rich in functional jewellery: tiny implements essential to daily use which are turned into miniature works of art. Such are the ear spoon and toothpick (*above*), and the little pick for piercing embroidered caps. The thorn pick (*below*) and its tweezers fit into a little silver sheath.

Firearms

The type of Omani match-lock seen on the right is known as the *gizail*. The match itself was of coconut or date fibre, bound with cotton thread. To fire the gun, black powder was measured and rammed down the barrel with a rod and wadding. The lead shot was poured in and rammed in tight with a further wad. Next, powder was poured into the powder pan, the cover was replaced, the match lit and firmly placed in the jaws of the cock. To fire, the powder pan cover was opened, and when the trigger was pressed, the match travelled forward in the cock, igniting the powder in the pan which in turn set off the powder in the barrel through the the touch-hole.

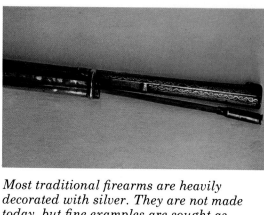

Most traditional firearms are heavily decorated with silver. They are not made today, but fine examples are sought as collector's pieces.

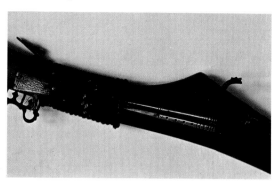

Such a decorative and jingling ornament is worn in the back of a plaited coil of hair.

Until recently, most men in the Interior carried a matchlock. The barrels were forged in eighteen-inch lengths, welded, and decorated.

particularly on the coast, but these are now giving place to more modern containers like tin trunks. Formerly seamen would decorate the chests with brass ornamentation to while away the hours on their long voyages on sailing ships. Floors are often covered with matting made from palm fronds or reeds; and rugs, sometimes locally made and sometimes imported from Persia, Afghanistan or Pakistan, are brought out for special occasions. The compounds of houses on the coast, particularly Sur, are spread with clean pebbles.

Agricultural Tools

The most common agricultural instrument is the spade which is used for light work in the gardens such as damming and undamming the water channels to irrigate each area or bed in turn. It is not used for turning the soil. The plough, which is made of wood with an iron tip, is small and light and is traditionally drawn by a single bull or cow, though tractors are now being increasingly used. A long, slightly curved and toothed sickle, *minjal*, is used for cutting lucerne, alfalfa, and other fodder and also for pruning the palm trees. A long chisel, *hib*, is employed to separate palm off-shoots from their parents. The date

Studded and coloured bandoliers are worn by Bedu *tribesmen.*

cultivators use the same sort of sling made of rope and leather, which is used in other date-growing areas in the Middle East and in the coconut groves of Africa to climb trees.

The powder horn from Sur (above) *lets out small quantities of powder by a spring catch.*
Below: *Bullet moulds and gunpowder scoops used to be essential.*

Dhofari Incense Burners

In Dhofar, incense burners are often made of brightly decorated pottery. One such pottery works in Salala has been in the same family for some five hundred years. Dhofar itself is the home of the frankincense tree, and for century upon century it was the centre of a vast international trade in frankincense. The resin is still used extensively in the Middle East and in Christian churches in the West.

Guns

Guns have for many generations been weapon, ornament and interest to the Omani man. In fact a gun had become, until very recently, virtually a badge of manhood. The most common and typical of these is the *gizail* or *abu futila*, which means the "father of the match" (the matchlock) and was in use until very recently. Many of these found their way into Oman through the Gulf from Ottoman Turkey in the eighteenth and nineteenth centuries, when the Ottomans traded such weapons with countries on the north-west frontier of India.

Many matchlocks are ornately decorated with strands of brass, silver or gold inlaid in grooves around the barrel, and some have attractive damascened patterns in gold or silver along the whole length of the barrel. Inlaying was a long operation. First the barrel was coated with an acid-resistant mixture of wax and resin. Next the design was either scratched in with a needle or painted into the coating with a stiff brush. Acid was then poured over the treated area to eat away the metal exposed, after which silver or gold was inlaid into the pattern of indentations either by hammering or with a dovetail cross-section. Each weapon is decorated differ-

ently – no two are alike – and each is an individual piece of craftsmanship.

The *gizail* always has a very long barrel, as most muzzle-loading guns had, and some barrels were six feet or more in length. The barrels were forged in lengths of about eighteen inches and welded together after the boring had been done; this was a long and complicated process involving the use of bamboo and iron borers. After the decoration had been completed the barrel was fitted to the wooden stock by a number of brass rings and a brass plate was finally fitted underneath to protect the woodwork and house the ramrod.

Different methods of producing ball for the *gizail* were employed and moulds might produce one or two at a time or as many as a dozen. The match itself was made of coconut or date fibres with cotton thread. The ordinary powder flasks were usually of hard wood, often ornately carved, but some were made of silver and gold.

Firing was a lengthy process. First, black powder was measured and poured into the barrel, after which a wad was forced down with the ramrod. Next lead shot was put in and finally a further wad, all of which was rammed home. A small quantity of black powder was then

poured into the powder pan, the cover of which was replaced, whereupon the match was lit and secured firmly in the jaws of the cock. When it was time to fire, the powder pan cover was opened, aim taken, and, when the trigger was pressed, the match travelled forward in the cock igniting the powder in the pan, which in turn ignited the powder in the barrel through the touch-hole.

Although the *gizail* was the commonest weapon, there were many other sorts of firearms carried by Omanis, such as the breech-loading Martini Henry, which was imported into the general area in large numbers at the end of the nineteenth century, and also the flintlock. These ancient weapons were the principal arms carried by the Omanis when they mustered at Sohar in 1952 to march on Buraimi after the oasis had been occupied by a Saudi force in that year. In the event, the march did not take place and the Buraimi dispute went to arbitration so that this antique weaponry was not put to the test at so late a date.

Pottery

The earliest pottery found in Oman dates from the Jemdet Nasr period (early third millennium BC) and utilitarian

Below: *Outside the kiln at one of the potteries at Bahla a row of pots await firing.* Right: *The slow kick wheel has been used since Sumerian times.*

Conscious pride in the craftsman's skill seems likely to withstand the common tendency elsewhere in the world for factory-made goods to diminish the call for things made by the hand of man. Metal, clay, yarn and wood are all wrought and worked in different centres throughout the land.

pottery has been made there since man first needed pots. The pottery still made in the villages is used largely for practical purposes and consists of items like porous water pots, cooking pots and cups. The standard of the finished product and methods used depends on the quality of the clay available and, where clay is poor, methods tend to be primitive.

Pottery is now produced quite extensively in Oman in such places as Bahla, Bilad Bani bu Hassan, Hayyil, Musilimat, Mutrah, Saham and Salala. In Bahla and Musilimat, where good quality clay is available, the craft is relatively sophisticated and the potters are highly skilled in their very ancient techniques. They use a simple foot-operated slow wheel and fire their work in large mud-brick kilns, fuelled with brushwood. Potters in northern Oman

are all men, but women also make pottery objects in Salala, where true clay is not available. Nevertheless colourful and attractive incense burners, water bowls and other practical items are made there by hand without a wheel, as well as decorative pottery including highly individual representations of objects such as small boats, cars and aeroplanes.

Bahla is the main centre for pottery in northern Oman and is noted for its large jars used for storing dates. Incense burners, roof gutterings, water jars, water cups, *laban* or yoghourt jars, and *halwa* bowls are among the other items produced there. Containers for food are glazed inside though the quality of the glaze now made is not as high as it was in previous centuries. For example glass made in Sohar in the tenth century was probably used for glazing in that era but the glaze now produced is from

The basic shape is formed.

locally ground substances of poorer material.

The basic materials for each product can be adapted according to the intended use of the finished article. For example, extra sand is added to the clay mix in order to make water jars more porous. A skilled potter can make up to fifty jars a day and the secrets of the craft are handed down from generation to generation usually within the same family. Some potteries have been in the same

Each pottery has its own skilled decorators (left). Below: *The large pot requires considerable physical effort from the maker.*

The neck begins to appear.

The crucial stage needs concentration.

The finishing touches are added.

family for several centuries and a potter in Salala informed a visiting expert that his business had been founded by forebears in the sixteenth century AD – a date which independent evidence established as correct.

Music

Music was not encouraged under Ibadhi precept, and what music there is tends to have an African quality. It is associated with joyful occasions such as weddings and Id holidays and in some places on the coast in northern Oman and in Dhofar, there is regular dancing on Fridays.

A distinctive character is given to the music by the beat of the drums and the players often move round and round in circles to encourage the dancers who may be both male and female. Other instruments include a type of trumpet made out of horn, a straight pipe, and a stringed instrument, a *rababa*, resembling those of east Africa. An entirely different sort of instrument is the curved horn, usually decorated with silver, used to summon the tribe together.

Sailors on their long voyages used to sing songs and chants, and the Omanis have their own versions of sea shanties. In some of the remoter areas too singing is quite common amongst the *Bedu* tribes but not among the town-dwelling people of the Interior. Special chants are sung for special occasions and some

147

tribes have distinctive airs for bringing camels to water, loading, or for trotting or walking them. There may be songs in praise of coffee, and, of course, love songs. The women sing in certain remote areas, but such conduct would be taken as most immodest in most places. In Salala there are special songs for lute and drum which are sung on holiday and festive occasions, and in some places there are special chants used for exorcism (*zar*).

One form of dancing still carried on at Ids in Oman is the sword dance. These dances were originally in the nature of exercises for war and the participants engaged in mock fights, armed with sword, dagger and target shield – small, round, embossed shields made of hippopotamus hide, wood, or sometimes of leather. Bertram Thomas in his book *Alarms and Excursions in Arabia* describes an Arab greeting in the Bani bu Ali country in the 1920s, though the scene contains many of the elements still to be seen at Id celebrations in various parts of the country. "Drums were beating, and the crowd swayed left and right to their rhythm; quivering sword blades flashed in the sun as sword dancers leapt hither and thither, and low chanting grew loud as we approached. Swinging round to form a

Overleaf: *Making pottery incense burners. The potter is fashioning the bases; behind her lie completed tops, which will be joined with clay.*

Delight in Ornamentation

Objects of common use are often charmingly wrought, like the floral box, the iron and brass lock and key, the Dhofari beaded bottle (made of horn and containing *kohl*), the Nizwa doorknob, and Bahla key, in these pictures.

Bahla is a centre of pottery.

firing their rifles at the same time, or racing in pairs down the straight, one rider standing upright on his stirrupless saddle, gripping only with his toes, and maintaining a parlous equilibrium by placing an outstretched arm on the neck of his more comfortably seated fellow rider. Reforming, the party would move past in close formation at a jog trot, chanting heroic verse, an ancient *Bada-win* custom deriving from the mighty Antar of antiquity. The leader gabbled his lines and at the end of each couplet, the rest of the party shouted in chorus 'Allahu Akbar'."

This description bears eloquent testimony to Omani horsemanship. The words of the heroic chant as translated by Thomas demonstrates the warriors' pride:

"We have filled every quarter with fear till mankind grovels before us.
Chorus: God is great!
We have excelled the Pleiades (Thuraiyya) in its zenith.
Chorus: God is great!
And whosoever approacheth us seeking trouble shall find us brave as lions.
Chorus: God is great!

"Drums were beating, and the crowd swayed left and right to their rhythm; quivering sword blades flashed in the sun as sword dancers leapt hither and thither. The tribesmen, holding their rifle butts to their hips for the feux de joie, *sent a hail of friendly bullets pinging over our heads."*

corridor for us, the tribesmen, holding their rifle butts to their hips for the *feux de joie*, sent a hail of friendly bullets pinging over our heads. We went on to where the Amir stood, before the fort, on a carpet placed in the large open square, a favourable position for witnessing the horsemanship and camel-racing that now took place . . . A dozen horsemen galloped past, now in this formation, now in that, curvetting and

149

The blue yarn is spun and wound on to racks to keep it tangle-free.

Great skill is needed to spin wool on the hand-held bobbin.

Weaving

Weaving is still carried on in many towns and villages, though most weavers tend now to be very old men. Carding and spinning are done on traditional implements made from palm-fronds, and the looms are of traditional design. The weaver sits in a kind of pit in front of his loom, the warp threads stretching some twenty or thirty feet in front of him. The cloth woven is mainly used for lengths of *wazara* or *lunghi* worn by men about the waist.

Weaving is often done under the shade of trees. Originally, the whole process of growing cotton, spinning and weaving was done in Oman, but little cotton is now grown, and raw cotton or thread has to be imported.

A distinctive cloak of black goat hair is woven in Bahla. It is a bat-winged garment with an embroidered design at the back, giving it something of an academic flavour.

Weaving and Dyeing

Weaving is still carried on in most towns and villages though weavers now tend to be very old men. Originally the whole process of growing cotton, spinning and weaving was done in Oman but relatively little cotton is now grown and consequently raw cotton or cotton thread has to be imported. Carding and spinning are done on traditional implements made from palm fronds and the looms are of simple design. When working the weaver sits in a kind of pit in front of his loom, the warp threads being stretched out over a distance of twenty or so feet in front of him. The cloth woven varies but is chiefly used for lengths of *wazara*, or *lunghi*, worn by the men round the waist. In Barka multicoloured cloth is woven for a greater variety of purposes.

Weaving is often done under the shade of trees and a distinctive cloak of black goat hair is woven in Bahla. It is a bat-winged garment with an embroidered design at the back which gives it something of the air of an academic gown. The women amongst the *Bedu* tribes make various articles such as lengths of cloth for adorning tents, camel and donkey saddle bags, and rugs which can be used either for tent making or for covering the floor. In the Ibri area rugs of a distinctive red and black striped design are produced. Goat and camel hair are the usual basic materials but sheep's wool is also used particularly for making the *bisht*, the traditional form of cloak with gold edging worn by men over the white cotton *dishdasha*.

Dyeing has been done for many generations in a few places, including Firq near Nizwa where indigo is the principal dye used. This indigo dye comes from the leaves of the indigo plant *neel*. When the Imam Said ibn Ahmad tried to make indigo dyeing a state monopoly in the eighteenth century it caused him considerable unpopularity.

Boatbuilding

Boatbuilding is a very ancient craft indeed and in the fifteenth century AD Ahmad ibn Majid, perhaps Oman's most famous seaman, even attributed its origin to Noah whose ship, he remarked, was put together in the form of the five main stars of the Great Bear.

There is still boatbuilding at Sur and Sohar and the trade continued until recently in Mutrah. The trade is confined to a few families who have always plied

Many of the craftsmen's materials are home-grown – the dyer's indigo and the weaver's goat hair. But the shipwright's teak comes from Malabar.

it and on the shore at Sur there are usually three or four boats being built at any one time. However, the boats built are only about a tenth of the size of the great ships of some 500 or more tons built earlier for sailing the oceans, though the traditional methods are still used. The boat is built, after the keel is laid, within a framework of poles like scaffolding and the wood used is mainly teak from India. The ribs and keels are natural grown timbers and the masts, a particularly expensive item, are Malabar teak trunks. The carpenters use the same tools as they have over many generations – adzes, saws, chisels, hammers and bow drills. Modern boats are put together with iron nails, the old method of sewing the planks together having virtually died out except for work on some parts of the ancient-shaped *badan*, a small craft propelled by oars. It is strange to reflect that when the Omanis made their greatest and longest voyages the planks of their ships were only sewn together: a system which had advantages in giving flexibility during storms, but at the same time led to a more rapid break-up in the event of shipwreck.

The traditional methods of Omani shipbuilders are described by Abu Said al Balkhi writing in the ninth century AD (third century AH) as follows: "There are people, at Oman, who cross over to the Islands that produce the coconut, carrying with them Carpenter's and suchlike tools; and having felled as much wood as they want, they let it dry, then strip off the Leaves, and with the Bark of the Tree they spin a Yarn, wherewith they sew the Planks together, and so build a Ship. Of the same wood they cut and round away a Mast: of the Leaves they weave their Sails, and the Bark they make into Cordage. Having thus completed their Vessel, they load her with coconuts, which they bring and sell at Oman."

The type of boat chiefly associated with Sur is the *baghala*, or its smaller version the *ghanja*, both of which had high poops and windows at the stern in the style of the old Portuguese galleon. Nowadays the craft are usually powered by motor, but until recently they moved under sail. The carpenters' responsibility ended after building the hull and

A lifetime of dyeing indigo cloth shows in this old man's hands.

caulking the ship, whilst sailors who were taken on in advance sewed the sails, rigged the ship and floated her away from the dockyard. Alan Villiers made a number of voyages on Arab craft in the 1930s and he describes one of the last really large *baghalas* built in Oman in his book *Sons of Sindbad*. It was called *Hope of Compassion* (Mercy) and was of about 200 tons with a capacity of 3,000 packages of dates. Even this was, however, relatively small compared with still earlier ships of 500 to 600 tons, which carried 400 men or more. By the 1930s the *baghala* was becoming extinct as *bums*, with their long-nosed distinctive prow, were preferred by the voyagers of that generation. *Baghalas* were thought to be less seaworthy and their carved sterns, though stately and picturesque, were reckoned to be dangerous in a pounding sea. The *bum* is a versatile craft.

The *Hope of Compassion*, Villiers says, was "beautiful from outside and beautiful on board with the picturesque romantic sweep of her ancient decks from the worn planks of the poop to the curved horn at the low bow. Her windowed stern was especially lovely. Its elliptical area of ancient teak was

Firq, near Nizwa, is well known for its indigo-dyed cloth.

The deep-blue garments dry in the shadow of a castle wall.

covered with intricate patterns of excellent carving and her curved bow swept up from the sea as gracefully as the breast of a swan. She was big for an Arab. Her oiled teak hull sat prettily in the water with a grace and strength and sweetness of line that sang of sea kindliness despite all Najdi's comments on the vulnerability of her stern. . . . She was very old – more than half a century – and dated back to the slaving days. Like so many Arab vessels, every line of her flowed and blended perfectly into a harmonious and lovely whole, though she had been put together on the beach at Sur by carpenters . . . [without] even an elementary paper plan. She was built by the eye and she was built beautifully though she was but a heap of indifferent teak poorly fastened with weak iron and here and there an ill-butted plank had warped and all her fastenings wept with rust stains from every pitted head. . . . Her quarter galleries were latticed delicately, like the narrow windows of a harim court: her five stern windows were protected by iron bars, and a teak shutter swung from the central window, richly carved in patterns of crescents and stars . . .''

She was indeed a craft of an earlier age, though life on local craft in the Indian Ocean and Gulf may not have changed radically even by now despite the powerful engines which have replaced the great lateen sail. Villiers described the scene on board: ''There was a carpenter working on his new dhow. There was a low forecastle head, heavy beams for belaying halliards and cables, a firebox over which a smoke-grimed cook crouched, wooden water tanks on either side, the great bole of the raking mainmast rising from the forward end of the long narrow main hatch. There were, too, a number of ringbolts and a big capstan that looked as if it might have come from Nelson's 'Victory'. Wherever carving and embellishments could be added they had been and the poop was liberally decorated in this way. In the after part of the spacious great cabin there was seven feet of headroom and the whole break of the poop was carved with a delicate tracery of involved patterns into which texts from the Qur'an had been worked. The reclining bench for the officers was an elaborately finished and well-joined piece of built-in furniture, protected by a carved teak railing. The poop had a small working capstan, rows of chests, a rising mizzen

155

mast towering above, binnacle, wheel and helmsman's chair. When the 'Hope of Compassion' sailed with a gentle breeze off the land, the sailors hove her short, raised the peak of the lateen main, broke out her hook and she turned on her lovely heel and went, a picture of grace and beauty as she turned her carved and galleried stern – a ship of romance, as the land wind filled her great sail. It took the sailors a long time to masthead the sail which fluttered out golden in the morning air. Her burnished hull slipped slowly through the blue water."

The daily life aboard a typical Arab craft was also described by Alan Villiers. "Our days began long before dawn and the muezzins began their calls to prayer some time before I could detect the faintest tinge of greyness in the eastern sky ... There are fairly well defined periods for the announcements of the five daily prayers – dawn with the first lighting of the sky; morning, a little after the sun has passed its meridian; third, or afternoon, when the sun has lost its glare and its redness is whitening and the shadows are long; fourth, or evening, immediately after sunset; fifth or night, any time between sunset and dawn, but usually, for the convenience of the ship, about two hours after sunset ... Prayers, breakfast, cooking, eating, sleeping, catching fish, cleaning fish, looking at what went on aboard the other vessels ... so the days passed. One bright morning I watched the scene on deck. It was typical of what I might have observed any morning. On the port side, upon the small forecastle head – which was really only a working platform for the anchors and the fore tack – Jassim the cook and a passenger were methodically killing and skinning a Somali goat, a large beast which had stood tethered to the port cable during the night. On the other side of the forecastle head, three sailors cleaned fish caught during the night by Hassan the helmsman and Mohammad Amiri, who, having fished all night, were now snoring in the lee of the firebox while the beduin milled all around them. When the fish had been opened and salted, they were threaded on a piece of light coir rope and hung in the sun.

In the meantime, the goat-slaughtering was completed, and Jassim and the beduin his mate were coiling the dead goat into a big pot. Watching them was a young beduin boy with long hair ...

Boatbuilding

Oman has a long and great tradition of boatbuilding, and her sailors were probably navigating the oceans from the third millennium BC. The craft is still carried on in Sur and Sohar, as it was until recently in Mutrah. Traditional methods have not been abandoned and the trade is confined to a few families who have always plied it.

The ribs and keel are of natural grown timbers, usually teak from India. The bum (below) *flies the flag of Oman to mark its near-completion.*

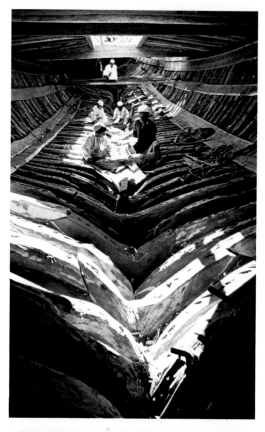

The carpenters use the same tools as their forefathers.

The keel is constructed within a framework of wooden poles.

The adze is one of the oldest tools, and one of the most difficult to use.

The bow drill, when skilfully handled, is the best tool for the job.

Of all Omani craft, the high-pooped baghala *has won the widest fame.*

He was a gentle boy and he and the old chief Aura were the quietest persons on board. He wore a silver bracelet on his right wrist, and a dagger was thrust into the folds of his sarong. I wondered what had brought him down on this long voyage . . . I gathered that there was a famine in his tribe, and not enough food for the young men. He had heard the elders speak of opportunities in Africa; therefore he came. He told me that he and some of the other young men brought frankincense on their camels from the borders of the desert . . . and sold both [before embarking].

. . . By the messy smoky firebox, Jassim, looking sadder and blacker than ever, squatted on the tiny fore hatch and stirred the goat-pot with a piece of wood . . . Abdulla Najdi and his gang, regardless of all else, continued their packing of 'best' Basra dates . . . We had sixty large packages of these dates.

Beneath the poop of the new dhow a tiny girl lay sleeping, a fat little mite in a long print dress with a black hood, her chubby small hands and her chubbier small face liberally decorated with lines of black and henna. From her ears hung silver ornaments, about ten to each lobe, which jingled as she walked. There were two heavy silver bangles round her ankles . . . Some made coffee, in long spouted brass pots designed to extract the maximum heat from the minimum number of embers. Some drank coffee. The poorer the coffee the more elaborate the manner of serving it, some of the beduin handing round the thimbles full . . . as if it were nectar from the gods, bowing and clicking the porcelain cups against the spout . . . Some answered the call of nature in the little pews along the ship's side . . . Old Yusuf

Although run aground, the boat still stands as a tribute to the builder.

Top: *Boats, too, are carved in Oman; this one shows a rope-pattern.*

157

The bum (centre, below) *is recognised by its high, beaked prow and its sharp stern. The projection at the stern of the boat* (bottom)*, is the mariners' privy – less precarious than it seems!*

Shirazi ... was making medicine ... Twisted pieces of weeds, odds and ends of leaves, dried and very ancient seeds, pieces of bark and lengths of something that looked like string – all these went in and Yusuf pounded and mixed them industriously ... I learned ... that the 'medicine' was a concoction for increasing the flow of milk from the breasts of beduin matrons. Yusuf wanted milk to bathe his eyes ..."

Careening

During many sea-voyages, the hull of a vessel inevitably becomes coated with barnacles, algae and debris. If allowed to accumulate it eventually slows the progress of the ship, and so it is necessary to careen the hull regularly. After scraping, the hull is treated with fish-oil to protect the wood.

Boats with sewn seams have been known since ancient times.

After careening and oiling, the smooth hull allows the boat to go faster.

The part-sewn badan *still survives.*

For off-shore fishing, a skilful assemblage of palm-fronds suffices in mild weather.

The shasha, *made from palm-fronds, is found on the Batina coast.*

Whether sailing a wooden boat or a simple shasha, *the Omani seaman remains an example to the world with his great maritime inheritance.*

Boats Found in Oman

There are many types of local craft other than the *baghala* and the more common ones are listed below. All the smaller boats may be rowed with a paddle as well as having a sail, though the *huri* very seldom has any canvas. The word *dhow*, which is applied to all sorts of local craft by Europeans, is never used. It was originally used to refer to a now extinct form of craft found on the east African coast.

Boat (general):	*khashab*
Boat (with engine):	*launch*
Boat with upright stem and transom stern. The word probably derives from the Portuguese *jalbuta* (cf. Jolly Boat):	*jalbut*
Larger boat with beak, prow and sharp stern:	*bum*
Pearling boat:	*sambuk*
Small high-pooped boat (partly sewn together instead of nailed):	*badan*

Small fishing boat
similar in shape to
sambuk: *shu'iy*
Small dug-out or dinghy: *huri*
Ferry: *abra*
"Pram":   *shahuf*
Palm-frond boat, found
on Batina Coast: *shasha*

A warship is still called *manwa*, a corruption of "Man of War" – a lasting tribute to the former strength and influence of the British Navy, long familiar in Omani waters.

Wood Carving

Beautiful carved doorways are a distinctive feature of towns and villages in Oman. These carved doorways greatly enhance the typical Omani house, whether it is a fine stone dwelling or merely built of mud. Some are great gates leading to palaces such as the gigantic and wonderfully carved doors in the fort at al Hazm. Others are more modest in size, but still ornately carved, perhaps opening into the houses of prosperous merchants. These often have little wicket gates like the bigger doors. Simpler doors to more humble dwellings are also frequently well carved.

The tradition of carving doors extends to the Gulf, and similar doorways are also found in Zanzibar and the other former Arab colonies on the coast of east Africa. Designs are floral or geometric and very often, particularly on the larger doors, a date is also inscribed. In Sur, a distinctive tradition of carving which includes palm tree patterns is still carried on, though modern doors are distinctly less ornate than earlier ones. The wood comes either from east Africa or India and the tradition of carving seems to have eddied round the Ocean between the Indian subcontinent, Oman and east Africa. No doubt trading and maritime connections between these regions caused the spread of this form of culture and it is natural, in view of the common tradition, that houses as well as doorways in Zanzibar should resemble those in Muscat so closely.

Carving also finds expression amongst Omani boatbuilders and various parts of Omani boats, particularly the poops, are still intricately carved. But in former times the scale was greater and the quality of the work higher, for there was an immense amount of carving on the much larger ships which the Omanis used.

Below: *A traditional Omani flower and leaf pattern;* (middle) *the carvings of Sur are distinctive;* (bottom) *ceilings, too, are decorated.*

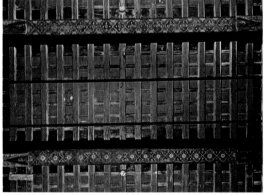

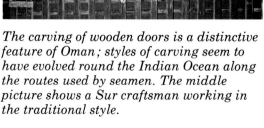

The carving of wooden doors is a distinctive feature of Oman; styles of carving seem to have evolved round the Indian Ocean along the routes used by seamen. The middle picture shows a Sur craftsman working in the traditional style.

160

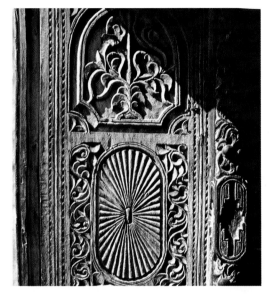

Sur produces possibly the finest examples of the woodcarver's art.

Flower patterns and geometrical designs characterise Omani woodcarving. The craftsmen still use traditional, simple tools, which in skilled hands produce work of the highest art and workmanship.

The Art of the Woodcarver

Art in Oman finds its highest expression, apart from in jewellery and silver objects, in woodcarving. Finely, and sometimes very ornately, carved doors are a feature of every Omani town and village, both in the Interior and on the coast. Similar doors are also found in the areas of east Africa where Omani influence prevailed.

Traditional local craft were, and still are, decorated by designs carved on the stern and poop. The art has not died in Oman and carving is still done to decorate both doors and boats, particularly in Sur and Sohar, where the method and style of craftsmanship has not changed for centuries. Doors frequently carry carved inscriptions from the Qur'an with the date of the work. The designs on doors and lintels are invariably Islamic designs of geometrical or flower patterns, and the flower and leaf motif is a common one.

When Sur was famous for the great ocean-going ships built there, the sterns and poops were beautifully, extensively and cleverly carved. It is sad that virtually none of these great ships survive and their beauty can only be appreciated from old photographs and drawings. However the ancient tools used by the carpenters and carvers – chisels, awls, adzes, hammers and bow drills – have survived and are still used by the shipwrights.

Scholarship

A considerable body of learning was at times preserved in extensive libraries of books and manuscripts. However, many of these have been destroyed in civil and other wars, and a difficulty faced by modern scholars has been the great reluctance of people who still possess manuscripts to disclose them. It is commonly supposed that a considerable amount of material was taken out of Oman by Omanis in the Jebel War of the 1950s. Fortunately, however, for scholars, a considerable number of manuscripts have been preserved outside Oman, and recently the Ministry of National Heritage has started a collection in the country. Omani books are not illustrated with the human figure, but calligraphy was practised and admired.

All learning in Oman has centred round religion and its interpretation and there have been many Omani scholars in past centuries as there are now. History and genealogy are secondary and closely connected with religious studies. Religious education was widespread in the settled parts of Oman and, until modern education was introduced in 1970, any place of any size and significance had its religious teacher under whom a knot of small boys – and sometimes girls – began their study of religion and the "three R's".

One of the earliest surviving Omani manuscripts dates from the ninth century AD, *as-Siyar al-Umaniya* (*Omani Ways*) by Abu'l Mu'thir as-Salt ibn Khamis al-Bahlawi. Salma ibn Musaalim al'Awtabi wrote *Ansab al Arab* (*Arab Genealogies*), a work of enormous value not only for its genealogy but for the details which help reconstruct the tribal pattern of his time. Awtabi, who was born near Sohar, seems to have lived and written during the late eleventh century AD (fifth century AH) and the Awtabis were important tribal leaders on the Batina. Awtabi's grandfather was author of a notable work on *fiqh* – Islamic jurisprudence.

Hisham ibn Muhammad al-Kalbi (ibn Kalbi) established the formal structure of Arab genealogy in early Abbasid times and he is an important source for early Omani history. The same applies to the *Qasida al-Himyariya* (*Himyaritic Poems*) by Nashwan ibn Said al-Himyari, though it has been alleged that he was responsible for creating a genealogical fabrication of a south Arabian unity stemming from Qahtan for political ends in the Kalb/Qais rivalry in Umayyad times. Another important writer is Abu Bakr Muhammad ibn al-Hassan ibn Duraid (ibn Duraid) who lived in Basra and who died in 933 AD (321 AH). His family came from Oman and he wrote a number of poems about affairs there. He and ibn Athir, who wrote the *Kamil*, are important sources on early Omani history.

A later writer of importance is al-Qalhati who probably wrote during the period of Qalhat's prosperity under the Hormuzis in the thirteenth to fifteenth centuries (sixth to eighth centuries AH). Of later historians, the most important are Salil ibn Muhammad ibn Razik the main content of whose work was translated by the Rev. G. P. Badger in *History of the Imams and Sayyids of Oman* and Sirhan ibn Said, the author of *Kashf al Ghummeh* (*Dispeller of Grief*). Sirhan came from Izki and belonged to Umbu Ali, a settled group of the Tai tribe, and both these authors are important sources for Ya'ruba and early history as well as chroniclers of the whole long history of Oman and of the Al bu Said dynasty.

Of modern authors the most important are Abdulla ibn Humaid as-Salimi, who wrote *Tuhfat al-Ayan bi-sirat Ahl 'Uman*, and died in 1914 at the early age of forty, and his son, Muhammad ibn Abdulla as-Salimi, who wrote *Nahdat al-Ayan bi-hurriyat 'Uman*, and is still alive. Also important is Salim ibn Humud as-Siyabi, who wrote *Is'af al-Ayan fi Ansab Ahl Uman*.

Language

Oman is unique in Arabia for the languages spoken by some of the inhabitants instead of, or in addition to, Arabic. The main instances are the Kumzar dialect amongst the Shihuh, which is an Iranian dialect and the four languages of the Southern Region, which Bertram Thomas first identified as "Four Strange Tongues – the Hadara Group", but better named the Modern South Arabian languages since they are related to Old South Arabian languages such as Sabaean, Hadrami and Qatabanian.

These languages are Jibali or Shheri (sometimes incorrectly rendered Shahri), Mahri, Harsusi and Bathari, and the language of Socotra is also one of this group. The ancient South Arabian languages are associated with the culture which stretched from the Wadi Najran to the Wadi Hadhramaut, from roughly the ninth century BC to the sixth century AD. All these languages, which are not written by the speakers, are Semitic, and bear resemblance to one another, though Mahri and Jibali are not mutually intelligible. There are two main groups; first the Jibali group, of which there are three major dialects identified, and a minor one used in the Kuria Muria Islands. The name "Shheri" indicates that it is the speech of a mountain people since *shher* means "mountain" in Jibali and it is probable that the "Shaharun" (Shhero or Shheris), early inhabitants of the area, were overcome by the invading Qara (probably Mahris), who reduced them to a class of serfs and herdsmen. The old city of these people is supposed to have been on Khor Rori in Dhofar, but Khor Rori in fact is much older, as the inscriptions there show.

The second group is Mahri, Harsusi and Bathari. Harsusi and Bathari are Mahri dialects and a speaker of one of these languages can understand most of what speakers of the other two say. Mahri is probably the closest of these languages to the Old South Arabian tongue, inscriptions in which have been found as far away as Delos in the Aegean and Ethiopia, and Idrisi, writing in about 1100 AD (494 AH) states that the Mahri language is a survival of the ancient Himyaritic. Trilith monuments all over the area are inscribed with rude characters bearing resemblance to ancient South Semitic characters, but there are also many inscriptions in Dhofar in Old South Arabian.

The southern tribes whose languages are of this group are: Mahra, Qara, Shhero (or Shheris), Batharis, Harsusis, Barahama, Bil Haf, Bait as-Shaikh and Afar. The name given to them by Thomas, *Ahl al-Hadara*, may be identifiable with the Hadoram of Genesis and the Adramitae of Pliny.

The Mahra are the most numerous group and are split into an eastern and a western section speaking closely related dialects of the Mahra tongue, though each section derives from a different ancestor. The eastern section are mainly nomadic and used to pick the frankincense during the harvest season whilst the western Mahra have long been largely settled and are coastal people.

The Qara, Shhero and Batharis are also settled tribes, the former two live in the Qara and Qamr mountains of Dhofar, whilst the latter live along the shores of the Kuria Muria bay. Local tradition, supporting etymological evidence, holds that the Shhero were once the exclusive possessors of Dhofar whilst the Batharis possessed the steppes, but that the Qara overcame and absorbed the Shhero taking their frankincense groves and herds, and that the Mahra drove the Batharis to the coast from the hinterland. The Qara also adopted the Shheri language now known as Jibali. In just such a manner the Bait Kathir, who were also later comers, have learnt the original Shheri language though their main language remains Arabic.

The Harsusis are a small tribe inhabiting the area between Dhofar and northern Oman and are associated with the Arab tribes of Awamir and Janaba. The small Afar tribe are also associated with them and speak their language. The Bil Haf live in the steppe land also occupied by the Bait Kathir and Mahra and, though an independent tribe, speak Mahri. The Bait as-Shaikh and Barahama speak Jibali (Shheri).

These Dhofari languages have features of pronunciation not known in modern Arabic, including lateral fricatives something like the "ll" in the Welsh pronunciation of Llanelly – and in Jibali nasalised vowels, resembling certain French sounds such as the nasal vowels *nom* and *matin* and glottalised consonation in place of the Arabic emphatics. The lateralisation of "dh" and probably also the glottalised consonants (which were taken many centuries ago to Ethiopia) seem to be old Semitic usages lost in modern Arabic and thus Oman demonstrates in yet another way the antiquity of its indigenous culture.

Archaic Cultural Evidence

It is perhaps strange that, despite the scale and undoubted antiquity of the frankincense trade, so few ancient settlements have been found.

Ruins dating from between the first century BC and the fourth century AD have, however, been found at various places in Dhofar – Hanun, Andhur and Khor Rori, now silted up but once the best harbour on the Dhofar coast. The city of Samhuram was built on Khor Rori with its Himyaritic fortress and a pre-Islamic temple dedicated to the south Arabian moon god, Sin, which contained an elaborate ablution system, two sacrificial altars, numerous bronze

coins, and ancient frankincense. An inscription found there in 1952 reads: "Shafsay and his mother Nadrat dedicated to their lord Sin, Him of (the Temple of) Ilum, in (the city of) Samhuram for the protection of their persons and of their king."

Other inscriptions found at Samhuram refer to King Ilazz of Hadhramaut, who is mentioned by classical authors as Eleazus, King of the Incense Country and Shabwa. It thus seems probable that Samhuram, which was referred to as the land of the Sachalites and called by the Alexandrine geographer Ptolemy Abyssopolis, the "city of the abyss", on account of the huge abyss above the city where the Wadi Darbat plunges precipitously, was a colony of Shabwa, 500 miles away to the west. At that time world consumption of incense was particularly high and the trade was largely in the hands of the people of Hadhramaut. The head of a bull with a triangular leaf on its forehead was also found at Samhuram. Amphorae from the Greek isles showed that the inhabitants had a taste for Greek wine and that lucrative trading contracts were well developed at the beginning of the Christian era.

Hanun, some thirty-six miles north of Salala, with an excellent water supply of its own, was also apparently associated with Samhuram. An inscription in the Old South Arabian script, found there in 1962, mentions Samhuram and the moon god Sin specifically and refers to the capital as Shabwa. It also calls Hanun Sa'nan, a name still used for it, and refers to Sa'kal or the country of the Sachalites. Hanun seems to have been a seasonal collecting station for frankincense which would have been taken from there either to Samhuram for shipment by sea, or overland to Shisur and thence by one of the camel caravan routes.

The style of a ruined fort or temple at Andhur, forty miles north of Marbat, suggests that it was contemporaneous with Samhuram. It lies in excellent frankincense country and was a very important place on the old caravan routes, leading to the Mediterranean and Gulf.

Rock Art

The human figure is not depicted in most art forms in Oman and there is nothing comparable to the Muslim paintings in Iran, India, Pakistan and Iraq. On the contrary, in Oman as

everywhere else on the Arabian side of the Gulf, the approach to art is simple, puritanical and fundamental. The only exceptions are the anthropomorphic figures which many women and children wear amongst their jewellery as a talisman and the depictions of the human figure, often in the shape of "stick men", in Omani rock art.

Artistic expression in Oman is mainly confined to utilitarian objects, but rock art is a notable exception and its origins go back to a time beyond calculation. Pictures and symbols are found in many places on smooth limestone boulders and rock walls, particularly in the main *wadis* between the interior of the country and the coast, such as the Wadis Bani Kharus, Sahtan and Aday.

Some features are fresh but others are weathered and old and it is difficult to date most of the pictures. It is clear that there are some modern reproductions of older themes and the appearance of aircraft and landrovers is obviously very recent. Nonetheless it is evident both from the state of the picture and the object depicted that some examples are of extreme antiquity.

The pictorial effect is obtained by "pecking" at the limestone surface with a hard, blunt or pointed implement according to the effect desired and figures found on rocks include all sorts of animals: horses, camels, ibex, oryx, dogs, goats, bulls, lions, leopards, foxes, snakes, scorpions, birds, and the now extinct Arabian ostrich and baboon.

The "stick" representations of people are stylised but others are more naturalistic and sometimes bas relief or hollow relief is found as well as "pecking". Men, women and children are represented in a variety of ways. Some ride or stand on horses or bulls. Some carry rifles or swords and shields and others fight with bows and arrows. Some are represented fighting and others hunting, herding or moving in caravan. One clearly old representation depicts a figure wearing a knee length dress with a wasp waist, bird head, long-fingered hands and a wrap around snake. In fact its whole effect resembles a figure on a cylinder seal of the Akkadian period in the third millennium BC in Iraq.

Words too are "pecked" out on rocks – mostly texts from the Qur'an but a short inscription in the old south Arabian tongue has also been found in the Wadi Sahtan.

بِسْمِ اللَّهِ الرَّحْمَنِ الرَّحِيمِ

الم ذَلِكَ الْكِتَابُ لَا رَيْبَ فِيهِ هُدًى لِلْمُتَّقِينَ

الَّذِينَ يُؤْمِنُونَ بِالْغَيْبِ وَيُقِيمُونَ الصَّلَاةَ

وَمِمَّا رَزَقْنَاهُمْ يُنْفِقُونَ وَالَّذِينَ يُؤْمِنُونَ بِمَا أُنْزِلَ

إِلَيْكَ وَمَا أُنْزِلَ مِنْ قَبْلِكَ وَبِالْآخِرَةِ هُمْ يُوقِنُونَ

أُولَئِكَ عَلَى هُدًى مِنْ رَبِّهِمْ وَأُولَئِكَ هُمُ الْمُفْلِحُونَ

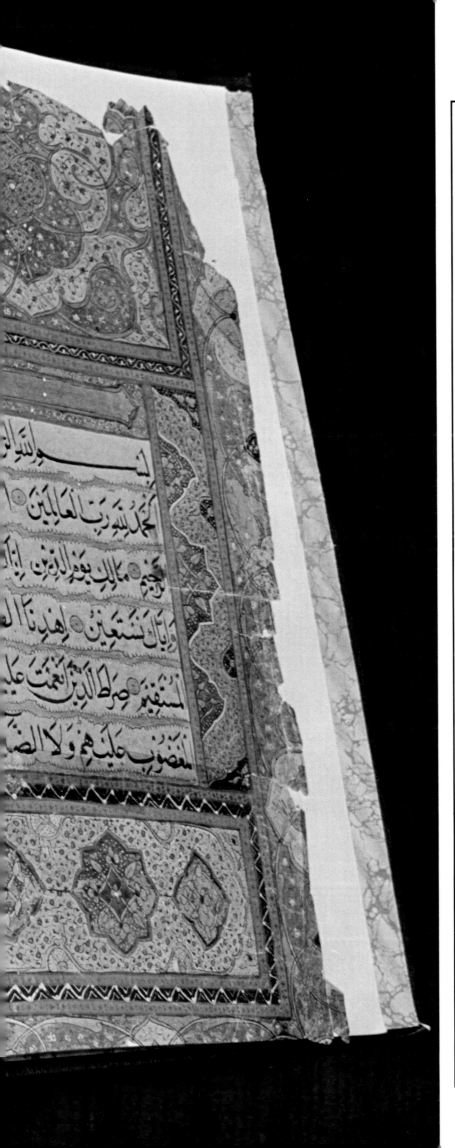

6 Religion

Islam came early to Oman, and has held the minds and hearts of the people ever since. The tolerance and straight-dealing for which Omanis are celebrated are outward reflections of an inner trust in God.

The message of Islam is enshrined in rich colours and glowing illumination in this eighteenth-century Qur'an (left) belonging to Imam Ahmad ibn Said. The new mosque in Muscat (above) is the religious centre of the city.

OMAN was one of the earliest countries to accept the doctrine of the Prophet Muhammad and was conquered not by the sword, as so many other countries were, but by the spirit. The Prophet, according to Omani tradition, said: "Blessed be the people of Ghubaira (an old name for Oman still used in Zanzibar) for they believed on me without seeing me."

The first Omani to embrace the new religion was Mazin ibn Ghadhuba of Samail, who was converted by the Prophet himself in Medina. However, it was Amr ibn al As, a prosperous merchant of Mecca of the Prophet's own tribe, the Quraish, and one of the first believers, who really won Oman over to Islam. Amr, who later conquered Egypt, came to Oman bearing a letter from Muhammad to Abd and Jaifar, the two brothers who then ruled the Arab part of Oman jointly. The letter was similar in tone to that sent to other rulers such as the Emperor Heraclius in Byzantium, the Kings of Persia and Ethiopia and the Governors of Egypt and of Yemen. It read: "In the name of God the most gracious, the most merciful. From Muhammad the Messenger of God to Jaifar and Abd, the sons of al-Julanda. Peace be upon those who follow the true religion. After compliments I call on you to embrace Islam – accept it and you will be saved, for I am the Messenger of God to all humanity. I have come to warn the living that affliction will befall unbelievers. If you accept Islam, as I hope you will, all will be well but, if you refuse to accept it, your Kingdom will vanish and my horses will trample your country and my religion will triumph over your Kingdom."

A council of the Azd tribe was then convened by Abd and Jaifar and they decided to embrace Islam. The main part of the Arab population followed the elders and apparently accepted conversion willingly but the Persians in the coastal towns did not and were subsequently driven out of the country. Amr stayed in Oman until the death of the Prophet in 632 AD, after which he left for Mecca, taking Abd with him to visit the Prophet's successor, Abu Bakr.

In his speech of welcome to Abd, Abu Bakr referred to Oman embracing Islam voluntarily and to Amr's mission there "without army or weapon". Amr's legacy to Oman was purely spiritual and he left no physical memorial such as the great mosque in Cairo named after him –

The saintly Bibi Maryam was commemorated by a mosque, which still stands among the ruins of the once prosperous city of Qalhat.

the most ancient of the many fine mosques in that city.

The five duties of Islam have been observed in Oman since the country's conversion. These are that the Muslim must:

1 say, with full acceptance: "There is no god but God and Muhammad is his Prophet."
2 Pray five times daily, facing Mecca, and say the Friday noonday prayers.
3 Give alms generously.
4 Keep the fast during the holy month of Ramadan, not eating or drinking between sunrise and sunset.
5 Make the pilgrimage – the *Hajj* – to Mecca and the holy places of Islam once in his life if he can.

In Oman itself the years following the first conversions were stormy and it must have taken some time for the whole country to become Muslim. Dhu't Taj Lakit, an Azdi who had previously tried to supplant the ruling Julanda

The Spread of Ibadhism

——— 700–900 AD
- - - 900–1200 AD

SPAIN

Kairouan

MZAB

JEBEL NAFUSA

Inscriptions found at Samhuram reveal that people living there in pre-Islamic times worshipped a moon god named Sin.

The Ibadhi doctrine which predominates in Oman has been compared to a bird: "its egg was laid in Medina, it hatched in Basra and flew to Oman."

from a woman descendant of Malik ibn Fahm, the legendary leader of the first Azd settlers in Oman. A dispute and a fight developed after the cry, "Oh Children of Malik" had been raised by the woman and her supporters. This cry was used before Islam as a tribal cry, and it was wrongly regarded by Hudhaifa's men as an act of defiance and apostasy. Consequently, the Caliph Abu Bakr realised that a mistake had been made and ordered the release of all the captives taken during and after the fracas.

Ibadhism

The Azd of Oman, after their early conversion, played a very important part in the formative days of Islam when Basra in southern Iraq became a very influential city and was the main base camp for Muslim conquests. It was here that the Ibadhi doctrine which predominates in Oman was evolved. As the Omani historian as-Salimi says: "The true religion has been compared to a bird: its egg was laid in Medina, it hatched in Basra and flew to Oman."

The Ibadhis derive their name from Abdulla ibn Ibadh who appeared on the scene in about 683 AD (64 AH), growing up in the Caliph Mu'awiya's reign and dying in Abdul Malik ibn Marwan's (685–705 AD: 66–87 AH). However, he and the early Ibadhis based their traditions on Abu Sha'atha Jabir ibn Zaid, an Azdi of the Yahmad clan, born at Firq near Nizwa. Sunnis and Ibadhis alike regard him as one of the most learned Muslims and of equal eminence with his friend the Mufti of Basra, Hassan al Basri. Abu Sha'atha was himself a *Tabi'* – a person in contact with the Prophet's Companions, the *Sahaba*, who transmitted doctrine directly from Aisha the Prophet's wife, ibn Abbas and others who had fought with the Prophet.

The Ibadhi ideal was to restore the pure Islamic state to what it had been during the time of the Prophet and the first Caliphs Abu Bakr and Omar. In their eyes it had become corrupted by Othman ibn Affan and the struggle between Ali and Mu'awiya for the succession. The Ibadhis believed that the Caliphate should not necessarily go to a member of the Prophet's family but that the best man available to lead the people at the time should be chosen. For a while they held a dialogue with the Caliph Abdul Malik ibn Marwan (685–705 AD: 66–86 AH), about the nature of

princes, is reputed to have rebelled during the Caliphate of Abu Bakr (632–634 AD: 11–13 AH), claiming himself to be a prophet. Abd and Jaifar thereupon retired to the Jebel Akhdar where they were joined by Hudhaifa ibn Muhsin and two other generals, Ikrima ibn Abu Jahl and Arfaja al Bariqi, whom Abu Bakr had appointed to suppress the rebellion. A battle was fought at Dibba, on which the rebel prophet had based himself, and ten thousand people were killed, Dibba itself, a wealthy town and the principal market of the area, being given over to the conquerors. This battle gave rise to and was commemorated in the Omani phrase, "The Day of Dibba", signifying the defeat of paganism by Islam.

However, Abdulla ibn Humaid as-Salimi refutes this story and gives another version of events at Dibba. Hudhaifa's tax collectors had been sent to Dibba to collect the *sadaqa* tax and one of them demanded a fully grown goat

the Islamic state but this ended in disagreement and the persecution which eventually drove the adherents of the Ibadhi precept to seek refuge in their original homes – Oman in the case of the Azdis and Libya, Tunisia and Algeria in the case of the north Africans.

At this old Muscat mosque the muezzin ascends by steps on the outer wall.

The Caliph Abdul Malik's failure to woo over the less extreme opposition to the Umayyad in Iraq led his governor al Hujjaj to clamp down on the power and influence of the Azd. Abu Sha'atha then became the hidden leader of the Ibadhis during this difficult period known as *Kitman*, when the political circumstances dictated extreme caution. Later, Abu Sha'atha withdrew to Oman, where his traditions as well as those of other early Omani *Ulema* founded the corpus of the Ibadhi law.

The Ibadhis held fast to the tenets originally formulated in Basra and, unlike the Sunni and Shia, never reckoned that there must necessarily be a permanent and visible head of the Muslim state or *umma*. They constantly maintained that when a suitable man is available, he should be elected by a prescribed process but otherwise the true Islamic state should rest in *Kitman* as in Abu Sha'atha's time in Basra. When

A continual reminder of Islam, the minarets of Muscat's mosque dominate even the suq.

such circumstances arose, they held that the community of true Muslims might have to conceal its actual beliefs.

The Ibadhis claim with justice that their school of thought, or *madhab*, had been evolved a century or so before those of the four orthodox schools, the

Hanbali, Hanafite, Malikite and Shafi'. Thus the Omani state has over the centuries been based on a very early and highly orthodox version of Islam – although Ibadhi beliefs have not prevented dynasties ruling Oman for long periods – and Shari'a law has been strictly followed in public and private matters. The isolation of the central part of the country has not infrequently centred round strict adherence to Ibadhism, which explains to some extent the dichotomy, so often apparent in Oman's history, between the Ibadhi Interior and the outward-looking Sunni and Shia seafarers of the coast.

Moderation and tolerance have always been essential elements in Ibadhism though, like most religions, it has had some fanatical phases.

This tradition of moderation dates back to the rise of Ibadhism in the later part of the first century AH (seventh century AD). Disputes then were as bitter and far reaching as those between Martin Luther and Pope Leo X or between King Charles I of England and the "Westminster Assembly of Divines". The Ibadhis were, however, sufficiently realistic to recognise that expediency must sometimes temper the ideal and that the means adopted to establish the ideal Islamic state must be reasonable. They were known as "quietists", qu'ad, in their approach, but as a result of perseverance nonetheless succeeded in establishing individual communities both in Oman and North Africa, living in a state of Zuhur, that is, living openly in what they regarded as a properly constituted state.

From the eighth century Imams exercising spiritual, political and military functions were appointed to rule in Oman. They were, however, strictly bound by the Shari'a and in general the Ibadhism of Oman has been characterised by puritanism without the intolerance which has marred other puritan sects in all faiths.

The essential simplicity of the Ibadhi approach is reflected in the quiet dignity of Omani mosques. They are beautifully proportioned but devoid of ornament apart from graceful stucco work around the mihrab niche and windows and from carving on the doors. The minaret is not a characteristic of Oman except on the coast, and the call to prayer is usually made from a roof top, or from a small set of steps on the mosque wall, in the same manner as in the earliest days of Islam. The traveller, ibn Batuta, who visited Nizwa in the fourteenth century admired the "splendid clean mosques" which were centres of community life, where the inhabitants ate their meals, each person bringing what he had to contribute.

Ibn Batuta also describes how the Friday service was conducted by the Ibadhis of Nizwa, saying that they did not – perhaps because the Nabhani Maliks, who then ruled Oman, were not regarded as Imams – use the canonical Sunni form of Friday congregational prayer, but the everyday form of noonday prayer. After the "bowings" the Imam read some verses from the Qur'an and then delivered an address resembling the sermon, Khutba, during which he used the formula "God be pleased with him" in respect of the Caliph Abu Bakr and Omar but not of Othman and Ali.

The austerity of Ibadhism is reflected in the almost total absence of music in the Interior of Oman, except for dancing to the drums during the Id holidays. Austerity is, however, sometimes relaxed in the mountain areas, where grapes are grown and wine made, for at times the people have been given a medicinal dispensation to drink alcohol on account of the extreme cold.

The Muslim Calendar

Oman with the rest of the Islamic world observes the main feasts and fasts of the Muslim calendar. The Muslim calendar, like the earlier Semitic and Arabian ones, is based on the movements of the moon, and the year comprises twelve lunar months. The Muslim calendar moves back approximately eleven days every year in relation to the solar year and thus every thirty-two and a half years it recovers its relative position.

In Oman the new month does not begin until the moon has actually been sighted in Omani territory. This sighting, known as ru'iya, is of particular significance at the beginning of the month of Ramadan – the month of fasting from sunrise to sunset – and Shawwal, the following month, which begins with the celebration of the Id al Fitr. Two reliable eye witnesses have to satisfy the chief Qadhi that the new moon has been seen. He then notifies the Sultan who declares the advent of the new month.

The twelve months of the Muslim calendar are: Muharram, Safar, Rabi' al awal, Rabi'al akhir, Jumada al awala, Jumada al ukhra, Rajab, Sha'ban, Ramadan, Shawwal, Dhu al qa'da and Dhu al hijja. The Muslim New Year on the 1st of Muharram is celebrated as a holiday. Muslim years have, since the time of the Caliph Omar, been counted from the hijra, the emigration of the Prophet

Muhammad to Medina in the year 622 AD, from which time he began his mission.

There are a number of other holidays in the Muslim calendar. The birthday of the Prophet (Mulid an Nabi) – it is not certain whether his birth was in 570 or

Portuguese Christians built this chapel at fort Mirani during their occupation.

"The Lord thy God is the only God" was the belief of the Portuguese, as well as of Muslims.

580 AD – is celebrated on the 12th of Rabi' al awal. Another holiday is the Night Journey and Ascension (*Leilat as asra' wa al mi'raj*) celebrated on the 27th of Rajab. This commemorates the Prophet Muhammad's night journey and ascent into heaven, which is referred to in the Qur'an. The Prophet's ascension differs from Christ's in that it occurred during his lifetime, shortly after his call as a Prophet. He is reputed to have met Allah (God) face to face in the Seventh Heaven and to have received instruction there about the obligatory prayers of Islam, which include the public prayers at Id festivals and the five daily prayers. He is also reputed to have

From the high tower of the mosque at Sur, the faithful hear the call to prayer.

travelled through all the other heavens accompanied by the Angel Gabriel.

The Id al Fitr, which follows Ramadan, denotes a breaking of the fast, and although it is strictly the lesser of the two major festivals, it is often celebrated more wholeheartedly as a result of the strain of fasting being relieved. It is referred to in some countries as Id al Kiswa, as it is the occasion for Muslims to wear new clothes. The Id al Adha means the feast of the sacrifice and it is celebrated on the 10th of Dhu al hijja, sixty-nine or seventy days after the first day of the Id al Fitr. All Muslims are bound to make a sacrifice at the Id al Adha and at this time the pilgrimage to the holy places of Islam – the *Hajj* – reaches its climax. For it is then that

those making the pilgrimage make their sacrifice of a sheep, camel, goat or ox at Thabir, the place in Saudi Arabia, where Abraham sacrificed the ram in place of his son Isaac.

At the two four-day Ids there is great rejoicing, involving not only dancing, including elaborate sword dances, but also singing and much firing of guns. On the coast there is much more dancing generally and playing of musical instruments, where celebrations have been greatly affected by African influences.

This completes the list of holidays kept by the majority of Omanis, but the Shia communities also observe the 10th of Muharram as a day of mourning for the death of Hussain ibn Ali at the battle of Kerbala in 680 AD (60 AH), for they regard him as having had the right to the succession to the Caliphate, being the last surviving grandson of the Prophet Muhammad.

Other Muslims

The orthodoxy and paramountcy of Ibadhism in Oman has not prevented other forms of Islam from taking root. The tribes of the Dhahira and of the area south of the Sharqiya, as well as some on the Batina coast, follow the Sunni precept, whilst the Bani bu Ali tribe in the Jaalan abandoned Ibadhism to become followers of the Wahhabi sect during the Wahhabi incursions from Saudi Arabia in the early nineteenth century. This puritanical and fundamentalist version of Islam, named after Muhammad ibn Abdul Wahhab, its eighteenth-century founder, spread considerably at this time, and fighting between Omanis and Wahhabis continued spasmodically as the century wore on without affecting Omani adherence to Ibadhism.

The Shia sect has a large following amongst the inhabitants of the coastal towns, particularly amongst the merchant class and there are also Khojas or Lutis – Shia originating from Hyderabad in Sind – who have been established in Mutrah for several generations. The Khoja community lives for the most part in a separate walled town within the town of Mutrah with its own mosque on the waterfront.

The mosques of the coastal dwellers in the past were often more elaborately ornamented than those of the Ibadhis, and ibn Batuta has left a description of the mosque in Qalhat: "The city of Qalhat . . . has one of the most beautiful

mosques. Its walls are tiled with *qashani*, which is like *zalij*, and it occupies a lofty situation from which it commands a view of the sea and the anchorage. It was built by a saintly woman Bibi Maryam, *bibi* meaning in their speech 'noble lady'."

The call of the muezzin may be heard throughout the city.

Religious Toleration

Despite the extinction of early Christianity and later the behaviour of Portuguese Christians, who brought the cruelty of the Inquisition and a fanaticism derived from anti-Islamic warfare in the Iberian peninsula, Omani religious tolerance extended to Christianity. Thus the treaty made between the Imam Nasir ibn Murshid and Philip Wylde in 1646 regulating trade between Oman and the East India Company at Sohar, provided specifically that the English should have licence to exercise their own religion. The same liberality has always applied to the Christian missions established at the end of the last century. Lieutenant Wellsted, who visited Muscat in 1835, noted the general tolerance extended to all persuasions by Sayyid Said ibn Sultan, including the Bani Israel, and both he and James Silk Buckingham, who visited the country in 1816, observed that a number of Jews, who had fled the persecution of Daud Pasha in Baghdad, had been permitted to settle. In earlier centuries a considerable number of Jews had been settled all round the coasts of Arabia and there was a large Jewish population in Sohar in the tenth century AD (fourth century AH).

Pre-Islamic Religions and Superstitions

The pre-Islamic Himyaritic kingdom which extended to Oman followed Old Testament precepts and the Hebrew religion. This is established by Omani oral tradition and an inscription found at Husn Ghurab on the coast of south Arabia west of Mukalla. This illustrates early religious practice in a song attributed to early Arabian Adites: "Over us, presided Kings far removed from baseness and stern chastisers of reprobate and wicked men. They noted down for us, according to the doctrine of Heber, good judgements in a book to be kept; and we proclaimed our belief in miracles, in the resurrection, in the return into the nostrils of the breath of life."

The religion of the Sabaeans, who worshipped sun, moon and stars, also had a strong hold. A second century AD temple at Samhuram, the Himyaritic city situated near Taqa in Dhofar, was dedicated to the moon god, Sin, and the triliths found in Dhofar as well as northern Oman may have been symbols of the south Arabian "Trinity" – sun god, moon god and Zahra, the Planet Venus. There may have been animistic aspects to religion too, for some early tribes took their names from animals, and there was for example the Dibba or lizard tribe and the Jaalan or water beetle tribe. Some worship of idols as well may have continued until comparatively recent times. A cave at Izki, which local people are afraid to enter, is said to contain an idol called Jurnan and Lieutenant Whitelock in the 1820s mentions the worship of idols which were smashed by the Wahhabis near Ras al Khaima.

Much of the Old Testament is the common heritage of both Islam and Christianity and it contains long and complicated genealogies of the Semitic people in the Book of Genesis which also mentions Mount Sephar, Dhofar and Obal after whom a place in Oman itself is named. One of Job's Comforters, Bildad the Shuhite, may well have come from the Shihuh tribe.

The crenellation along the walls of this mosque shows the Mogul influence.

The mosque is outlined against the sky at Sur (left).

The new mosque in Muscat serves as the "cathedral" mosque for the capital city. Simple gravestones mark the final resting-places of the people of Salala.

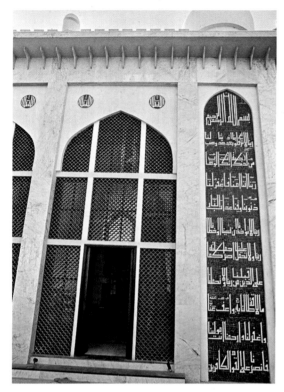

The keynote of Ibadhism is its simplicity – a characteristic reflected in the quiet dignity of Omani mosques. The Ibadhi school of thought can claim, with justice, to have evolved a century or so before other schools of Islamic thought.

Other Religious Manifestations

Miracles are attributed by the chroniclers to several Omani historical figures. The first Imam of the Ya'ruba dynasty, for example, was credited with several, the most noteworthy being that a basket of dates and rice provided enough to feed a hundred men for several days. He was also credited with curing a she-camel which had broken out in pimples after eating food belonging to the Bait al Mal, and he may have had the gift of an aura, for it is related that a corner of the mosque at Rostaq where he was sitting appeared to be lit up as if by a lamp.

On the other hand belief in the *djinns* has not completely disappeared and there are still places to which people will not go for fear of them. In some *wadis* in Oman figures or rock features representing a devil have been pelted with stones since time out of mind. In recent times this has taken the form of shooting with a gun, and it still seems to have some religious significance. Around Bahla, belief in a witch who inhabits the Jebel Khumaila still persists and mothers, as a protection from her, give their children small quantities of mercury.

172

Belief in possession by an evil spirit called *zar* is still prevalent amongst some sections of the population as has been remarked on by, among others, Wilfred Thesiger in *Arabian Sands*. "One night, near Mughshin, when sleeping on the open plain, I was awakened by

The tradition of moderation – established early in Islamic Oman – has allowed the presence of other faiths throughout much of Oman's history. Records of a Christian community, for example, reach back to 424 AD

a long-drawn howl. Again and again the uncanny sound quavered across the camp, sending shivers down my back. It came from a group of figures sitting twenty yards away. I called out: 'What is wrong?' and bin Kabina answered, 'Said is possessed by a *zar*.' I got up, walked round some camels, and joined them. By the light of the setting moon I could see the boy, one of the Bait Kathir, crouching over a small fire. His face and head were covered with a cloth, and he rocked himself to and fro as he howled. The others sat close to him, silent and intent. Suddenly they began to chant in two parts, while Said thrashed himself violently from side to side. More and more wildly he threw himself about, and once a corner of the cloth with which he covered his face fell into the embers and began to smoulder. Someone leant forward and put it out. Steadily the chanting rose and fell about the demented boy, who gradually became calmer. A man lit some incense in a bowl and held it under the boy's nose beneath the cloth. Suddenly he began to sing in a curious, strained, high-pitched voice. Line by line the others answered him. He stopped, grew violent

again, and then calmed once more. A man leant forward and asked him questions and he answered, speaking like someone in his sleep. I could not understand the words, for they spoke Mahra. They gave him more incense and the spirit left him. A little later he lay down to sleep, but once again he was troubled. This time he sobbed bitterly and groaned as if in great pain. They gathered round him once more and chanted until he grew calm. Then he slept. In the morning he was all right."

Christianity
There were a considerable number of Christians in Oman before Islam, though the Julanda princes did not profess Christianity themselves. The second Caliph, Omar, indeed appointed a former Christian, Kaab ibn Sur al-Laqiti, as *Qadhi* in Basra in 639 AD (18 AH).

The Christian population around the Indian Ocean held a strong tradition that Christ's Apostle St Thomas brought Christianity while visiting Oman and places in the Gulf *en route* to India where he suffered martydom. The Indian Sibyl is also reputed to have advised King Perimel of Ceylon to meet

The new Islamic centre at Wattaya was built in 1970–71 as a focus for Islamic affairs.

the two other Kings in Muscat on their way to worship the Infant Jesus. This is not inherently unlikely, for Dhofar is the source of frankincense, myrrh comes from south Arabia, and gold from Ceylon. King Perimel was buried in Coulan in a religious house founded by the disciples of St Thomas.

Christianity in Oman centred round Mazun and Sohar, where there was a Nestorian bishop from at least as early as 424 AD when Bishop John was appointed. His representatives used to travel to church synods in Mesopotamia and Mazun is frequently mentioned in Nestorian records. This bishopric almost certainly fell within the area known as Bait Qatraya and probably came under the Metropolitan of Revi Ardashir, the Sassanid port on the coast of Pars. Nestorian missionary activity, in which the flourishing Nestorian community at Sohar was heavily involved, extended as far afield as Malaya by the seventh century AD. The last recorded bishop, Stephen, was alive in 676 AD but

173

On the 10th of Dhu al Hijja falls the Id al Adha, sixty-nine or seventy days after the Id al Fitr. All Muslims are bound to make a sacrifice at the Id al Adha, and the pilgrimages to the holy places of Islam (Hajj) reach their climax; it is the duty of the Muslim to make the Hajj once in his life if he can.

The two Ids are occasions of great rejoicing, including sword-dances and much firing of guns.

Nestorian Christianity had completely disappeared from Arabia by the ninth century AD.

Christianity was brought back to Arabia by the Portuguese who established two churches in Muscat, one of which was the See of the Vicar and the other the church in the Convent of the Augustinian Friars. Both churches were dedicated to the Virgin Mary and another small chapel, which still stands, was built in fort Mirani, then known as fort Capitan. These churches were still standing in the early eighteenth century when Alexander Hamilton visited them and commented: "A cathedral built by the Portuguese still retains some marks of its grandeur and is now converted into a palace for the King," the Sultan's palace on the water front. The earlier presence of the church is also commemorated in the name of the large and elegant house known as the Bait Graiza, a local corruption of the Portuguese word "igreja" meaning church, which still stands nearby.

Christianity again died out with the expulsion of the Portuguese from Oman in the middle of the seventeenth century and it was not until 1891 that Christian-

ity returned to Oman with the arrival there of Bishop Thomas Valpy French, a former Bishop of Lahore – a remarkable man, described as "a Christian Fakir" and "the most distinguished of all Church Missionary Society missionaries". He ended his dedicated life in Muscat a few months after his arrival, and was buried in the Christian cemetery in the cove near the British Embassy. A poem in his memory by Archdeacon Moule, in somewhat Victorian vein, begins:

"Where Muscat fronts the Orient sun
'twixt heaving sea and rocky steep
His work of mercy scarce begun
A saintly soul has fallen asleep."

The American Mission in Muscat was started at about the same time and their work has continued on an ever-growing scale since then. This mission, whose work has lain mainly in the educational and medical spheres, has had amongst its dedicated staff such notable figures as the Reverend S. M. Zwemer, the author of *Arabia, the Cradle of Islam* and several outstanding doctors like Dr Sharon Thoms and his son Dr Wells Thoms.

The Id al Fitr, the end of the fasting month of Ramadan, is celebrated with music, dancing and feasting. The lesser of the two Id festivals, it is nevertheless celebrated with great vigour, perhaps as a result of the strain of fasting being relieved. It is the occasion for Muslims to wear new clothes.

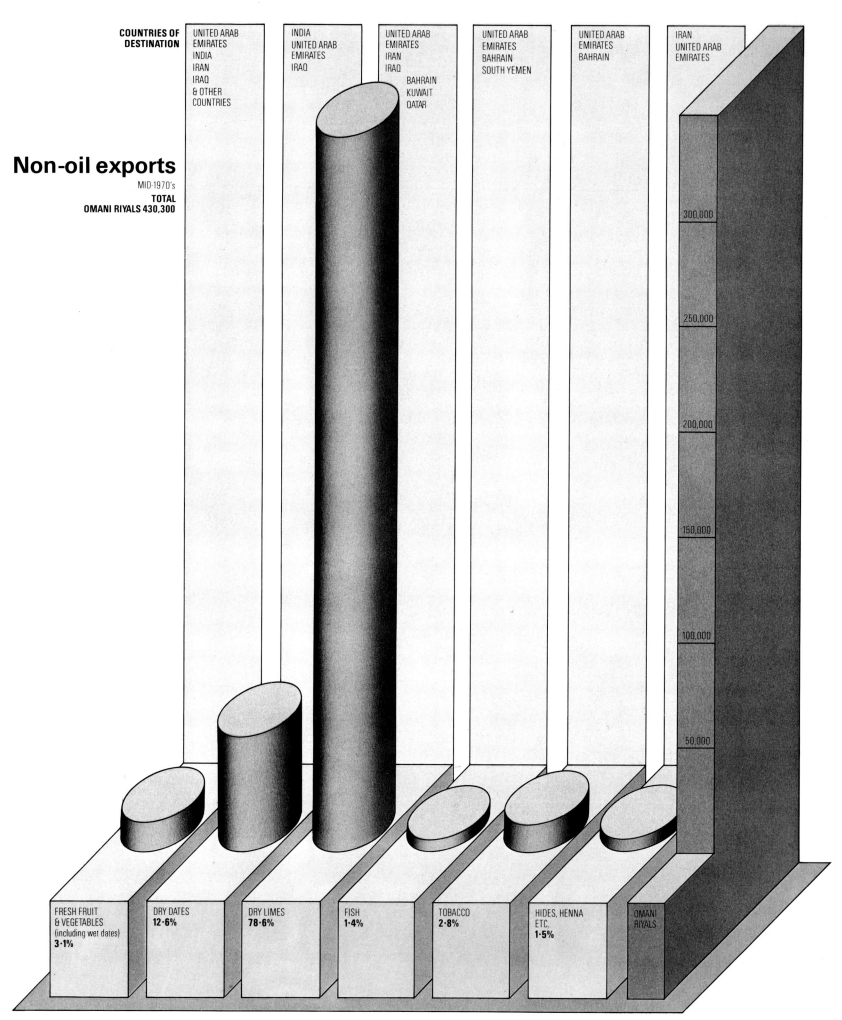

Non-oil exports

MID-1970's
**TOTAL
OMANI RIYALS 430,300**

**COUNTRIES OF
DESTINATION**

UNITED ARAB EMIRATES INDIA IRAN IRAQ & OTHER COUNTRIES	INDIA UNITED ARAB EMIRATES IRAQ	UNITED ARAB EMIRATES IRAN IRAQ BAHRAIN KUWAIT QATAR	UNITED ARAB EMIRATES BAHRAIN SOUTH YEMEN	UNITED ARAB EMIRATES BAHRAIN	IRAN UNITED ARAB EMIRATES	

300,000

250,000

200,000

150,000

100,000

50,000

| FRESH FRUIT & VEGETABLES (including wet dates) **3·1%** | DRY DATES **12·6%** | DRY LIMES **78·6%** | FISH **1·4%** | TOBACCO **2·8%** | HIDES, HENNA ETC. **1·5%** | OMANI RIYALS |

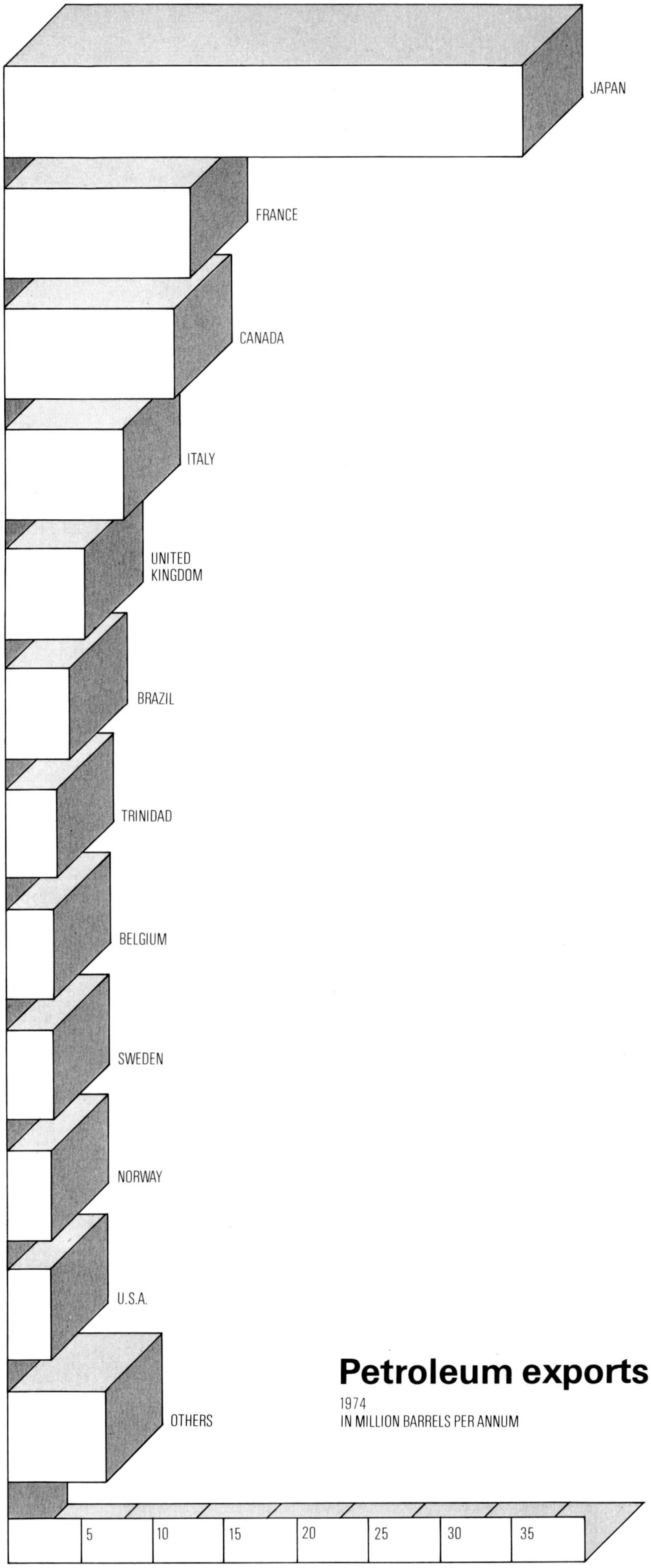

Petroleum exports

1974
IN MILLION BARRELS PER ANNUM

JAPAN

FRANCE

CANADA

ITALY

UNITED KINGDOM

BRAZIL

TRINIDAD

BELGIUM

SWEDEN

NORWAY

U.S.A.

OTHERS

5 10 15 20 25 30 35

Figures since 1974 are not available

7 Commerce

As it was in the Phoenicians, with whom they may have some connection, commerce is in the bloodstream of Omanis. Their mercantile empire has straddled the Indian Ocean. As formerly their sailors and merchants probed the furthest corners of the known world, so today Oman's latest and most important product, petroleum, is sold from Japan to the West.

Petroleum and the other products of mineral oil are only the latest among a wide variety of exports for which Oman has been known. Throughout the centuries Oman has been famous for frankincense, for limes, dates and other fruit and for the entrepôt *trade.*

177

The Jebel Fahud looked promising but was reluctant to reveal its treasure.

OIL has transformed the economies of many countries in the Gulf area, and Oman, though production and prospects there are modest compared with Kuwait or Abu Dhabi, is no exception (*see also* Section 8: Petroleum).

The Anglo-Persian Oil Company Limited carried out a geological exploration in 1924–25, a time when there was considerable competition to obtain concessions in Arabia. However, the Company gave their concession up when the results of the survey proved disappointing.

In 1937 Petroleum Development (Oman) – P.D.(O.) – obtained concessions or options for Oman and the southern province of Dhofar. The company was then a subsidiary of the Iraq Petroleum Company, the ownership of which was: BP 23.75 per cent, Royal Dutch Shell 23.75 per cent, Compagnie Française de Pétrole 23.75 per cent, Near East Development Corporation which comprised the Standard Oil Company of New Jersey and Sacony Mobil Oil Company 23.75 per cent and C.S. Gulbenkian – later Partex – 5 per cent. The area was by then of considerable potential interest to the oil companies as the western slopes of the Oman mountains had been shown to contain well-folded sedimentary rock masses and to lie on the fringes of a great geosyncline. However exploration was interrupted by the 1939–45 war, and in the immediately following years was confined to a visit to Dhofar in 1948 and work of a few weeks' duration in 1950.

In 1951 the Dhofar concession was given up, which enabled the Sultan to interest other oil companies in possibilities there. But in northern Oman between 1953 and 1960 P.D.(O.) partially explored and test drilled their concession area though they had great difficulties over access owing to differences between the Sultan and the Imam, Shaikh Ghalib ibn Ali who, unlike his predecessor Shaikh Muhammad al Khalili, claimed independence for the Interior of Oman. Nonetheless a well was spudded in on the promising Jebel Fahud structure

in 1956 and a supply of men and materials was organised from the coast at Ras Duqm and Azaiba near Muscat. Though drilled to 12,250 feet, the Fahud well did not live up to expectation and was abandoned in May 1957. Another well was sunk at Ghaba eighty-five miles south-east, but though drilled to 12,660 feet, it also proved to be dry. Similar disappointments over wells at Haima and Afar dashed the hopes which the region had seemed to hold on tectonic grounds. Accordingly, three of the major participants in the Petroleum Development Company (Oman) – B.P., Near East Development Corporation and Compagnie Française de Pétrole – decided to withdraw, leaving Shell with 85 per cent and Partex with 15 per cent, though C.F.P. later rejoined the venture in 1967 by purchasing 10 per cent of Partex's 15 per cent.

The reformed P.D.(O.) Company continued exploration and in March 1964 announced plans for production following discoveries at Yibal in 1962, Natih in 1963 and Fahud in 1964. It was ironical that the successful Fahud well was drilled only a very short distance from the original dry well. A new and revised agreement was signed on 7th March 1967 for the unexpired period of the 1937 concession, incorporating the more modern terms already applying in other parts of the Middle East.

In Dhofar, Cities Services obtained a blank concession for the 30,000 square mile area in 1952 and formed an *ad hoc* subsidiary called Dhofar-Cities Services Petroleum Corporation. Soon afterwards they accepted the Richfield Oil Corporation as an equal but non-operating partner. In early 1954 the first well – at Douka, 140 miles inland from Salala – was spudded in. Though drilled to 12,000 feet it proved dry as did the next two holes in the same area. In 1957 small quantities of oil were found at Marmel, forty miles from the coast, but the initial flow of only some 2,000 barrels a day fell off rapidly. By May 1960 a dozen wells had been drilled, with geological and seismic work going

on simultaneously, but no prospect of a major strike had eventuated and the companies abandoned hope.

In 1962 the Dhofar oil rights were taken up by the John W. Mecom Company with which the Pure Oil Company joined in 1963. Mecom, however, withdrew in 1964 and in 1965 Continental took over a one-third share in the Mecom/Pure Oil enterprise. In 1969 P.D.(O.) resumed the concession in Dhofar under an agreement similar in terms to the revised agreement which they made in 1967 for northern Oman. This agreement was, however, for a six-year period only, unless oil was found in commercial quantities during that time.

In 1970 the Sultanate's share of profit was raised from 50 per cent to 55 per cent. From 1st January 1974 the Oman Government acquired a 25 per cent interest in the Company's (P.D.(O.)'s) concession under an agreement similar to those current elsewhere at the time in the Gulf area. At the same time 35,000 square miles of the concession were relinquished and the area retained in Dhofar was integrated into the main concession. In July 1974 agreement was reached whereby the Government interest was increased retrospectively from 1st January 1974 to 60 per cent. A Joint Management Committee was set up in the same year with two members appointed by the Government and four by the Company. Further production wells were discovered in the early 1970s at Ghaba, al Huwaisa, Saih Rawl, Habur and Lekhwair.

Total production figures were 20.9 m. barrels in 1967, 87.9 m. in 1968, 119.7 m. in 1969, 121.3 m. in 1970, 106.25 m. in 1971, 103.18 m. in 1972, 106.85 m. in 1973, 105.8 m. in 1974 and 124.6 m. in 1975. Payments to the Government by the Company were £1,366,625 in 1967, £25,461,784 in 1968, £38,518,356 in 1969, £44,391,937 in 1970, £47,738,978 in 1971, £51,045,000 in 1972 and £73,665,000 in 1973. In 1974 payment of taxes and royalties amounted to £136.1 m. However, this figure was not comparable with the 1973 figure as it related to the 40 per cent remaining

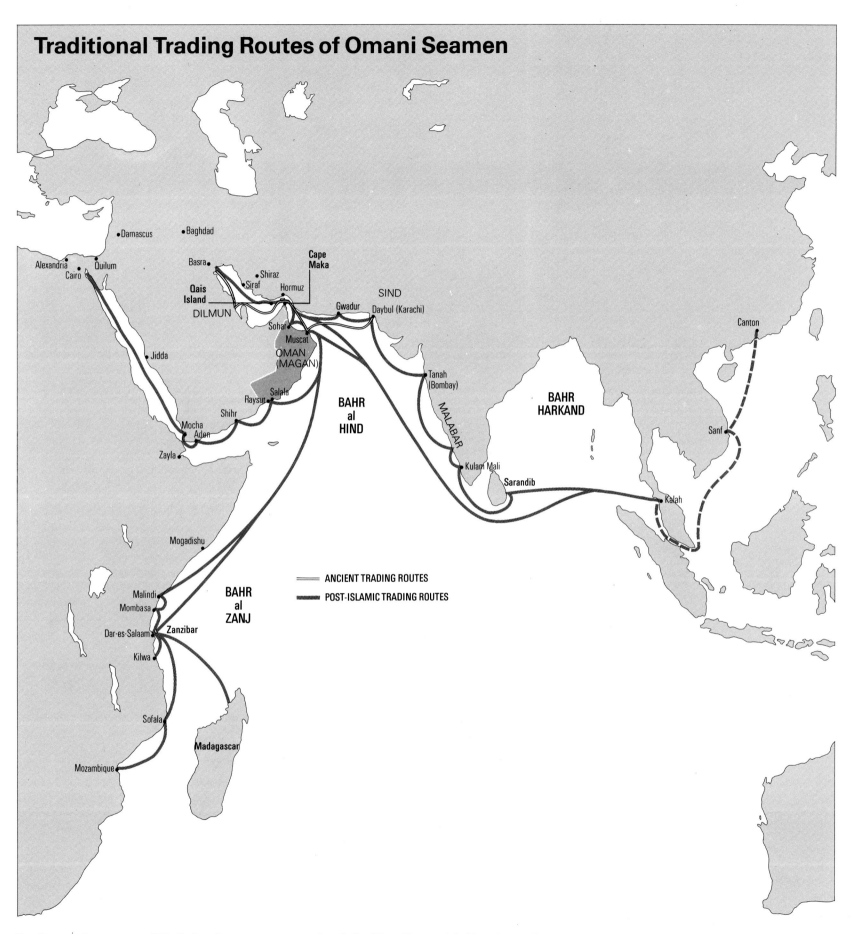

In the tenth century AD Sohar's commanding position near the Straits of Hormuz brought prosperity to the enterprising seamen of Oman. Through Muscat and Sohar passed the exotic trade of the Far East with Persia and Arabia, and southwards their sailors were carried to the African coast by the monsoon winds.

179

In 2200 BC, copper, ivory, ochre and jewellery were main trade items.

private company interest and not to all the oil produced and exported. Taxes and royalties averaged $7.58 per barrel compared with $1.83 per barrel in 1973. The Government also received revenue from sales of their 60 per cent of the crude oil.

These figures well illustrate how it has been possible to finance the material renaissance of Oman.

The Early Entrepôt Trade

The exotic has always played an important part in Oman's trade, and the expensive gifts of the East – gold, myrrh and frankincense – have all featured as well as monkeys, mynah birds, ivory, slaves, coffee, cloves and spices. The *entrepôt* trade has throughout history been the main plank in the Omani economy, but shipbuilding, shipowning and privateering, agriculture and horse breeding, copper mining, and latterly oil have all contributed in large measure.

In the fourth and third millennia BC Oman was probably called Magan and was already renowned as a seafaring and mercantile nation. Magan's trade centred largely on copper, and the extensive copper workings near Sohar indicate a likely source. Sumerian inscriptions refer to copper from Magan and list the goods sent in return for this most sought after of metals – barley, garments of high and medium quality, skins, wool, sesame oil and "merchandise for buying copper".

The recorded exports of Magan, apart from copper, were wood, diorite – both used for example in building the temple of Nin-Gir-Su by Gudea of Lagash in about 2200 BC – ivory, precious stones, red ochre (perhaps brought from the islands of Abu Musa or Henjam), "Magan onions", and bamboo. Other Magan exports were multicoloured beads and wooden curiosities. There were also Magan chairs and tables. Could the stools inlaid with ivory and gold, which astonished Vasco da Gama when he was entertained by the Arabs of Malindi in 1498 have been latter day versions of these? Whether the wood for this furni-

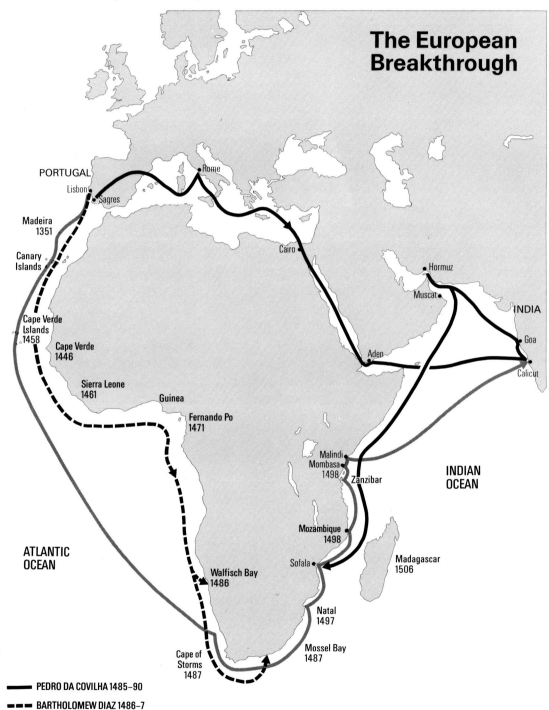

The European Breakthrough

━━━━ PEDRO DA COVILHA 1485–90

■ ■ ■ BARTHOLOMEW DIAZ 1486–7

━━━━ VASCO DA GAMA 1497–8

ture came from Magan itself or from Malabar to Oman, like the teak exported in subsequent generations, remains obscure. But some of Magan's trade with Mesopotamia was certainly founded on imports from Maluhha, which at this period was probably India, for example

The kernel of the trade with Europe was the export of spices from the East to Portugal, passing through the entrepôts.

Sohar was "the hallway to China, the storehouse of the East".

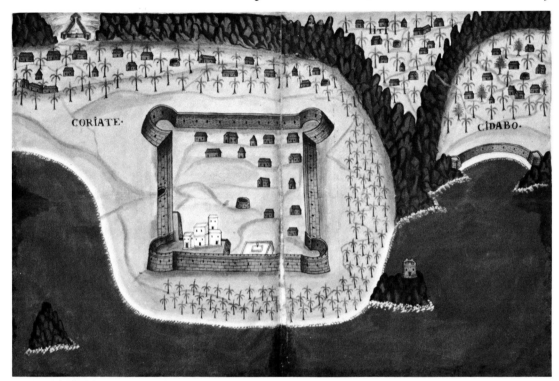

Sohar

During the tenth century AD, the fourth century of Islam, Sohar was richer in fine buildings and foreign merchandise than any other port in the Islamic world. Ibn Hauqal claimed that "its traders and commerce cannot be enumerated" and al-Muqadassi called it the "hallway to China, the storehouse of the East and Iraq, and the stay of the Yemen". It was the greatest sea port of Islam and yet its fame is relatively unsung. Ibn Hauqal himself said that the rest of Islam hardly knew it existed and a modern visitor finds it hard to imagine its past glories. These rivalled those of Siraf, which was world famed in its day.

Sohar's importance was attributable to a number of factors. First it is conveniently situated on the eastern coast of Oman which looks outwards towards the coasts of Africa and India and the Far East. Secondly its hinterland is very fertile and was much more so in the past. Thirdly its situation at the end of the Wadi Jizzi gives it easy access through the mountains to Buraimi and to the northern coast in the present United Arab Emirates. Finally historical circumstances in the tenth century gave its enterprising and cosmopolitan people opportunity.

In the tenth century, and probably subsequently when the Omani coast was under the suzerainty of Hormuz, the goods passing through Sohar and Muscat were very varied. Omani seamen brought aloes, wood, bamboo, camphor, sandalwood, ivory, tin and spices of all kinds from Kalah, an important trading city on the coast of Malaya, which became the neutral meeting place between Arab and Chinese merchants after the foreign community in Canton had been massacred in 878 AD (265 AH). Earlier Omani and Gulf merchants had taken their ships to China itself to trade and Chinese ships had come to Oman and the Gulf. There was a vast trade in chinaware, and other imports from China included musk, silk and jewels. The exports to the Far East included costly

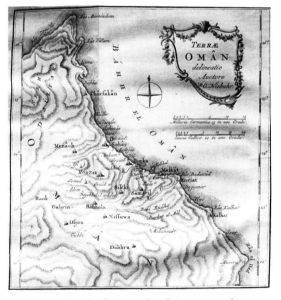

Carsten Niebuhr made this map of Oman in the eighteenth century.

gold, wood, ebony, ivory and monkeys. Magan may also have exported goats on the hoof, for the country was famous for these and its goddess was called Nindulla, "Queen of the Flocks".

Omani copper was produced at small smelting sites in many parts of the

Forts like that at Quriyat helped to defend the trading ports.

country, particularly in the Wadi Jizzi, and it is not hard to imagine a sea port at Sohar even at this early date with a route through the Wadi Jizzi to Buraimi and on to Umm an-Nar on the north coast, near the present Abu Dhabi. Shortly after 2000 BC, at roughly the same time as the Indus Valley civilisation was wiped out, sea trade broke down and did not revive until the middle of the first millennium BC. Copper was then exported from Oman again but it was not until Sassanid and early Islamic times that copper was mined on a vast commercial scale. The scale of the operation is indicated by slag heaps at Lasail in the Wadi Jizzi which contain 100,000 tons and are comparable in size with modern slag heaps. The widespread workings were used for some centuries subsequently and copper smelting was certainly an important industry in Sohar's heyday in the tenth century. Supplies of copper were indeed so plentiful then that broken pots were mended with copper rather than iron staples.

Every sea captain had a home among Sohar's 12,000 houses.

fabrics of linen, cotton and wool – perhaps from Persia – rugs, metalwork, iron or bullion and possibly dates. From Africa Omani seamen brought ivory, tortoiseshell – though some of this may have come from the island of Masira, to which several of the world's known species of turtle resort – leopard skins, ambergris and slaves.

The Omanis of Sohar in its heyday were building on a well established foundation. The spread of Islam in the seventh century led to the Arabs occupying all the coasts of the Gulf and re-uniting the great economic area of western Asia, first united politically under the Achaemenids, split by the successor of Alexander the Great and reunified under the Sassanids. The Gulf and Red Sea were no longer rival routes to the markets of Rome or Byzantium, but parallel routes to the nearer lands of the Caliphate. In fact the Muslim countries of the Middle East dominated and controlled the lucrative trade between the Far East and the West until the arrival of the Portuguese in the Indian Ocean in the sixteenth century, lying across this great belt like a "Moslem Colossus".

Omani mariners of the tenth century were remarkable for their skill, courage and endurance. The planks of their ships were only sewn together with yarn spun from the bark of the coconut palm and yet they sailed as far as China to the east and Madagascar to the south. The beginnings of this renaissance for Omani shipping was – strangely – attributable to the Persian Sassanid dynasty. Sohar, which was called Mazun during the Sassanid period, already boasted notable seafarers in the third century AD and Ardashir, the founder of the Sassanid dynasty, moved some sailors of the Azd tribe from there to Shihr, thus perhaps establishing the long sea-faring traditions of the Hadhramaut. There is little evidence about the size of the ships used during this period but a clear distinction was drawn by the Arab geographers between the great seagoing ships, which carried as many as 400 men,

and those used for coastal traffic in Gulf waters. In the years before Islam, Nestorian Christians amongst the inhabitants of Sohar were active in trade with India and beyond, and their missionary activities – after the establishment of the Nestorian bishopric in about 424 AD – extended even as far as Malaya.

Lucrative sea trade between the Gulf and China was made possible by the simultaneous existence of great empires at each end. The whole Muslim world from Spain to Sind was united under the Umayyad Caliphs from 660 to 749 AD (40 to 132 AH) and, with the exception of Spain and North Africa, for over a century, 750 to 870 AD (133 to 257 AH), under the Abbasids in Baghdad. The Ta'ng dynasty ruled over a united empire in China from 618 to 907 AD (–4 to 295 AH). Thus conditions at either end of this long trade route were relatively stable and the Omanis profited for by the middle of the eighth century AD an Omani called Abu Ubaida Abdalla ibn al Qasim made the first recorded voyage to China, taking about two years to cover the distance of some 4,350 miles. It is no coincidence that *Kitab Aja'ib al Hind* (*The Book of the Wonders of India*), the forerunner of the Sindbad stories, was produced during Sohar's heyday.

Al-Muqaddasi described the port of Sohar in detail. The anchorage was about a *farsang* – four miles – in length and breadth and was always busy with ships. Near the shore was a great mosque with a high minaret and a magnificent many-coloured *mihrab* on a spot where, according to tradition, the Prophet's camel had knelt. It is hard now to reconstruct this Sohar in the mind's eye, but it is possible that the two creeks were open to the sea and that there was a mole built out into the sea. The town, which consisted mainly of red brick buildings, was then four times as large as it now is. There were 12,000 houses and each sea captain lived in a separate dwelling. The agricultural land was also about four times as large as it is now and covered thirty-eight square miles compared with the present eleven

Sohar – Historic Port

The port of Sohar was so splendid in the tenth century AD that it became for a short while the first city of Islam. The anchorage was about four miles in length and breadth, and was always teeming with ships. Sohar was then about four times as big as now; built largely of red brick, it contained 12,000 houses, and each sea captain lived in his own house. The cultivated area was also four times as extensive in the tenth century, covering thirty-eight square miles as opposed to eleven square miles now, and producing dates, bananas, figs, grapes, subtropical fruit and citrus varieties from India. There was then a thriving brick industry, ascribed to the Jewish community whose strength is indicated by the large number of ancient Jewish graves. Copper smelting and glass-blowing were also important industries.

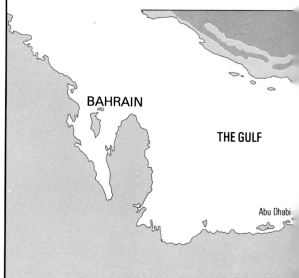

BAHRAIN

THE GULF

Abu Dhabi

Sohar & the entrance to the Gulf

Sohar lies on the low, sandy Batina coast. The nearby Wadi Jizzi provides natural links with the Interior.

0 Kilometres	100	200	300
0 Miles		100	200

Ships of the day, bound with yarn, plied to China and Madagascar.

Sohar Fort 1500 AD

The fort at Sohar guarded a major port and, because of its strategic position, helped to command the Straits of Hormuz, a vital seaway.

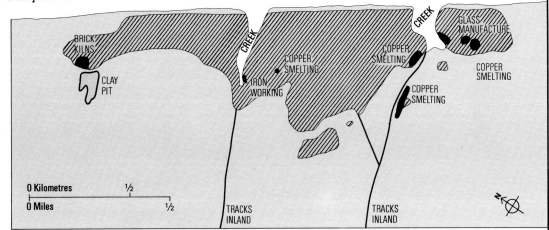

Sohar in the 4th-10th centuries AD

Brickmaking from local clay, copper smelting and the making of glassware were the main industries of Sohar during this period.

Sohar Today

Sohar today is linked by a new asphalt road to Mutrah, some 148 miles away. Completed in 1973, this road not only turned two principal towns into neighbours, but simultaneously began to serve many villages along the Batina coast, giving new opportunities for the distribution of goods, and linking the entire coast to the fine harbour at Mutrah, Port Qaboos. A new port is planned for Sohar to handle the recently-discovered deposits of copper in the surrounding regions; Sohar may thus once again become a major port.

Over the centuries, Sohar's coastline has changed. The creeks which once sheltered boats are now sealed off and the ancient jetties destroyed.

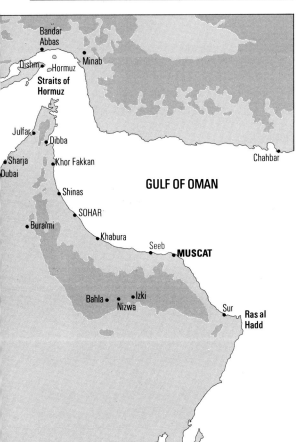

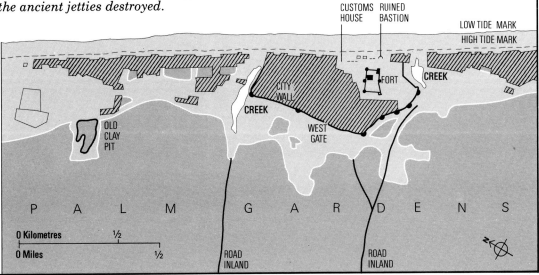

de Stadt MUSCHAT
in Arabia.

Besides Sohar, Muscat, Qalhat and Quriyat prospered. Glassware and copper smelting were among the local industries.

All trade had to pass through Muscat to take on water and limes.

square miles, and produced dates, bananas, figs, grapes, subtropical fruit and citrus varieties from India. The old kilns still survive on the northern edge of the town and tradition ascribes this brick industry to the Jewish community, whose strength at this period is attested by the large number of Jewish graves. Copper smelting, glass manufacture and shipbuilding were amongst the most important industries. Sohar's prosperity was, however, largely built on the *entrepôt* trade and it was this which caused Istakhri to write: "... it is not possible to find on the shore of the Persian Sea nor in all the land of Islam a city more rich in fine buildings and foreign wares than Sohar."

Later Entrepôt Trade

After the fall of Sohar, Oman never had an *entrepôt* port so magnificent. However, Sohar, which rose again, Qalhat, Quriyat, Muscat, and Khor Fakkan were all prosperous during the period of Hormuzi supremacy on the coast, as Marco Polo and ibn Batuta noted. Albuquerque himself commented on

Dutch ships outside Muscat (left).

185

their prosperity when he reduced them to Portuguese sovereignty and Oman became part of the pattern of Portuguese overseas trade. During the same period Balid in Dhofar was also flourishing under its own Sultan.

Before the advent of the Portuguese, Omani sailors, who were to be found all over the Indian Ocean, had evolved a

different routes safe in every wind and possesses fresh water and a hospitable and sociable people who love strangers."

Ahmad's father and grandfather were also well known navigators and his work is based on their writings and experience as well as those of the "three lions" of the sea, Laith ibn Kahlan, Muhammad ibn Shadhan and Sahl ibn

those of the Omani coast, stretching from Hormuz to Sofala in the west and to the Moluccas and Macao on the edge of the Pacific. Pepper came from Malabar and Indonesia; gold, silks and porcelain from China; gold from Sumatra and south-east Africa; horses from Persia and Arabia and cotton textiles from Gujerat (Cambay) and Coromandel. The various

The 72-gun Imaum *(third from left), a gift to King William IV of England.*

Ahmad ibn Na'man, Oman's first trade envoy to America.

sophisticated system of navigation. Navigational theory, and indeed the whole gamut of seamanship, are the subject of a nautical book, by Ahmad ibn Majid, the most famous navigator of his day, called *Kitab al-Fawa'id fi usul al-bahr wa'l-qawa'id (The Book of Benefits on the Principles of Seamanship).*

Ahmad, who may have piloted Vasco da Gama from Malindi to Calicut in 1498 (904 AH), was born in Julfar but his home town was almost certainly Muscat. At least he described Muscat in glowing terms as "the most well-known port in the world" and went on: "Muscat is a port the like of which cannot be found in the whole world. There can be found business and good things which cannot be found elsewhere. There is a rock at the head of the port which the traveller to and from any place sees, whether he aims for India and Sind or Hormuz or Makran or the West, and North West by West of it is a high red island called Al Fahal and these are landmarks sufficient for even the ignorant man when he comes across them night or day. Muscat is the port of Oman where year by year the ships load up with men, fruit and horses, and they sell in it cloth, vegetable oils and new slaves and grain and all ships aim for it. It is a cape between two

Abban, all of whom were also famous for voyages of exploration. Ahmad's navigational and intellectual successor Sidi Celebi, the Ottoman sailor who took command of Sultan Sulaiman's fleet after it had been abandoned in Basra by Piri Rais, the Captain General of the Turkish Navy, carried the Indian Ocean version of the art a step further forward.

The pilots of the Indian Ocean relied on compass bearings and on taking the altitude of the stars whereas the early Mediterranean method depended on the compass and on measuring the distance travelled through the sea. As ibn Majid and other captains in the Indian Ocean calculated latitudes by reference to stellar altitudes and there is no evidence that they ever "shot" the sun, their measurements must always have been taken by night. However during the day they relied on *isharat*, that is, the physical signs such as tides and discoloured water to which they attached great importance, to help their navigation and keep them on course.

After the Portuguese seaborne empire was established in the sixteenth century, Portugal held a chain of forts, including

items of merchandise which originated in Asia either passed through the local *entrepôts* or were shipped round the Cape of Good Hope to Lisbon. The kernel of this trade was the export of pepper from the East to Portugal and of silver bullion to Goa.

The pattern of trade, during the later reign of the Imam Ahmad ibn Said, is illustrative of the type of commerce which prevailed in the area for long periods. The carriage of coffee from Mocha in Yemen to Basra was an important feature at this stage, and in 1765 about fifty vessels formed the annual "coffee fleet" which sailed every year from Muscat to Basra, Oman's principal trade at this juncture lying with Turkish Iraq. The mariners of Sur also played an important part in the coffee trade. By 1775 Muscat had become the principal *entrepôt* for trade between the Gulf, India and the Red Sea and by the last decade of the eighteenth century about five-eighths of the total trade of the Gulf passed through Muscat. Sayyid Sultan ibn Ahmad then claimed the exclusive right to protect navigation in the Gulf and tried – though without ultimate success – to make a preliminary visit to Muscat obligatory on all vessels proceeding up the Gulf, a stratagem which had made other great *entrepôts* in the area, Hormuz, Qais and Siraf, prosperous in their own heydays. During Sultan's time half the produce of Yemen flowed through Muscat.

Oman's own exports during the latter

The great Sayyid Said ibn Sultan sent Ahmad ibn Na'man to America.

half of the eighteenth century, apparently coming from the Interior, were gums – perhaps frankincense from Dhofar; ostrich feathers – presumably from the now extinct Arabian ostrich, though it is possible that they came from east Africa; hides, skins, honey, beeswax and live cattle and sheep. Re-exports from Persia were copper, drugs, rosewater, dried fruits, raw silks, raw cotton, sulphur and rock salt; from Iraq: dates, copper, gall-nuts, tobacco, gum, catgut, pen reeds and horses. Oman's own export of horses too was for many generations very considerable. Imports from abroad for Omani home consumption included: Indian piece goods, pepper, ginger, rice, tobacco, coffee, sugar, English cloth, cutlery and toys. Apart from coffee, all sorts of other goods flowed through the Omani *entrepôts*.

In Sultan's time in the last years of the eighteenth century, Muscat alone had fifteen ships of 400 to 700 tons, along with three brigs; and Sur was the headquarters of a fleet of a hundred seagoing vessels trading directly with Bengal, Batavia and Malabar, whilst smaller ships traded with the Gulf,

east Africa and Abyssinia. In fact Suris and Omanis from the Sharqiya area played a considerable part in the Omani exploitation and opening up of east Africa. From the 1830s Europe was developing steamboats, railways, telegraph systems and other engineering skills. Nevertheless, about five-eighths of Gulf trade still touched at Muscat in the 1840s and as late as 1854 Muscat-owned ships carried about half of the trade. Thus Muscat remained important as an *entrepôt* well into the nineteenth century and its *entrepôt* trade was estimated to be worth £1.8m in the 1830s. By the 1870s, however, the situation had changed and Muscat's trade dwindled to £425,000 in 1874–75.

Trade in the western Indian Ocean began to interest the Americans in the 1820s and the first American vessel, the *Laurel* from Salem, called at Zanzibar in July 1825, a time when Sayyid Said was becoming increasingly preoccupied with his east African possessions. This preoccupation was heightened by the action, subsequently disavowed, of Captain William Owen in provisionally declaring a British protectorate over Mombasa at the request of the Mazrui shaikhs, the dominant Omani group there who had renounced Omani suzerainty on Said's accession.

Edmund Roberts of Salem, New Hampshire placed American trade with Said on a sound and formal basis. After obtaining letters of credence addressed to Said from his kinsman, Senator Levi Woodbury, Secretary of the Navy, Roberts took a small naval squadron to conclude treaties with Siam, Cochin China, Japan and the powers of Arabia on the Red Sea as well as Said.

Roberts travelled on the United States sloop of war *Peacock* and arrived in Muscat in September 1833. A Treaty of Amity and Commerce was signed on 21st September which stipulated *inter alia* that American traders would only pay 5 per cent import duty in the Sultan's dominions. Unfortunately there were discrepancies between the English and Arabic texts, which later gave rise to misunderstanding, but at the time Roberts carried away not only the signed treaty but also a friendly letter from Said to President Jackson expressing his determination that the treaty should be faithfully observed "as long as the world endures"; this echoed the provision in the 1800 treaty with Britain that the friendship of the two

states should "remain unshaken till the end of time, and till the sun and moon have finished their revolving career". The treaty was ratified in 1834, and thereafter American commerce with the Sultanate rested on a most favoured nation basis.

Trade between Americans and Oman grew, particularly after the appointments as Consul of Richard Waters in Zanzibar in 1837 and Henry Marshall in Muscat in 1838 – though the latter appointment was short-lived. Cotton sheeting, crockery, muskets, gunpowder, ships' stores, clocks, shoes and spices were brought from America, and return cargoes consisted of gum copal, copra, cloves and ivory.

Said, who was personally one of the largest importers, decided, on the advice of Edgar Botsford of New York, to add a new dimension to relations by sending one of his own vessels to the United States and purchasing munitions – for he still aimed to drive the Portuguese from Mozambique. The *Sultana*, named after his first consort the Sultana Azza bint Saif, who came from his own family, was designated for the voyage to New York and Said tried to persuade Richard Waters to go too, as he had no Omani navigator to pilot the ship across the Atlantic, all his crews being experienced in the Indian Ocean only. Waters did not take up Said's invitation and William Sleeman, a Britisher who had previously commanded the Omani frigate *Prince Regent* and was a good navigator though he had an unfortunate addiction to the bottle, was instructed to sail the vessel as sailing master, leaving early in February 1840.

Said's confidential private secretary, Hajji Ahmad ibn Na'man, was chosen to represent him in the United States and he too sailed on the *Sultana* via St Helena. It was he who stole the limelight in New York, for, perhaps on account of Sleeman's bad conduct, he announced that he was in command and that his name rather than Sleeman's should appear on official port documents. Ahmad was small and slightly corpulent, his complexion tawny, and his eyes black and piercing. He wore a gaily-coloured turban on his head, a bright cashmere shawl around his waist, and a splendidly embroidered *qaftan* trimmed with gold over his long white undergarment. He was the first Omani envoy to the United States and he made a great impression. His upbringing was as cos-

For a while Omani-controlled Zanzibar rivalled the motherland's wealth.

A century ago, the Omani-ruled island of Zanzibar was a major trade centre.

mopolitan as that of many Omanis. Of the Bani Kaab tribe on his father's side, with a Persian mother, he had been born in Basra. Having joined Said's service in 1820 he travelled to China, Cairo and Europe on his behalf, and also made the pilgrimage to Mecca.

Amongst the passengers on the *Sultana* were two young Englishwomen – Mrs Robert Norsworthy, wife of an English trader in Muscat and Zanzibar and her maid Charlotte Thompson. They were closely guarded in their cabin to ensure privacy, a security precaution which gave rise to rumours in the United States that Said had sent "two or three Circassian slaves of outstanding beauty" to present to the President!

Ahmad and the crew were fêted in New York and he was entertained by the Mayor of Brooklyn as well as Commodore Renshaw of the Navy Yard, who had been instructed by the Secretary of the Navy to pay every attention to him. Ahmad carried no letters to the President, however, and so no arrangements were made for him to meet President van Buren. Nevertheless gifts between Said and the President were exchanged. Said had sent two fine Najd stud horses, jewels, attar of roses, rose-water and a beautiful gold-mounted sword. The return gifts included a fine pleasure barge beautifully fitted out and four five-chamber rotary repeating pistols and two eight-chamber repeating rifles made by Colts.

The *Sultana's* cargo grossed 26,157 dollars. It consisted of 1,300 bags of

dates, 21 bales of Persian carpets, 100 bales of Mocha coffee, 108 prime ivory tusks, 81 cases of gum copal, 135 bags of cloves and 1,000 dry hides. The whole cargo was sold on Said's account and the return cargo comprised 125 bales of grey sheeting called "Mericani", 24 bolts of scarlet cloth, 13 cases of red, white and blue beads, 20 dozen prints, 300 muskets, gunpowder and china plates. There were also items for Said's own use, such as candles, gold thread, perfumes, vases, musical boxes, mirrors, rifles, paper, glass and plates.

On the return journey the *Sultana* ran into bad weather, but under an American master, Captain Sandwith Drinker, who replaced Sleeman, the ship was brought safely back to Zanzibar ten months after it had set out. Thus Ahmad ibn Na'man accomplished his

The arrival of the steamship was to alter traditional east–west trading patterns.

The Dutch East Indiamen brought trade and prosperity.

unique journey, the first Arab diplomatic mission to the United States.

The years 1862 to 1872 in fact brought about the destruction of the formerly flourishing *entrepôt* system. The introduction of European steamers immediately affected the Omanis who did not have the capital or the knowledge to acquire the new invention for their own use. Though Gulf trade expanded considerably during this time, the Omanis did not benefit. On the contrary, the trade formerly carried in large Omani ships was increasingly carried by steamers calling at ports in the Gulf, bringing prosperity to them and taking it away from Muscat.

The large Omani ships which had carried trade over the oceans began to disappear and by the late nineteenth century the largest ships built in Oman were of 100 to 200 tons, whilst even smaller craft of only some ten tons were in greater demand.

The pattern of trade also changed. Whereas there was a great variety of items, including luxuries, to be had in Muscat as long as it remained an *entrepôt*, the trade was confined largely to staples and necessities in the last quarter of the nineteenth century. The decline was marked by a drop in the population; Muscat was estimated to have 55,000 inhabitants in the 1850s and Mutrah somewhere between 8,000 and 20,000 inhabitants. By the 1960s, Muscat's population had dropped to a mere 5,000 or 6,000. Mutrah was only a little larger and the trend was not reversed until the change of regime in 1970 when prosperity returned to the area.

Limes

Small round green limes have been one of the agricultural products of Oman, particularly the Batina, for many generations, and as an export they have been second only to dates. The drying and packing of limes has always been an important supplement to the income of people in the coastal towns. The dried limes were, and are, mainly exported to

Limes were a protection against scurvy, especially for sailors.

The Frankincense Trade

The frankincense trade was responsible for Dhofar's fame and prosperity, and its origin is in the mists of antiquity. Vast quantities of incense were used in the ancient world and the Roman Emperor Nero burnt more than the whole annual average production of Arabia at the funeral of his wife, Poppaea. Frankincense trees are confined to Dhofar and certain other parts of South Arabia and Somalia. The best quality is *najdi*, from the Najd to the north of the Dhofar hills. The next quality is *shazri*, from the Qara mountains; and the poorest is *sha'abi*, from the coastal plain. The frankincense tree rarely grows more than eight or nine feet high, and the incense itself is collected in the form of olibanum globules which ooze from incisions made on the tree. The incisions are made when the trees are three or four years old, and the globules are collected in March, April and May before the monsoon.

Above: *A tribesman cuts into the frankincense tree to release the fragrant gum. The cut must be made to exactly the right depth.*

Talking mynah birds were one item of exotic Omani merchandise in the tenth century.

The most constant of exports has been frankincense, and for thousands of years Oman's region of Dhofar has supplied the fragrance which the world has sought. But the country's other products of nature have played a role of significance.

the Gulf area and large quantities of them found their way to southern Iraq, from where they were distributed throughout the country. In Iraq they are still known as *Lumi Basra* and are made into a drink like tea called *shai hamudh* – sour tea – which is usually taken with sugar. By the early 1970s limes were the most important export apart from oil, and contributed a considerable amount to Oman's income; in 1971 they were worth 333,300 Omani Riyals.

Dates

The date tree flourishes in all parts of Oman, except Dhofar, even at a height of 2,000 feet. The plantations on the Batina were in the past sometimes seven miles deep along the coast and the number of palms in the Wadi Samail was estimated at 600,000 at the turn of the century. The best dates in Oman are known as *mibsali*, *fard* and *khalas*, and dates have throughout history been one of the country's main exports. In the late nineteenth century date exports increased in absolute value until they became Oman's single most valuable export, and by 1880 AD (1298 AH) they were exported in increasing quantities to India and the United States, the *fard* being preferred by American importers. Sales of wet dates were increased by the railways in India, which took them from Karachi to the populous Punjab, and other varieties were shipped dry for distillation into spirit. In an average

year in the 1890s the value of Omani date exports reached some 750,000 Maria Theresa dollars. However, by the middle of the twentieth century the trade had greatly declined and in 1973 date exports were only worth 118,000 Omani Riyals.

Frankincense

Dhofar's fame and prosperity, which emerges from the mists of antiquity, arose from the trade in frankincense, of which truly vast quantities were used in the ancient world. The famous visit of the Queen of Sheba – the Sabaean Kingdom – to King Solomon in the middle of the tenth century BC was probably to secure an agreement on frankincense and myrrh advantageous to both parties. Herodotus, writing in the sixth century BC, records that about two and a half tons of it were burnt annually in the temple of Bel at Babylon alone and it was used in the temples of Egypt and Mesopotamia from the earliest historical times. Frankincense, together with myrrh and gold, was brought as a gift to the infant Jesus, and the Roman Emperor Nero burnt more than the whole average production of Arabia at the funeral of his wife, Poppaea.

Frankincense is the exudation of olibanum from the incense tree, *Boswellia Carterii*, caused by deliberate incisions which lead to the formation of globules of gum resin. These are then collected by the tribesmen who have marked the trees earlier. The trees, which are rarely more than eight or nine feet high, are incised when they are three or four years old and the globules are collected in March, April and May before the monsoon. "The mount of myrrh and the hill of frankincense" mentioned in the Song of Solomon may well refer to Dhofar. For, though myrrh grows extensively throughout south Arabia, Somalia and Africa, frankincense trees are confined to Dhofar and certain other parts of south Arabia and Somalia. The best area for frankincense is the home of the Bait Kathir tribe in the Najd or steppe area to the north of the Dhofar hills, which the Book of Genesis refers to as

Mount Sephar. *Najdi* is the highest quality of frankincense. *Shazri*, which is collected in the Qara mountains, is the next in quality and *sha'abi*, collected on the coastal plain, is the poorest.

In antiquity some of the incense was no doubt shipped by sea, but much of it was carried by the camel caravans to the markets in the north. There were three main routes, all of which led across the Wadis Mitan and Fasad. One route went across the Empty Quarter, the Rub'al-Khali, in a north-westerly direction; a second route, which according to Pliny was accomplished in sixty-five stages, skirted the sands and went to Hadhramaut to join the major land route which began at the city of Shabwa, from which it went to Timna', Marib, Ma'in, Yathrib (now Medina), Dedan and Gaza. A third route, which took forty days by camel, joined the route leading from Hadhramaut across the middle of the Arabian peninsula to the Chaldean city of Gerrha on the Arabian shore of the Persian Gulf opposite Bahrain. By the late third century BC Gerrha had become the principal commercial centre in the Gulf and it seems to have remained so for several centuries, for Pliny (23–79 AD) describes its walls as being five miles in circumference.

Other Exports

A small quantity of tobacco has long been grown along the Batina and in a few other places in Oman. Some of it has been consumed locally but a certain amount has always been exported, mainly to the United Arab Emirates, and the trade was worth 34,800 Omani Riyals in 1973. In the past, Oman provided considerable quantities of vegetables and fruit for visiting ships and exports, particularly to the U.A.E. However, no statistical record was kept. With the change of regime in 1970 a new impetus was given to agriculture, and fruit and vegetable exports were worth 160,000 Omani Riyals in 1973. A trade in dried, salted and wet fish such as sardines has flourished on a small scale for generations.

8 Oman's Renaissance

Destiny kept her secret during many years of apparent decline in Oman. For in the 1970s, with newly found wealth and under fresh leadership, Oman experienced a rebirth; and the people were inspired to build on ancient foundations a modern and forward-looking state.

The new royal palace rises on Muscat's waterfront.

The Liberation & its Consequences

"A new spirit was abroad in the land." Omanis responded at once to the lifting of restrictions and the fresh and open-hearted relationship between ruler and the ruled. Released from its isolation from the international community, the country was swift to make its mark in the world; and at home young people reacted to the stimulus of a modern-thinking future with energy.

ON 23rd July 1970 a new page of Omani history was turned. After a short, sharp engagement in Salala, the young Qaboos ibn Said became Sultan in place of his father, who left the country. As the news spread, dancing broke out spontaneously in the streets, both in the north and the south of the country. After several generations of decline, the people of Oman thus hailed a new era.

Nearly three years earlier, the flow of oil from the fields at Fahud and Natih had begun to transform Oman's financial position. But a combination of extreme caution, inaction and excessively auto-cratic rule stifled the benefits which might otherwise have been received by

The accession of Sultan Qaboos in 1970 began a new era in Omani history.

the people. In the south the future of the country was threatened by rebellion, which, though later encouraged by Oman's neighbour, the People's Democratic Republic of Yemen, had started merely as opposition to the former Sultan's policies. The heir to the Sultanate, who was denied contact with the people and unable to persuade his father to change his policies, was thus forced to act to replace him. His motive was love of his country and faith in Islam both of which he saw imperilled in the Southern Region and his action

was immediately successful.

Sultan Qaboos had been trained for his role as heir to the Sultanate by private education in England, followed by military training at the Royal Military Academy, Sandhurst. He had then done a spell in local government at Warwick, after which he travelled in many countries during a world tour. Thus, before his period of enforced idleness in Salala which began in 1964, after he had failed to persuade his father of the need for change, he acquired a knowledge of international affairs. From 1964 until 1970 he also had plenty of time to read. Through having a Dhofari mother, a lady of the distinguished family of the Bait Mashani, the new Sultan understood the problems and needs of the people of the Southern Region.

On his accession Sultan Qaboos issued a proclamation promising to set up as quickly as possible a forceful and modern government whose first aim would be to remove unnecessary restrictions under which the people suffered and to produce as rapidly as possible a happier and more secure future for everyone. Initially he appointed his uncle Sayyid Tariq ibn Taimur as Prime Minister, but had to assume the premiership himself when the latter resigned in December 1971.

On the same occasion, Sultan Qaboos declared that, though yesterday was dark, tomorrow would dawn bright for Oman and all her people. That long-hoped for dawn became reality as the Sultan proceeded to fulfil his promises and he was himself the instigator and symbol of the new era of hope and development. He made tours throughout the country among his varied and scattered subjects which helped to revive the Omani spirit and sense of purpose, and by spending part of his time in the capital and part in Salala he sought to bind the Northern and Southern Regions of the country closer together. In Muscat he built a spectacular new palace on the site of the old one as evidence of national renaissance. The Al bu Said family is already the longest reigning dynasty in any Arab country and the palace was conceived to provide a worthy seat not only for the present sovereign of Oman, but also for generations to come. It was thus fitting that it should have been the site for the celebrations on the occasion of Sultan Qaboos's marriage to his cousin Sayyida Kamila, the daughter of Sayyid Tariq in March 1976.

Sultan Qaboos made it plain, very

By National Day on 18th November 1975, His Majesty was able to proclaim the end of the protracted struggle in the south, which had eaten up so much of the country's wealth. "While I congratulate our heroic army and friendly forces," he told the nation, "I see hope on the faces of this people who use force only for

shortly after his accession, that he wished to end the isolation in which Oman had for so long been kept. He offered an amnesty, and many exiled Omanis returned to serve their country in various capacities. When a new government under Omani ministers was set up, diplomatic relations were exchanged with an increasing number of countries in the Arab and Islamic worlds, the West, and the "Third World". Financial confidence was evidenced by the investment of foreign capital and expertise.

Schools, hospitals and clinics, roads and modern housing were built at an increasingly rapid pace. The benefits of an electricity supply were greatly ex-

tended and Oman leapt straight into the second half of the twentieth century by introducing colour television. Surveys of Oman's resources in minerals, water, soil and fish were carried out and the economy planned on an organised basis. A new spirit was abroad in the land.

For over five years peaceful development took place simultaneously with the waging of war in the south against the tenacious rebels. The Sultan brought his own military training and judgement to bear on the problem and the military situation improved as year followed year and the Sultan built up a sense of personal devotion by frequent visits to the battle areas and his forces elsewhere.

H.M. Sultan Qaboos has given these children the benefit of education.

defending a faith and to preserve their gains which they achieved in their noble march.

"We have waited a long time, during which the agents of Communism have committed the most terrible crimes against our peaceful citizens in the mountains of Dhofar . . . We extend the hand of peace from a position of strength."

The price of Oman's liberty would be vigilance. But from then on military expenditure need not be so predominant and the bulk of Oman's resources could be devoted to peaceful development.

Communications, Trade and Industry

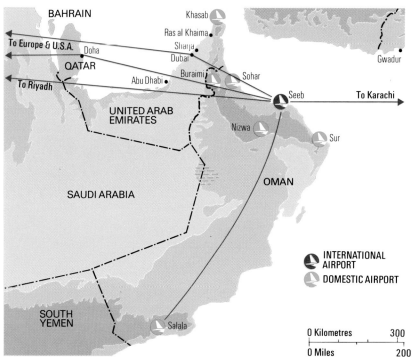

PERHAPS it is understandable that Oman, at certain periods of its history, has tended to become inward-looking. It is a country of many scattered communities, isolated from one another by mountain ranges and long reaches of desert. Certainly Oman had become an inward-looking nation by 1970. There was little to discourage it from such introversion: the roads were few, the transport on them negligible; there was no international airport; docking facilities for big ships carrying international cargoes did not exist.

As a result, contact between town dwellers on the coast and their fellow countrymen was very limited. There was nothing in the nature of a national press and news was passed by word of mouth, with all the dangers of distortion. The postal system worked well, but was confined to Muscat and Mutrah; the few telephone lines in operation existed mainly for the use of the Sultan's household, high government officials and some of the merchants.

Success in implementing the new programmes of development postulated the provision of an adequate communications network as the essential first step. The first new roads were begun in 1970, while plans were made for an international airport, new airfields were created, ports at Mutrah and Raysut were projected, and telecommunications systems gradually extended over the country. In the space of a few years, links never known before were provided between the capital and the less developed areas of the country and it had become possible to diffuse accurate information among the people and draw communities together. Thus Oman emerged once more as a centre of regional, and even global, trade, for the aim of the planning was to regain for Oman her position as an internationally important trading centre. Placed at a natural cross-roads of trade between east and west, and strategically dominating the Straits of Hormuz and the northern Indian Ocean, Oman was well placed to resume her historical role, which was so well known in the past to the merchants of Europe, Africa, India and the Far East.

Oman is as air-conscious as it was once sea-conscious. Salala (left) is Oman's second major airport. Since the installation of sophisticated landing systems in 1976, it joins Seeb (above) as an international airport capable of handling the most modern jets, and Concorde.

The new Government gave responsibility for land, air and sea communications to the Ministry of Communications. Roads were an early priority for at the end of 1970 there were only six miles of asphalt roads in the country between Muscat and Bait al Falaj. By 1979, this figure had risen to 1,600 miles, and by the early 1980s it was possible to drive from Muscat to Salala on tarmac. Graded un-surfaced roads had also increased to over 12,500.

The earliest development in the field of major roads was the construction of the asphalt surface link of some 145 miles between Mutrah and Sohar. This, starting in 1971 and completed in 1973,

not only turned two of Oman's principal towns into neighbours, but also served the many villages along the Batina coast, facilitating the distribution of goods and linking places along the entire coast to the fine new harbour at Mutrah, Port Qaboos. A link road north-wards from Sohar to the United Arab Emirates was built, dividing at Shinas to join the U.A.E. road network at the frontier points at Aswad and Khatmat al Malaha (*see road map on page 198*). In Mutrah itself, a new seafront "corniche" was built on reclaimed land and opened in 1973, creating a by-pass along the rim of the city and connecting the Mutrah–Sohar highway with a new Mutrah–

Muscat road which cuts across the knuckles of rock and the sea inlets separating Muscat from Mutrah.

Seeb International Airport was built on the Muscat–Sohar road, twenty-eight miles from the capital, and from Seeb an asphalt highway running some eighty-six miles inland to the ancient capital of Nizwa was constructed. This passes through the Wadi Samail and forms the most important link between the capital area and the Interior. A further link with the countries of the southern Gulf was forged by the extension of this road from Nizwa to Ibri, and thence over the eighty miles between Ibri and the Buraimi Oasis, where Oman meets the United

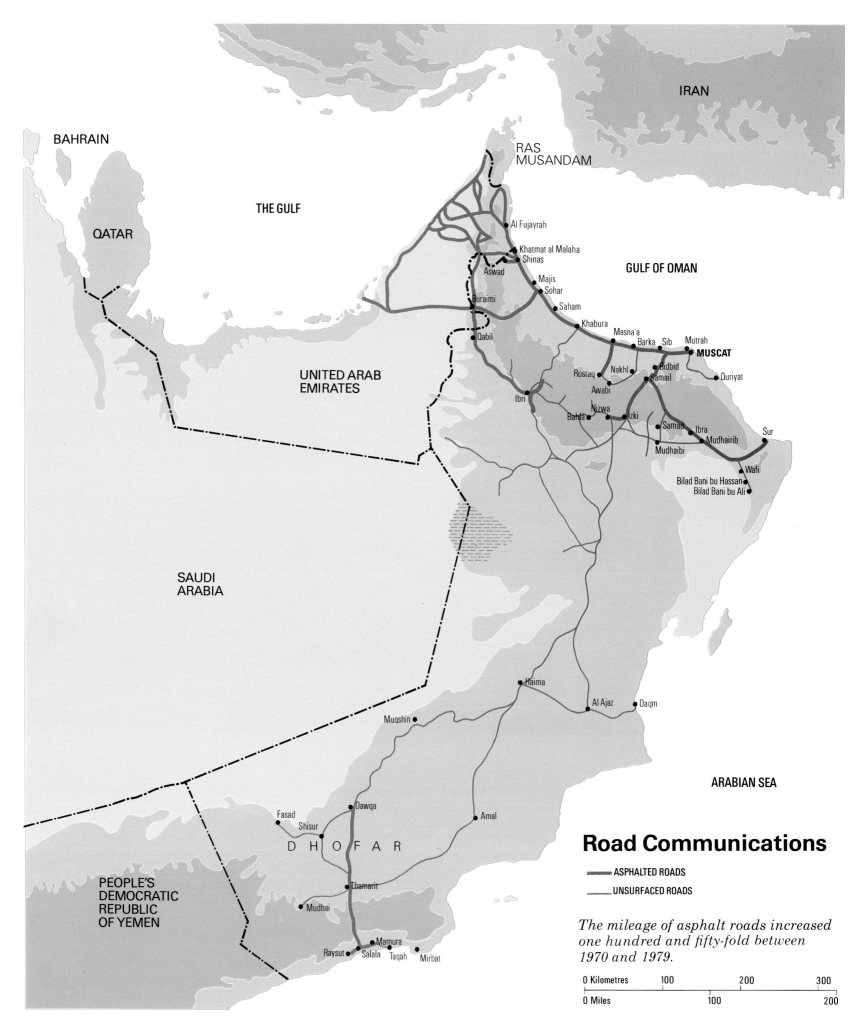

IRAN

BAHRAIN

RAS
MUSANDAM

THE GULF

QATAR

Al Fujayrah

Khatmat al Malaha
Shinas

GULF OF OMAN

Aswad

Majis
Sohar

Buraimi

Saham

Khabura

Masna'a

Barka Sib

Mutrah

UNITED ARAB
EMIRATES

Qabil

Rostaq

Nakhl

Bidbid

MUSCAT

Samail

Quriyat

Awabi

Ibri

Nizwa

Izki

Samad

Ibra

Bahla

Mudhairib

Sur

Mudhaibi

Wafi

Bilad Bani bu Hassan
Bilad Bani bu Ali

SAUDI
ARABIA

Haima

Al Ajaz

Daqm

Muqshin

ARABIAN SEA

Fasad

Dawqa

Amal

Road Communications

Shisur

D H O F A R

ASPHALTED ROADS

UNSURFACED ROADS

PEOPLE'S
DEMOCRATIC
REPUBLIC
OF YEMEN

Thamarit

*The mileage of asphalt roads increased
one hundred and fifty-fold between
1970 and 1979.*

Mudhai

Mamura

Raysut

Salala

Taqah

Mirbat

| 0 Kilometres | 100 | 200 | 300 |
| 0 Miles | | 100 | 200 |

Arab Emirates on her north-west border. From Buraimi/al Ain a dual carriageway runs direct to Abu Dhabi. Another important road was begun in 1974, which passes through the Sharqiya and links Sur with the Muscat–Nizwa road near Samail.

In the Southern Region, rapid road building, often undertaken in the teeth of obstacles and dangers from mines and ambushes was a major factor in extinguishing the rebellion and reconciling the people. The only main road existing in 1970 was that between Thamarit and Salala, which runs on to northern Oman. It was cut for several years by rebels, but was realigned and surfaced in 1975. Earlier tarmac roads had been built to Raysut to the west of Salala and Taqa to the east. Graded roads were then driven into the Qara mountains, linking Taqa to Medinat al Haq and Tawi Atair, and the northern Jebel to Jebel Halqaut. Imaginative road building both in the north and south facilitated the bringing of amenities such as health services, schooling and shops to remoter and previously inaccessible places. The development of roads inevitably brought hazards and accidents to man and beast, for thousands of vehicles appeared on the roads within a very short period of time. A mere 840 road vehicles were registered at the end of 1970, but by 1979 this figure had risen to over 70,000 and thousands of Omanis by then held driving licences. A few privately-run local bus services began during this period.

One of Oman's great needs in 1970 was a modern international airport to replace the strip at Bait al Falaj, which could only take relatively small aircraft, and which necessitated a dangerous approach between rocky mountains. Seeb International Airport was therefore constructed twenty miles north-west of Muscat on the coastal plain. It was completed in 1973 with a runway long enough to take every type of modern aircraft, including the supersonic Concorde, and several major international airlines began to run regular scheduled services direct between Seeb and the outside world. But already the airport has had to be enlarged and improved to cope with a rapidly growing volume of air traffic. In 1978 it handled over half a million passengers, and over 12,000 metric tons of cargo. The Oman Government's stake in civil aviation was increased by the acquisition of 25 per cent

in the equity of Gulf Air, the airline in which several Gulf states participate. The airstrip at Salala was considerably modernised and Gulf Air scheduled flights ran with increasing frequency between Muscat and Salala as well as Muscat and the rest of the Gulf, and Europe. Sophisticated landing systems were installed both at Seeb and Salala, which was once used only by military aircraft. By 1976 large modern jet aircraft could land at Salala, which was designed as Oman's second international airport. Air services were also planned between these two principal airports and smaller airfields at Sur, Khasab, Sohar,

Nizwa and Buraimi.

Oman also needed one or more sea ports to handle the greatly increased cargo traffic which the country's development brought in. A new harbour, Mina al Qaboos at Mutrah, was planned at a cost of about $40m. and opened in 1974. It has ten deep-water berths and by 1979, despite a growing transhipment traffic to other Gulf ports, its constantly expanding range of modern cargo-handling and storage facilities enabled it to handle as many as two million freight tons of cargo a year. There is also a small inner harbour for local *dhows* and fishing boats. Before the new port was

The new corniche at Mutrah is just one example of the rapid road-building which took place in the '70s. By 1979, over 70,000 road vehicles were registered to drive on over 14,000 miles of road, stretching from Raysut to the United Arab Emirates.

built ships had to unload offshore on to barges at Muscat itself or at the Refinery Terminal at Mina al Fahal. Cargoes were often damaged, and it was a slow method, particularly during rough weather. Previously all goods had had to be ferried ashore by lighters, and the monsoon prevented any discharge of cargo between May and October.

In the Southern Region another new port at Raysut, twelve miles west of Salala, was opened to shipping in 1973. Originally designed for small trading and fishing vessels, Raysut was connected by an asphalt road to Salala and thus became the port for the whole of the Dhofar region. After expansion, the port

Top Left: *Road construction in the Salala area.* Bottom Left: *Funjah road-bridge on the new Nizwa road to the Interior.* Right: *The Satellite Earth Station at Al Hajar which provides radio links with the rest of the world.*

was capable of handling tankers of up to 35,000 tons. *Dhow* berths were constructed at Khasab and at Bukha, in the Musandam peninsula, and plans were drawn up for small harbours at Sohar and Sur.

On the Sultan's accession small radio stations were immediately installed in Mutrah and in Salala. They came under the Ministry of Information and Tour-

ism, and were gradually developed. A still more exciting development, however, was the commencement of colour television services both in the north and the south. The first television broadcasts took place in the capital area around Muscat in 1974, from transmitters erected on the heights at Qurm. This project was completed in the record period of nine months and a full colour service for the whole of the northern area was provided. Public television sets were installed in the capital and main towns. In 1975 a new radio and colour television broadcasting station was completed at Salala. This, together with three relay stations, was able to cover the whole of the Dhofar region. Regular programmes in north and south included local and international news, live outside broadcasts and documentaries, and feature films from other Arabic-speaking countries. Television also began to be used extensively for educational purposes. Radio broadcasts in the north were improved by a new transmitting station at Seeb and this in turn was linked with the powerful new radio station at Salala, which broadcasts to the whole of the Dhofar region and can be picked up in neighbouring countries.

In November 1975 a new earth satellite station, sited in the Hajar Bowl, was opened a short distance from Muscat, providing both telephonic and audio-visual links with the rest of the Middle East, Europe and the United States, by means of communication satellites. This new station replaced a small transportable station set up temporarily earlier the same year at Wattaya. Previously all international communications had had to be made *via* high frequency radio channel to the earth station at Bahrain, where they were connected to an international switch system.

With the earth satellite station, direct dialling to neighbouring Gulf States, and later Western Europe, was made possible, and an automatic telex system was operating by the end of 1979. Internally, telex lines between Muscat and Salala were installed. In the mid-1970s telephones were being installed at a rate of three thousand a year to provide a network of 23,000 telephones by 1980, and new switch systems had to be introduced at the telephone exchanges in Muscat, Mutrah and Salala to cope with overloaded circuits. Telephone facilities were also brought to all but the most isolated parts.

1970, which grew into the Ministry of Information and Tourism; this office issued a daily news circular (distributed in the streets free of charge) and also gathered news for the radio stations. An independent newspaper, *Al Watn*, was started in 1971 and the national newspaper, *Oman*, which rolled off new presses in Muscat in 1972, was soon being circulated nationally and internationally. In addition, *The Times of Oman* was published as a weekly English language newspaper, and there were other English and Arabic newspapers.

The improved facilities for travel by road, sea and air greatly assisted the flow of trade. The transport of imports from port to town and village was speeded up, and facilitated the opening up of fresh markets, and the small-holder's modest crops and the local craftsman's handiwork became available in shops outside his own immediate area.

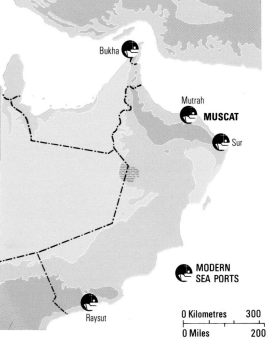

Posts as well as telecommunications were the responsibility of the Department of Posts, Telegraphs and Telecommunications (P.T.T.), now a Ministry. A system of numbered post boxes was introduced in the mid-1970s, and mail was delivered to these by the P.T.T. service. Where no post box existed, mail was delivered by special messenger. In 1970 there were two post offices in Oman, but no sub-post offices; however, by the late 1970s there were four major post offices, and thirty-eight sub-post offices. Regular international flights ensured an efficient airmail service abroad, and internally the Sultan's Air Force carried mail to the smaller, local airfields from

The development of ports was of great importance to Oman's expansion. Muscat itself yielded to Mutrah's broader anchorage, where the new port of Mina al Qaboos (right) was opened in 1974. In the Southern Region, Raysut (above) was opened in 1973.

where it could be easily delivered. The P.T.T. took training seriously and sponsored programmes at home and abroad in telecommunications and posts.

The desire to foster a sense of national unity at home and promote the country abroad led to the establishment of the press in Oman for the first time. A basic information service was established in

Trade and Industry

Laying the foundations of a modern state brought about a tenfold increase in imports in the first half of the 1970s, the major items being machinery and transport equipment, manufactured goods, and textiles. Food, especially dairy products, cereals, in particular rice, fruit and vegetables, were next in importance.

The United Kingdom, Japan, West Germany, India, the United States and the United Arab Emirates, which acted as an *entrepôt* for re-exports, were the major exporters to Oman, between them being responsible for seventy per cent of Oman's imports in 1978. Import duties were low, originally at a rate of 5 per cent, *ad valorem*, except in the case of any kind of alcoholic preparation where the duty was 75 per cent, and a duty of 25 per cent on potatoes and bananas. There was no duty on essential foodstuffs, books, and other goods required for infrastructure projects.

By 1979 gross domestic product had reached RO 950 million, with a growth rate of 5 per cent. The main contributing sectors were oil and natural gas, construction, agriculture, fisheries and manufacturing. Oil and agricultural produce remained Oman's most significant export, with oil by far the most important both in value and tonnage. In fact oil has, since 1967, contributed well over 90 per cent of Oman's revenue. These oil earnings were used to invest in income-generating projects as a safeguard against diminished oil production in the future. The Sohar copper complex was one such project. However the possibility that the decline in output, which began in 1977, would continue has not materialized due to new finds in the Southern Province.

Cargoes of dry limes constituted the major item of Oman's non-oil exports. The United Arab Emirates took the largest share of this commodity, most of which was destined for re-export elsewhere, particularly to Iraq. Dried dates were second in importance to limes and India was the largest market for them. Tobacco, fresh fruit and vegetables, fresh dates, fresh, salted and dried fish, hides, henna and palm fronds remained on Oman's list of exports, though these brought in only small foreign exchange.

The modern economic and social development of Oman can be divided into two periods – from 1970 to 1975, when there was massive investment in building an economic and social infrastructure which was non-existent before 1970; and from 1976 onwards, when development was governed by a Five Year Plan.

Oman's budget rose considerably between 1970 and 1976 and the five-fold increase in oil prices in 1973–74 gave a welcome fillip to development plans. In 1971 government expenditure was 46.0 million Omani Riyals (RO) against

a revenue of RO 50.1 million; in 1973 it was RO 92.9 million against 68.5 million; and in 1974 it jumped dramatically to RO 201.0 million while revenue went proportionately higher to RO 220.0 million.

By 1975 a sizeable infrastructure of roads, ports, airports, telecommunications, water and electricity supplies, had emerged making further economic growth possible. In 1976 the first Five Year Plan was launched. Its main objectives were, first, to lessen the Sultanate's heavy dependence on oil by diversifying the economy into industries based on non-oil natural resources – minerals, agriculture and fisheries – and into manufacturing; secondly to shift the pattern of investment from the public to the private sector; and thirdly, to provide more equitable opportunities for employment.

With a total investment of RO 1,356 million, 30 per cent of which was private, the Plan succeeded in achieving a gross domestic product of RO 950 million, and a growth rate of 5 per cent, by 1979. Both income from, and investment in, the

This new grain silo (top) *and flour mill* (above) *at Mina Qaboos demonstrate one of Oman's expanding industries.*

manufacturing sector far exceeded the targets set. The growth rate in agriculture and fisheries was also higher than anticipated. But, of course, oil continued to be the mainstay of the economy contributing RO 482 million to the Government's estimated revenue of RO 532 million.

Although no industry in Oman is at present equal to oil in importance or scale, plans were set in hand to harness

natural gas, an alternative future source of power which in the mid-1970s still remained largely untapped. Oman has four trillion cubic feet of known natural gas reserves, quite apart from the large quantities associated with oil production, which until now have been burnt off. A 331 km pipeline was completed in 1978 to bring gas from the gasfields of Yibal in the Interior to the Capital for use in the production of

At first, nearly all the raw materials essential to building and other projects were imported, and the local demand for cement rose dramatically. However good quality limestone is available within the country, and consequently a cement factory was planned near Port Qaboos, with an annual capacity of one million tonnes, sufficient quantities for home export markets. The building materials sector also includes asbestos, cement products, concrete blocks, building aggregate, marble quarrying, tarrozo products and paint manufacture.

Most of the existing food industries are domestic market-orientated, utilizing natural resources like dates, or processing imported materials, such as reconstituted milk and dairy products and poultry farming. Amongst smaller scale industries, a tile factory was built, a flour mill was begun in Dhofar in 1976 to process locally grown and imported wheat, two soft drinks plants were built and, as a consequence, the importation of some soft drinks was banned. Plans were made for the development of a furniture industry, and for the manufacture of aluminium products.

By making favourable investment and tax concessions, Oman was also seeking joint industrial ventures with countries which had management and technical know-how and finance. As it is, less than one-third of the 4,350 manufacturing jobs were filled by Omanis in 1980, and Oman employed nearly 100,000 expatriates in that year.

Nevertheless for Oman's population of 1.5 million the country's economic growth resulted in a nine-fold jump in per capita income from RO 67, before the accession of Sultan Qaboos in 1970, to RO 586 in 1977. The coming of the 1980s brought a still higher standard of living.

However, old established crafts have not died out. Fine silver ornaments and weapons, copperware and woven textiles, camel and goat hair carpets and rugs, palm-frond baskets and mats, earthenware pottery and traditional wooden or palm-frond boats have for centuries been flourishing industries in Oman. These traditional crafts were preserved and revived. Improved equipment and techniques were introduced, experimental units established and production encouraged. It was characteristic of the spirit of Oman's renaissance that the techniques and styles of their past were not allowed to be swamped as the modern age began to pervade Oman.

The new Al Gubrah desalination and power plant near Muscat (above), *with its ultra-modern control room* (left), *was opened in 1975.*

various kinds of fertilisers, assorted petro-chemicals and also rubber, in the generating of electricity, and finally and most importantly, for running the new Al Gubrah desalination and power plant near Muscat, which was opened in 1975. Surplus capacity fuels the country's copper, cement, and industrial estate projects. The water supply is, of course, important for industry as well as agriculture. Consequently the needs of industry are borne in mind by the Water Resources Council in their surveys.

Petroleum and other Minerals

FROM 1954 when prospecting began in earnest Oman gradually acquired one of the most highly automated oil industries in the world. Although production and known reserves are modest when compared with neighbouring producers in the Gulf, wealth from oil has given Omanis new life and hope, revived Oman's stagnant economy and made ambitious development programmes possible. How long Oman can remain dependent on oil is not certain, but the steady rise in world oil prices since 1973 has made it possible to produce oil previously not available in commercial quantities. New discoveries in South Oman mean that Oman will still be producing oil in the year 2000. Meanwhile natural gas is being conserved for local industry and power generation.

1st August 1967 was a landmark in Oman's history, being the day on which the first tanker laden with crude oil sailed from the terminal at Mina al Fahal. But the road had been long and difficult to reach this point. For, although the first concessions had been granted as early as 1937, it was not until 1962 that oil was struck by Petroleum Development (Oman) Limited, in potentially commercial quantities. The difficulties were unexpected as Fahud had presented an apparently perfect structure to geologists and consequently, when exploration centred on this area began in the 1950s, hopes of an early and successful strike were high.

As time went on and no oil was struck, despite the Fahud area continuing to show all the evidence of subterranean

promise, hopes were dashed and B.P. and the American companies withdrew from Petroleum Development (Oman) Limited, eventually leaving Shell holding 85 per cent, Compagnie Française de Pétroles 10 per cent and Partex 5 per cent. The faith and persistence of those who remained in the venture was rewarded when, after a series of further seismic tests, oil was struck at Yibal in 1962. Within two years oil had also been found at Natih and Fahud.

Within two years, enough oil in the Fahud area was found to make commercial production certain. A fourth oil field, fifteen miles south of Yibal at al Huwaisa, came on stream in 1971 and was connected to the pipeline system established for earlier fields in 1967. This, the first productive area in Oman,

The high point in the Oman mountains to which the oil is pumped from the oil tanks in Fahud (right). *From here it flows under its own gravity to the coast for export.*

was situated on the far side of the Hajar mountains from the coast on the edge of the Rub' al-Khali. This is the traditional area of the Duru tribe, whose animals graze its scanty pasture and drink from the scattered wells. Care was taken to protect the traditional rights of the Duru, and to offer them adequate jobs on the oil installations in their area. The same policy was applied to other tribes such as the Harasis whose territory was affected by oil exploration or development.

The oil was extracted from beneath the

ground by standard techniques. It was then pumped to a gathering station where the oil was separated from the gas, which was blown off. The oil then flowed to tanks and was pumped through a mainline pumping station into the main trunk pipeline to the coast. This pipeline, 172 miles long, was built through the mountains to storage tanks at the terminal at Mina al Fahal, just north-west of Muscat. The oil was piped from these tanks through submarine pipes to the waiting tankers.

By the end of 1967, 20.9 million barrels of crude oil had been exported and the quantity exported rose from 88.2 million barrels in 1968 to 119.2 million barrels in 1969 and 121.3 million barrels in 1970. But the following two years showed a decline in production, despite the intro-

duction of the al Huwaisa field in 1971. and exports fell to 106.3 million barrels in 1971, and to 103.2 million barrels in 1972. After 1973 production was on an up-swing again, after the discovery of oilfields south of the Fahud area at Saih Nihayada, Saih Rawl, Qarn Alam, Ghaba north and Habur. Production sank to 300,000 per day in the late 1970s, but with additional new fields in southern Dhofar and at Sahmah, and the use of secondary recovery techniques, was expected to rise again to 350,000 in the early 1980s.

Meantime seismic exploration was carried on year after year in the field in the search for new oil. Crews generally used a 48-channel recording and weight-dropping method which proved the most effective one for Oman's terrain.

Oil Exports: destination countries

1978
IN MILLION BARRELS

U.S.A.
18.3

Oman's oil is exported worldwide. The map (right) indicates distribution. On reaching the coast from the oil-fields, the oil is stored in tanks to await pumping into the tankers which supply the world market.

The geological structure of the country is complicated, particularly in the north where the volcanic upheavals which produced the Hajar mountain range seriously disrupted the strata and caused major faults. This explains why one potential oil-bearing structure may be separated from another by a mere hundred yards.

There is promise of further oil production, and in South Oman at Amal high quality oil was found in 1976. In the 1950s the American oil company, Dhofar Services, prospected extensively in the area, known as Marmul, but found only thick oil, which was not considered worth exploiting commercially. The site was, therefore, abruptly abandoned and equipment, prospecting data and even typewriters with half-finished letters still in them were left in the desert. Some twenty-five years later, P.D.(O.), following seismic tests, decided to return to the area, and drilled to far deeper levels and through a layer of salt, below which it is extremely rare to find exploitable oil. However, oil of relatively good quality was found, and if this can be exploited, it will be the oldest extracted

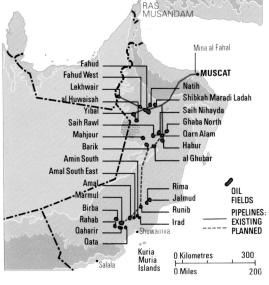

RAS MUSANDAM

Mina al Fahal

Fahud
Fahud West
Lekhwair
al Huwaisah
Yibal
Saih Rawl
Mahjour
Barik
Amin South
Amal South East
Amal
Marmul
Birba
Rahab
Qaharir
Qata

MUSCAT
Natih
Shibkah Maradi Ladah
Saih Nihayda
Ghaba North
Qarn Alam
Habur
al Ghubar

Rima
Jalmud
Runib
Irad

Shuwaimia

OIL FIELDS

PIPELINES:
EXISTING
PLANNED

Kuria Muria Islands

Salala

0 Kilometres   300
0 Miles   200

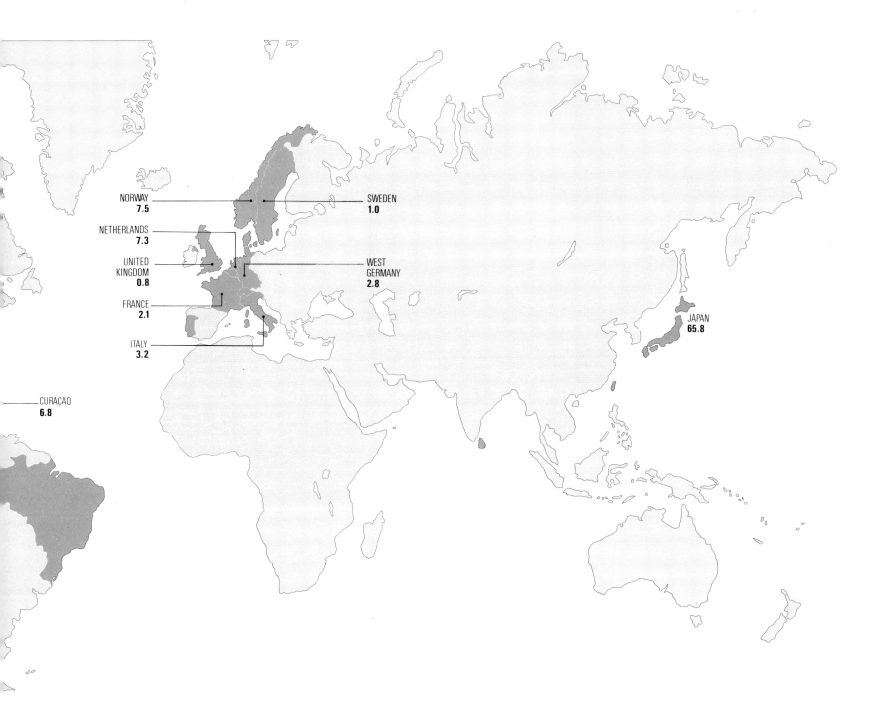

NORWAY
7.5

SWEDEN
1.0

NETHERLANDS
7.3

UNITED
KINGDOM
0.8

WEST
GERMANY
2.8

FRANCE
2.1

JAPAN
65.8

ITALY
3.2

CURAÇAO
6.8

oil in the world.

The agreement between the Government and P.D.(O.) provided for the progressive relinquishment of territory within the concession area and accordingly 48,000 square miles were surrendered in 1974. Prior to this P.D.(O.) had from 1969 held the concession for the whole of the land area both in the north and the south. However, they had no similar concession in the offshore areas, though Shell was associated with the German company Wintershall in the offshore concession off northern Oman in the Indian Ocean, in which unsuccessful prospecting had been taking place up to 1973. The offshore concession for the Dhofar area had been granted to Wendell Phillips by the former Sultan but this

was granted in 1973 to a consortium led by the Sun Oil Company of the United States. The concession for the offshore area of the Musandam peninsula was granted in 1973 to the French concern E.L.F./E.R.A.P. who found natural gas, which raised hopes that oil might be found in this area.

By the later 1970s, Japan was Oman's largest consumer of crude oil, taking some 60 per cent of the total exported by the late 1970s. Other major purchasers were the United States, Norway, the Netherlands and lesser quantities were exported to Italy, West Germany, France, Sweden, and the United Kingdom.

Petroleum Development (Oman) Limited remained the largest concessionary in Oman despite the relinquishment of

parts of the original concession. In 1974 the Government acquired a 25 per cent interest in the concessions and assets of the Company, and a joint management committee with four Government-appointed members and four Company-appointed members was set up within P.D.(O.) to administer a national oil programme. Later the same year, the Government's holding was increased to 60 per cent, thus making it the major shareholder. The Government's share of the oil produced was partly sold back to P.D.(O.) and partly sold direct to third parties overseas, and its income from oil revenues in 1979 comprised approximately 90 per cent of its revenue from all sources which amounted to an estimated 482 million Omani Riyals. On the other

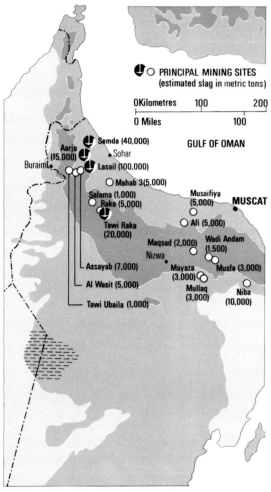

PRINCIPAL MINING SITES
(estimated slag in metric tons)

0 Kilometres 100 200
0 Miles 100

GULF OF OMAN

Semda (40,000)
Aarja (15,000)
Sohar
Buraimi
Lasail (100,000)
Mahab 3 (5,000)
Salama (1,000)
Raka (5,000)
Musaifiya (5,000)
MUSCAT
Afi (5,000)
Tawi Raka (20,000)
Maqsad (2,000)
Wadi Andam (1,500)
Nizwa
Assayab (7,000)
Mayaza (3,000)
Musfa (3,000)
Al Wasit (5,000)
Mullaq (3,000)
Niba (10,000)
Tawi Ubaila (1,000)

Recent prospecting work and the examination of core samples (top) *have suggested that copper deposits are Oman's biggest asset after oil and gas.*

side of the balance, government costs for oil operations constituted 11 per cent of its total expenditure. Revenue increased with the rising price of oil – the price per barrel multiplied seven times between 1967 and 1976 – but prices for purchases, increased exploratory activity, and

higher salaries also became inflated.

The Mina al Fahal–Ras al Hamra area became the centre of P.D.(O.)'s operations, and offices, a school, a hospital, houses and recreational facilities were built there near the terminal. The crude oil was stored in six tanks, each with a capacity for 320,000 barrels, and a further, larger tank built in 1970, with a capacity for 900,000 barrels. By 1973 there were three single buoy moorings off Mina al Fahal. These have been improved and replaced to handle the largest super-tankers in the world.

Inland a drinking-water plant capable of producing 20,000 gallons of fresh water a day by the osmosis process was built at Fahud; over 1,000 miles of road were graded. P.D.(O.) looked after the welfare of its staff and sponsored home ownership and house improvement programmes by providing loans to Omani staff. It established clinics and held regular safety meetings to help reduce the number of accidents. Training centres were established to provide courses in preliminary technical and electrical technician work, radio operating, basic skills, English language and commercial work. P.D.(O.) also sponsored trainees on courses outside Oman, and provided scholarships, through the Ministry of Education, for higher studies abroad.

Although a member neither of O.P.E.C. nor O.A.P.E.C. Oman received the benefits secured for the producing companies through the efforts of these organisations. Thus Oman was able to obtain the maximum benefit from her oil assets and this helped to enable her to fulfil her ambitious programmes.

Minerals

The mineral deposits in the mountains of Oman may become her most valuable asset after oil and gas, for the deposits of copper, chromite, iron, magnesite, manganese and nickel offer potential for development. The prospects for copper production looked bright in 1976.

It seems likely that Oman, then known as Magan, was a copper-producing country as far back as 2500 BC when a shipment of twenty tons of metal was recorded. Ancient copper artefacts have been found and Magan was a major supplier of copper to Ur and other Sumerian cities. The Samail complex of igneous rock in Oman resembles the great copper-bearing Troodos Complex of Cyprus geologically, though the Samail igneous complex covers over 8,000 square miles,

compared with the 800 square miles of the Troodos Complex. The Troodos is renowned for its massive, rich copper-gold ore bodies, found by the Romans and then lost, rediscovered and again mined in modern times. These factors, together with geological data accumulated and evaluated since 1971, aroused the interest of Prospection Limited of Canada and in February 1973 H.M. the Sultan granted concessionary rights to this company and to Marshal Oman Exploration Inc. (U.S.A.) (acting jointly) to "prospect, develop, process and sell" minerals in two areas totalling over 34,000 square miles. These rights excluded radioactive materials, asbestos, cement limestone, natural gas and oil.

Prospecting showed that the main mineral-bearing area was in the Hajar mountains along the Gulf of Oman. But the mountain areas proved difficult of access to the prospectors until helicopters were brought in. In the north of the concession area, between Sohar and the Buraimi Oasis, flaming orange, red and yellow surface gossans marked the presence of volcanogenic sulphide copper, and possibly zinc-rich deposits of pyrites. The black slag-piles and clusters of buildings marked the sites of ancient mines developed in the pre-Islamic and Islamic periods. Mineralised shear or fracture-zone occurrence of copper deposits were found to be widespread in a mainly gabbroic, partly peridotite environment, particularly in the eastern Hajar. Malachite or azurite copper oxides were also found at the surface in these sites, along with the ubiquitous ancient slag-piles.

Investigations continued until the end of 1973. In 1974, the Oman Government took up its option to participate in the enterprise with the two prospecting companies and acquired a 51 per cent stake in the operation. The first diamond drill pierced the first orebody, at Lasail, by the end of January 1974 and revealed massive copper-bearing sulphide mineralisation. Airborne electro-magnetic surveys, totalling over 1,000 line miles, were then made of selected regions, and 119 mineral finds were made. By January 1976 fifteen of these had been fully investigated.

Three of the prospects, lying adjacent to each other, aggregated more than 11.5 million tons of ore, with a minimum content of 2.1 per cent copper. Plans were drawn up to produce 3,000 tons of ore daily by the end of 1978, by which time

Sophisticated prospecting has revived ancient sites. The Geophysical Survey team works on the receiver console at the Ghuzayn site, in the Sohar area.

processing facilities, roadways and the new port at Sohar would be completed.

In the same region deposits have also been found of chrome, lead, zinc, nickel, iron ore and minor minerals, but by 1976 it was not plain whether extraction would be commercially viable. In 1976 a feasibility study on various asbestos production schemes was carried out including the possibility of manufacturing asbestos cement.

Although large deposits of manganese were found in the mountains near Sur their commercial viability has not yet been proven. Coal seams have also been found in this region and estimates in mid-1976 suggested that 10 million tons of coal could be mined. Production of coal on a commercial scale naturally depends on ancillary facilities being available, and tentative plans were made to build a modern port at Sur, which, despite its historical importance, only had its ancient *dhow* port in the creek.

High-quality limestone was found in the north of the Hajar range and the Dhofari mountains. To utilise the limestone a cement plant was built in 1980. Plans were approved for a factory to produce glass, bottles and containers from proven deposits of quartizites. Future possibilities include quarrying the large deposits of fine marble in the Hajar mountains and mining phosphate deposits in Dhofar.

Many old mining sites were discovered in the course of survey work and sites of great archaeological importance have been found in the Wadi Jizzi region in a good state of preservation. Although these were useful indicators of likely mineral-bearing sites it was government policy that sites of historical value should be protected from destruction. Features of the old mine-workings stimulated expert curiosity, particularly unusual patterns of arches and pillars first noted by prospecting geologists.

The mineral deposits in Oman gave ground for optimism that the country's economy would become better balanced. Copper was the best short-term prospect for major production and confidence grew that a target of 3,000 tons of ore daily might be reached which would make Oman a copper-producing country of considerable importance. There was also cause for hope that other minerals, particularly coal, asbestos and manganese might be exploited commercially. Thus Oman might become a major mineral producer by the 1980s.

211

Construction

PART of the sad but singular charm of Oman before 1970 was that for the most part it was a country of traditional buildings, some very old. With the exception of a few modest buildings in Muscat no modern buildings clashed with the fading harmony of the old, and many buildings which had been fine in the past, particularly those built of mud, had deteriorated into ruins or near-ruins.

From 1970 onwards the face of the country changed with startling rapidity. The greatest change took place in the capital area itself. Then the twin towns of Muscat and Mutrah, connected by a narrow coast road of considerable beauty, both retained their individual and traditional character. It was not long, however, before the capital area came to be regarded, by planners and public alike, as the whole area from the fishing village of Sidab to the west of Muscat to Seeb, where the new International Airport was situated from 1973 onwards – a long narrow coastal strip of some twenty-eight miles in length.

Muscat itself remained the true political capital and it was therefore here that a new and impressive palace was built for the Sultan on the waterfront between the sixteenth-century forts of Mirani and Jalali perched on their barren rocks. Muscat remained the location of the Ministry of Foreign Affairs and some other ministries as well as of some of the embassies. The best of the traditional houses were preserved and new gates and buildings, including government offices, erected in the style of, or in harmony with, the well proportioned buildings of the past. Thus the old walled city of Muscat retained much of its character even after new construction had changed its physical aspect markedly.

Nonetheless change elsewhere was widespread and rapid, and the breakdown of old barriers was symbolised by the sudden collapse in 1973 of the ancient city gate of Mutrah. Until then the great wooden gate within its lofty portal had solemnly been opened at dawn and closed after dark even though a motor road had been driven through the city wall a few yards away. And it was almost certainly the vibrations caused by the motor traffic which caused the collapse of material and of tradition. Indeed the rapidly increasing number of motor cars

and lorries was responsible for many of the changes to the country's appearance and way of life as the 1970s proceeded, for prior to 1970 only a handful of cars had been permitted and even in 1971 the drivers of saloon cars could be numbered on two hands. As the main road was pushed out from Mutrah in the direction of Seeb and Sohar, building took place on an ever growing scale in the Ruwi valley behind Mutrah, where areas were allocated for commercial and industrial premises, for housing and government development, as well as for hotels and other amenities. The aim was to create a community of some 35,000 instead of the previous 17,000.

So eager were the Omani authorities that the new areas should be intelligently planned that many consultants – British, Swedish and French among others – were employed. Despite the number involved and the changes made over responsibility within the Government for physical planning, few visitors to Oman were unimpressed with what had taken place. In particular the high standard of architecture and building both in the public and the private sector was often remarked upon. A department of lands was set up in 1972 and the title to property in Muscat and Mutrah and the new development areas was systematically registered.

Shortly after coming to power the new Sultan made grants of land in the Ruwi valley and elsewhere to the people on a considerable scale. Subsequently grants were made through the Ministry of Lands to ensure that this fitted into zoning plans. The criteria were first that an applicant should be a native of the area in which he wished to build, though this was interpreted liberally; secondly that he should possess no other residence, if applying for a residential plot, and thirdly that he could show sufficient means to build in accordance with the building standards specified in the regulations. Likewise an applicant for land for commercial or industrial purposes had to prove his financial capacity to construct premises which met the specifications and standards of the area.

The speed of development was so rapid that it was understandable that some anomalies should have arisen in the field of physical planning and the administration of lands policy. Consequently

The changing face of Oman: a new high-rise development at Ruwi (right).

steps were taken in 1976 to rationalise the situation by grouping municipal affairs, planning and lands under a single minister, by constituting the Ministry of Land Affairs.

One of the early priorities of the new Government after 1970 was a large office block initially designed to house nearly all the ministries. It was, however, scarcely surprising, in view of the rapid expansion of government activity, that further accommodation was needed almost as soon as the building was completed. Flats for government officials, including qualified Omanis who returned from exile, were also speedily built, and schools, hospitals and health buildings also had very high priority.

At Qurm on the coast to the west of Mutrah a whole new complex was built, known as "Information City", comprising colour television transmitters and studios, a new radio station, offices, housing and the Oman Museum in temporary accommodation. An area nearby next to the sea was allocated for foreign embassies. Two new hospitals were completed near Wattaya.

The International Airport at Seeb not only had an excellent runway, which took any type of aircraft including the Concorde, but also terminal facilities which in design and efficiency were the envy of countries with far longer established international airports. The new sports stadium built at Wattaya near another complex commissioned by the Royal Omani Police was equally impressive and became the venue for the splendid parade traditionally held on the Sultan's Birthday.

A small palace at Seeb for the Sultan's early occupation was completed in 1972. The palm tree formed the basic inspiration for the design and the building therefore fitted very harmoniously into the palm garden where it was sited.

Inland the traditional aspect of a number of towns was changed not only by the advent of tarmacadamed roads and private building but also government schemes such as the school/hospital complexes. The first of these were at Nizwa, Rostaq, Samail, Buraimi, Sohar and Sur, and the modern construction

contrasted strikingly with the old part of these places, proclaiming the benefits of the new era.

Housing was one of the most pressing problems facing the new Government when it took over in 1970 and three main approaches were used to overcome the shortage. First the Government itself built flats and houses for its employees as rapidly as construction could be organised. Secondly the Government commissioned low cost housing units and by 1975 over 1,000 had been erected. Thirdly the private sector was encouraged to build houses for all sections of the population. The Oman National Company for Housing Development, a joint venture between banks and the Government, provided loans for private individuals; there were loan schemes for government employees; and similar schemes were run by companies for their own staff.

A prestigious new housing area was developed at Medinat Qaboos at Qurm twelve miles to the west of Muscat. The scheme was first announced in 1972. By 1973 the first show houses were open to the public and options on the first thousand houses were quickly taken up. The aim in the buildings was to marry contemporary designs with traditional Arab styles of architecture and the result was very successful both visually and in terms of comfort for the householders. There were two separate housing areas, each designed and constructed by a different concern, with plans for linked common community areas, shopping and recreational facilities.

If development took place at a startlingly swift pace in northern Oman it was equally rapid in Dhofar. The sleepy town of Salala with its dusty roads quickly came to life when tarmacadamed roads were built in the town and pushed out to the port of Raysut on the west and to Taqa on the east. New housing was a high priority here also and houses of various standards were soon under construction. Special consideration was given to those who had to move their place of residence on account of the war, including widows and orphans, and 700 low cost houses were built at Salala and Taqa in the years 1972–73 alone. By 1976 the look of the place had changed greatly though Salala retained its unique character as a garden city where the cultivated areas as well as buildings were extended. There were new schools, a new building for the

Contemporary designs marry with traditional Arab styles of architecture in a prestigious new housing area developed at Medinat Qaboos in 1973.

Provincial Administration and for the Information Department, television and radio stations, greatly improved airport facilities, hotels and barracks and a 300-bed hospital was opened in 1976 to replace the smaller one built in 1971. By this time too the careful planning which had begun in previous years was taking more definite shape and the town centre project was set in hand. This catered for 400 shops, fruit and vegetable markets, supermarkets, offices, housing, show-

*One of the more adventurous develop-
ments in housing is Medinat Qaboos on
the eastern side of the capital area.*

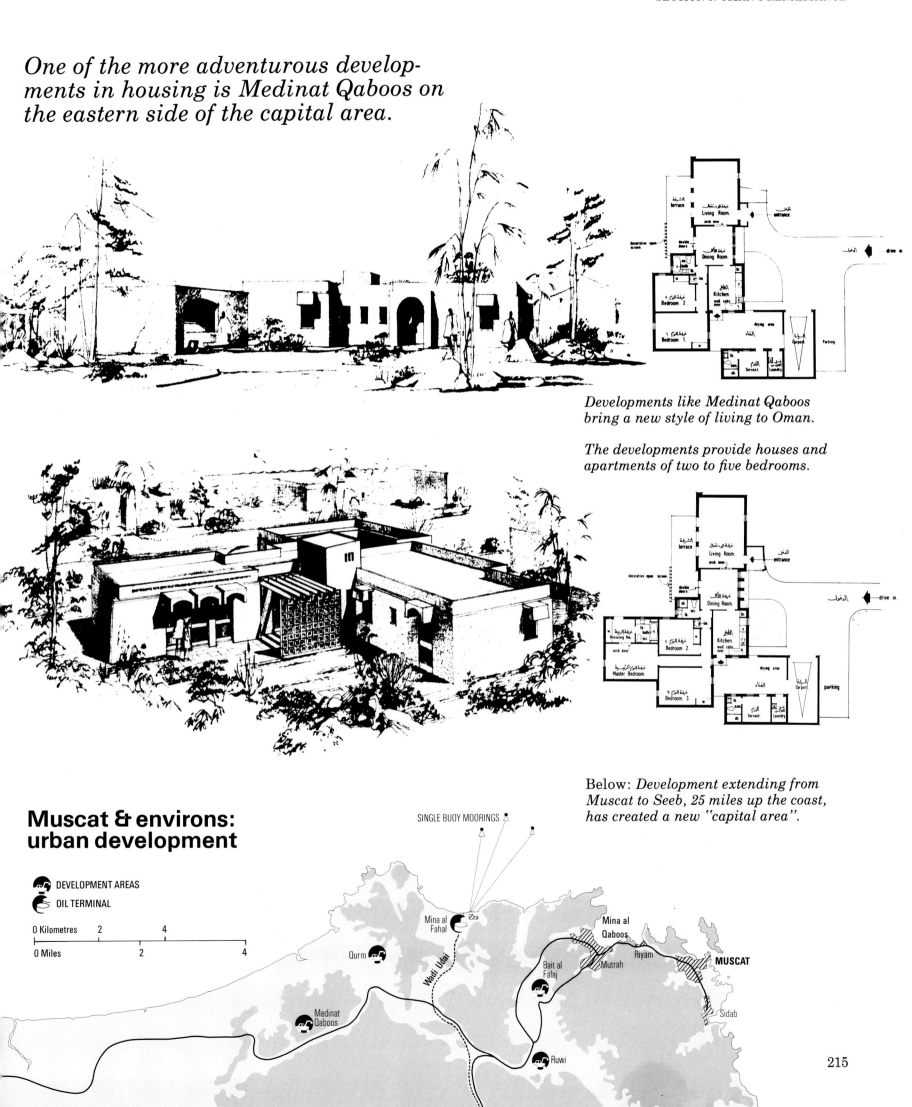

*Developments like Medinat Qaboos
bring a new style of living to Oman.*

*The developments provide houses and
apartments of two to five bedrooms.*

Below: *Development extending from
Muscat to Seeb, 25 miles up the coast,
has created a new "capital area".*

Muscat & environs:
urban development

DEVELOPMENT AREAS

OIL TERMINAL

| 0 Kilometres | 2 | 4 |
| 0 Miles | 2 | 4 |

SINGLE BUOY MOORINGS

Mina al
Fahal

Qurm

Wadi Udai

Mina al
Qaboos

Bait al
Falaj

Riyam

Mutrah

MUSCAT

Medinat
Qaboos

Ruwi

Sidab

rooms, cinemas and hotels.

Meantime development was not neglected in the coastal towns of Taqa and
Marbat which grew in size and sophistication as Salala did, or on the Qara
mountains. Government centres were
established at suitable places where
water bores had been sunk, within the
different tribal areas on the Jebel, and
complexes of various sizes built, including schools, clinics, mosques, housing
and workshops.

Oman's other extremity, the Musandam peninsula, was not forgotten either,
and schools, clinics, airstrips, housing
and other facilities were built at Bukha,
Khasab and Baia and improved port
facilities for small vessels were constructed at Bukha. Similar attention was
given to the Island of Masira.

Central, of course, to all this building
development was the provision of adequate water and power supplies. In
most of the country water could be
supplied from traditional sources or
from newly installed pumps, but more
complicated arrangements were necessary both in the capital area and Salala.
Water surveys were, therefore, amongst
the earliest government projects to cater
both for domestic water supply and
agriculture.

Until the 1960s, the people of Muscat
and Mutrah obtained their water from
local wells and it was still on occasion
being supplied on donkeys in the early
1970s. In 1968 a Water Department was

set up and water for the capital was piped
from a large and previously untapped
well field at al Khod, thirty-four miles
from Muscat where the Wadi Samail
debouches on to the Batina plain. By
1970 there was an adequate supply for the
whole of Muscat and Mutrah as they
were then, but it was not sufficient for
the needs of the ever-growing capital
complex after Sultan Qaboos's accession.
Consequently new wells were sunk and
a desalination plant constructed in the
Qurm area in 1975 to supplement the
older system based on wells which
depended on sufficient annual rainfall
to recharge the aquifers.

The water supply for Salala, which
was first established in 1972, depended
on bore holes sunk on the Salala plain,
though in the past much of the water had
been led down to the inhabited and
cultivated area by *falaj* from the Wadi
Arzat. This source had been interfered
with by the rebels and consequently it
was found more satisfactory whilst the
rebellion continued to depend on nearer
bore holes which were also considered a
better permanent source of supply for
the whole system, which covered the
area from Mamura to Raysut.

The origins of Oman's power supply,
like the water supply, preceded Sultan
Qaboos's accession in 1970, for a Muscat
Power Company was established in 1967.
A power station was built at Riyam,
between Muscat and Mutrah, with a
capacity of three megawatts, which was

*Modern and traditional are blended in
the building of the bank* (above).
Downtown Ruwi after dark (below) –
modern facilities for a modern city.

sufficient to supply the whole of Muscat
and Mutrah. However, it was insufficient
for the needs of the capital as it expanded
rapidly in the 1970s. In 1971 the Company
was taken over by the Government and
became the Government Power Corporation, though it continued to draw on
expatriate expertise. Additional plant
was installed which increased capacity
tenfold and costs were reduced by con-
verting the generators to operate on
fuel oil, which was pumped from Mina
al Fahal to Riyam. The next phase was to
install plant capable of generating electricity as well as powering the desalination process and by 1976 it was planned
to modify installations to work on

natural gas as an alternative to crude oil, and thus to utilise Oman's energy resources which were otherwise going to waste. Sufficient capacity to supply electricity to the coastal towns of the north as well as the capital area itself was also envisaged. Additional smaller generating plants were installed from 1971 onwards to provide electricity for the towns and government establishments in the Interior.

Developments in the north could be of no direct benefit to Dhofar, 600 miles away, but separate arrangements for the supply of electricity were made there. Until 1970 Salala had no general power supply. However by mid-1971 a small

power station was functioning at Salala and a new and considerably enlarged power station run on diesel fuel was put in during 1974 under the auspices of the newly constituted Dhofar Electricity Board. This generated electricity sufficient for the needs of the whole of the Southern Region.

In this way the face of Oman was changed within a short span of years, but despite the change in physical appearance and the greatly improved general standard of living, the force of Islam remained strong. This was demonstrated by construction of new buildings for an Islamic Centre at Wattaya and a fine new mosque in Muscat on the site of the

The Finance Ministry in Muscat (top). *The Intercontinental* (above and left) *is one of many fine hotels in the capital area.* Overleaf: *the new mosque gleams in the Dhofar mountains.*

mosque where prayers have traditionally been said at Ids and holidays – in a sense the cathedral mosque of Oman. Indeed the Ministry of Endowments and Islamic Affairs was also active in the building of mosques and improving the facilities of others all over the country. The message that "There is no god but God" still permeated Oman even in a more materialistic age and phase of its own development.

Education

WHEN Sultan Qaboos committed Oman to taking its place among the nations of the modern world, it was natural that attention should immediately be focused on the youth of the country. The aim was to inspire the youth, grant them the opportunities which the late twentieth century offers, equip them to face its challenges and master its techniques, so that Oman could surge forward.

In such a spirit was the new education programme conceived from 1970 onwards, and the pace of educational development accelerated year by year. Learning was seen both as the foundation of a bright future for the younger

generation, and as a means of helping older people to come to terms with the rapid material and social changes which the new era would bring. The Government, therefore, stated that one of the basic rights of all Omani nationals, irrespective of race or creed, was "free and accessible education", not only for children, but also for the adult population which had previously been denied opportunity.

The eagerness to learn, and indeed thirst for knowledge soon characterised Omanis of the younger and older generations. There was a total absence of bitterness amongst the older generation

and fathers in no way resented the opportunities for education suddenly given to their children. On the contrary they were proud that their children learnt to read and write, and many were encouraged thereby to learn themselves. Once the young would sit at the feet of one elderly master to learn the Qur'an by rote and gain some slight knowledge of "the three R's" but now the old sat at the feet of younger and better educated teachers, many of whom came, at least for the first phase of Oman's education programmes, from other friendly Arab countries.

The Ministry of Education and the

New schools quickly sprang up as at Taqa (above). From the beginning girls' education was central: Mutrah girls' school (right).

Ministry of Social Affairs and Labour both had a role in the educational sphere. The Ministry of Education was responsible for primary, intermediate, secondary and general education, for teacher training, the abolition of illiteracy campaign and for adult education as well as supervision of non-governmental institutions. The Ministry of Social Affairs and Labour on the other hand was concerned with vocational, industrial and commercial training.

The Ministry of Education was by the mid-1970s made up of Departments for Education, Planning, Scholarships and Cultural Affairs, Research and Development, Illiteracy Abolition and Adult Education, each of which was responsible to the Under Secretary of the Ministry. There were also seven regional Ministry offices, each headed by a Superintendent with administrative, technical and religious assistants, and a Higher Council for Education was projected.

The expansion of education in Oman was explosive. Before Sultan Qaboos's accession in 1970 the standard of education was good but the number of govern-

ment schools had been deliberately restricted to three – one in Muscat, one in Mutrah and one in Salala. These schools were open only to boys and did not consist of any classes above intermediate level. In the autumn of 1970, however, tented schools sprang up all over the country and enthusiasm amongst teachers and pupils alike was intoxicating as education was opened to increased numbers of boys, and was available to girls for the first time.

By 1979 things had vastly improved. Education was free and actively encouraged, but not compulsory: 43 per cent of Omani children of primary school age

221

were receiving education and plans were
ready for primary places for all children
in this age group by 1980. In the short
period of nine years the number of schools
had grown from three to 353 and the
pupils from 900 boys to 88,000 of both
sexes. There were 257 primary, eighty-
six preparatory, and nine secondary
schools. In addition there were 700
students studying abroad at higher
levels. The overall pupil-teacher ratio
had dropped from 35.4 to 1 in 1971 to
23.3 to 1 in 1975. The table below illustrates how rapid the expansion was:

Academic Year	Pupils	male/female
1969–70	900	all male
1970–71	6,941	5,805 male
		1,136 female
1974–75	49,229	36,851 male
		12,378 female
1978–79	88,000	61,000 male
		27,000 female

Meantime there had been a building
programme and several new permanent
schools were built. Thirty-seven new
school buildings had been completed by
early 1977, of which ten were in Dhofar.
It was only in the remoter areas that
schools remained under canvas. Boarding sections for children from inaccessible mountain regions or from the outlying islands, and for orphans and those
children who had lost their fathers
during the fighting in Dhofar, were
created in some schools. The new system
provided for four or six years at the
primary level, according to the age of
the pupil. This was a transitional arrangement made in order not to disappoint
children – and their parents – above the
normal starting age in the primary grade,
which was reckoned at between five and
seven. The six-year course was the first
norm and the four-year course was for
older pupils. Examinations were set on
six subjects: Arabic language, religious
studies, English language, mathematics,
science and social studies.

Intermediate education in these early
years covered the age bracket of twelve
to eighteen, and consisted of a three-year
course in either general or religious
studies. The secondary level course also
lasted for three years and was available
to children from the age of fourteen
upwards. They could choose between:

*Mathematics, languages, sciences and
religious studies are the important
parts in the education of Omanis.*

a general education, with the option at the start of the second year to follow either literary or scientific courses;

b religious education for those pupils who were in the religious stream at intermediary levels;

c vocational education in agriculture, technical and commercial subjects, or teachers' training.

A pass at secondary level entitled a student to enter any Arab university. Nor were Omani students discouraged from study abroad and by 1979 there were over 700 Omani pupils in other countries at elementary and intermediary levels (mostly in the United Arab Emirates) and nearly 200 at secondary level (mostly Qatar).

Prior to 1970 no state education had been provided for girls; the very first school for girls was opened in the 1970–71 academic year, with 650 pupils. By 1979 there were more than 27,000 schoolgirl pupils comprising nearly one-third of the total school-going population at that time. Thus the country's great enthusiasm for girls' education was clearly demonstrated. Intermediary schools for girls were introduced in 1972, and the first girls' secondary school was opened in 1973. In the girls' *curriculum*, particular emphasis was placed on home economics and a development of the traditional arts such as weaving and embroidery, but languages, mathematics, sciences and religious studies played just as important a part as in the boys' schools. Girls like the boys were taught drama, music and crafts.

The expansion of education in the Southern Region of Dhofar was of particular significance in the latter stages, and in the aftermath, of the rebellion there. The one school in Salala in 1970 did little to satisfy the aspirations of the people but by 1979 there were 7,000 pupils, boys and girls, in fifty-six schools in the Southern region, most of these in the village centres away from the coast. A boarding school called the Qaboos School, for war orphans and the sons of people who lived on the Jebel a long way from the coast, was opened in 1973.

Although Muslim tradition remained as strong as ever in Oman, the Qur'an no longer formed the basis of all teaching but religious studies became one essential part of the total *curriculum*. And indeed, since the Omanisation of Education in 1978, new attitudes have made

A six-year course became the norm for the younger pupils. The curriculum included the Arabic language, basic science and social studies. Then came a three-year course, and, from the age of fourteen, children could choose between general education (including literary or scientific options), religious education, or vocational schooling in such areas as commerce, agriculture or teachers' training.

223

linguistic skills, and in particular the learning of English, the main priority. Religious affairs continued to be the concern of the Ministry of Endowments and Islamic Affairs, who not only encouraged eminent and religious scholars to lecture in Oman, but also stimulated religious teaching throughout the country.

In the field of further education, subsidies were awarded by the Government for students to attend foreign universities and specialised institutions, mainly in the United Kingdom. As Oman caught up with the modern world, it became increasingly important that adequate vocational training should be provided by the Ministry of Social Affairs and Labour to meet new needs. For this purpose a Technical School was established at Mutrah. This had had its beginnings in the trade school started by Petroleum Development (Oman) Limited, which was handed over to the Government in 1972. Training courses were given in mechanical engineering, carpentry, bricklaying, science and electronics. An Institute of Public Administration was also opened in 1973 to provide one-year courses in mathematics, book-keeping, language studies, particularly in English, typing and other secretarial skills. By the mid-1970s the Technical School had a capa-

Good village schools are the grass-roots of the educational system and have led to a huge increase in literacy; youngsters are often better informed than their parents. The continuing growth of such education is intended, for with these children lies the future of Oman.

Boys returning home from school in Bahla carry their homework in modern briefcases.

city of 180 and the Institute one of sixty of both sexes. U.N.E.S.C.O. and the World Bank contributed in the supervisory and financial fields to the development of various further educational projects: basic education centres in Muscat and Sohar, an agricultural school at Nizwa, a teachers' training college at Mutrah, and technical colleges at Sohar, Salala and Sur.

In 1972 the Ministry of Education started a programme of two-year in-service teacher training courses for Omani teachers, who were in short supply compared with the country's needs. A teachers' training college was set up in Mutrah in order to increase the number and improve the standard of Omani teachers, for rapid expansion had entailed the employment of teachers from well-disposed Arab countries, notably Egypt and Jordan, on a large scale. In 1975 there were only 335 Omani teachers out of a total of 3,570 teachers. Advisers from U.N.E.S.C.O. and U.N.I.C.E.F. helped to establish the training courses, and student teachers were also sent on short training courses in neighbouring Arab countries. Regional training centres were established, and a further two teacher training colleges, one for male and the other for female students, were built in 1975.

Most of the text books used in the schools before 1970 came from abroad, mainly from Qatar and Kuwait, but with the assistance of the U.N. Agencies concerned *curricula* and text books specifically suited to Oman were prepared and a centre for educational aids and a teaching laboratory planned.

In the fight against illiteracy seventy classes, catering for some 5,000 students, were established between 1971 and 1973. These were later supplemented by a further 200 classes as part of an intensive drive to spread education. The importance of adult education was emphasised by the creation of a special department within the Ministry of Education, and self-education was encouraged by broadcasting networks and specialised publications, and also by home study and correspondence courses. A further important aspect of the adult education department's work was the institution of specialised schools for the blind.

Importance was attached to welfare

and leisure activities for young Omanis and this became the specific responsibility of the Ministry of Youth Affairs. The Ministry planned to build a sports city at Khwair and an art gallery, as well as publish a magazine on youth affairs. Such activities were additional to what the schools provided in the way of sports, especially hockey, football and volleyball for boys and table tennis, volleyball and basketball for girls. The Scout movement became active and there were 3,000 Scouts, 200 Cubs, 128 Girl Guides and 504 Brownies in Oman by the end of 1974. The armed forces have provided many Omanis with educational opportunities of an academic and technical as well as a general nature. A school was established in 1973 at the S.A.F. Training Regiment at Ghalla for young cadets and facilities were later extended to the Air Force and Navy. The academic *curriculum* followed that prescribed by the Ministry of Education. A training school for apprentices in aircraft engineering was opened in 1975 under the auspices of the Air Force.

The building of schools, educational institutions, and teachers' accommodation were given high priority, but the provision of suitable premises could not keep pace with the expanding educational services. Some schools had to work on a shift system in order to make

Gymnastics are a special feature of the present curriculum; great attention is paid to this form of education.

the maximum use of buildings and teaching staff, and some classes were held in temporary or rented accommodation. Despite all the difficulties, however, Oman made astonishing strides in the educational sphere in the years after 1970 and many opportunities, unimagined only a few years ago, awaited Omani boys and girls.

In fact progress in providing free primary and secondary education was so rapid in the first nine years that, by 1979, the Government was able to slow down its school-building programme and devote more attention to improving standards, preparing young Omanis for future requirements of trained manpower and "Omanising" the *curriculum*; the object of this is to instil national and Islamic consciousness among schoolchildren from different social and tribal backgrounds, in effect producing through the schools young people who are distinctly Omani, and yet feel members of the wider Arab world.

Health services have been a priority since 1970.

The al Nahda Hospital was begun by Sultan Said, and improved and modernised under Sultan Qaboos.

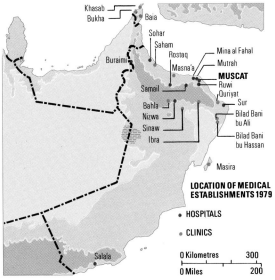

LOCATION OF MEDICAL
ESTABLISHMENTS 1979

• HOSPITALS
• CLINICS

| 0 Kilometres | 300 |
| 0 Miles | 200 |

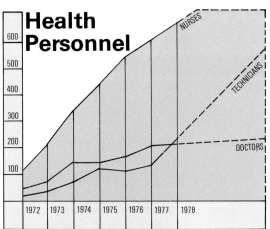

Health Personnel

Health

OMAN should be a healthy land, and its people, living as they do in uncluttered communities along its coastline and among its mountains and deserts, start with an advantage. There are no slums, no swamps, no overcrowding, no gross shortage of food. Life is hardy and outdoor. Yet for a variety of reasons the general state of health of large sections of the community was very poor up to 1970, particularly in the Interior where trachoma, glaucoma and other eye diseases were widespread. Malnutrition and vitamin deficiency were rife, as much through lack of knowledge about diet or internal parasites as through true poverty. Malaria epidemics could devastate a community, and ailments resulting from poor hygiene were ubiquitous.

Until 1970 modern medicine had only scratched the surface of the problem despite the devoted work of doctors and others in the American Mission Hos-

pitals. Estimates suggested a ratio of one doctor to 28,000 citizens in 1970. Five small clinics existed then and three others were under construction.

Oman's medical ills have not been eliminated. But the Ministry of Health, set up in 1970, whose task was regarded as of paramount importance to the people's welfare boldly attacked the problem of disease and malnutrition, and by the mid-1970s there was a noticeable improvement in the people's health and well-being. Instruction in child care brought a sharp drop in infant mortality.

The complement of doctors and dentists increased six-fold in the first five years of the 1970s, and the number of other trained medical staff quadrupled. Many Omanis were training in medicine abroad, including, in 1979, a number of nursing and paramedical staff, and five fully qualified doctors, undergoing courses in different fields of specialization. The Al Rahma

School of Nursing was Oman's first to open in 1970, and then still further plans were made for the training institute of nurses, midwives, sanitary assistants and laboratory technicians. The Department of Public Health in the Ministry ran a nationwide school health service, to give children protection against malaria, trachoma, tetanus and diphtheria.

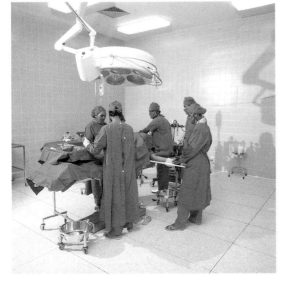

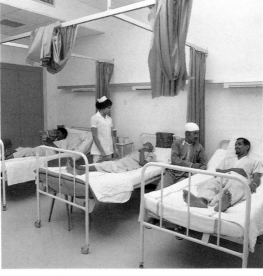

The programme of public health began by tackling widespread malnutrition, and a high incidence of disease. The hospital at Bahla (above) *was one of many hospital-school complexes which were launched as part of this development programme. Salala's Qaboos hospital* (left) *opened in 1976.*

operating by 1976, each with in-patient facilities for twenty-four patients, together with about forty dispensaries year. Twelve rural health centres with in-patient facilities for twenty-four patients, and 47 dispensaries were operating by 1979. Together with Mobile Medical Teams visiting remote villages, this integrated rural health service has put modern medicine within reach of virtually the whole population.

Assistance was forthcoming from the World Health Organisation and qualified staff came from overseas. It seems expatriate help may well be needed for some time to come but within a very short period Oman acquired a professional, competent and enviable health service.

Mass programmes of vaccination against smallpox and inoculation against cholera were completed.

By 1979, thirteen hospitals, and various health centres, clinics, maternity and child care centres together provided 1,656 beds. Al Nahda hospital in Ruwi specialised in eye disease, internal medicine and dentistry, ar-Rahma hospital at Mutrah in pulmonary cases and al Khoula at Wattaya in surgical and maternity cases. Salala's largest general hospital, with a separate maternity wing, was opened in 1976. The hospitals in hospital-school complexes at Nizwa, Rostaq, Sohar, Samail, Sur and Buraimi, could by then handle 100,000 patients a year. The nine rural health centres

Hospitals for Villagers

The biggest planned expansion in the health field has been the provision of health centures and dispensaries (*see lower picture*). The centres, consisting of about twenty-four beds, staffed by two doctors and ten nurses, will have reached 26 by 1982. Dispensaries should have reached 80 by that year.

A mobile medical centre for the Jabali tribe in the Dhofar mountains.

Jabali schoolgirls also receive medical care in Dhofar.

Agriculture

THE main aim of the agricultural policy introduced after 1970 was to utilise Oman's natural resources and to make the country more self-sufficient in food and the products which can be grown in Oman, as well as to increase production for export. For Oman has the advantage of being the only country on the Arabian side of the Gulf where agriculture has been practised on a large scale in the past and where there is scope for expansion in modern circumstances. Indeed with the exception of Yemen Oman has the highest rainfall of all the countries in the Arabian Peninsula.

The monsoon, which affects Dhofar, produces enough rain on the mountains to provide good grazing for the small cattle of the Southern Region and to sustain subsistence level grain crops. However, agriculture on the Salala plain depends on irrigation just as it does everywhere in the north. Thus agriculture throughout Oman depends on careful exploitation of water resources and the widespread *falaj* system which has been operating in Oman for two thousand years and more, is a sophisticated way of doing this. Along the

Cutting grass to feed cattle in the Salala area (top). *Experimental farming includes the installation of sprinkler systems as on this farm in Dhofar* (above), *dependent on irrigation.*

Batina coast on the other hand water traditionally has been raised by *shaduf*, a gallows-like structure at the apex of which is a wooden wheel. Over this a long rope is pulled by a donkey, bull or camel, thus drawing the water up from the well in a bucket attached to the rope. However over the last twenty years this traditional system has been gradually

Agriculture in Oman today is a strange amalgam of change and changelessness, of opportunities and of climatic constraints. It is an important key to her future.

replaced by small modern pumps operated by diesel engines.

In the past the cultivated area was considerably larger than it was in 1970 when only about half of Oman's potentially cultivable 250,000 acres was being worked. Of this, 37 per cent was under date cultivation whilst the remaining area was under wheat, lucerne, onions, limes and other citrus fruits, bananas, mangoes, pomegranates and other fruits, tobacco, and, in the south, coconut palms.

The new Government saw its general task as five-fold: the proper use and

231

New areas of cultivation have vastly changed the physical appearance of the Oman landscape, nowhere more so than in Salala (above).
Water is crucial in Dhofar (left).
Frankincense trees (bottom left).

exploitation of water; introducing improved strains of crops and animals and new techniques; eliminating crop disease; assisting with the distribution and preservation of food; and harvesting Oman's seas. All involved research. In 1970 there were only two experimental farms but by 1979 Oman had eighteen and there were also thirty-five "extension centres". Thus ordinary farmers, who comprised some 80 per cent of the working population, gained knowledge of the new strains of crops and agricultural methods which had been found successful on the experimental farms. Tractors were hired out, fertilisers and crop sprays supplied, and instruction, financial credit, marketing facilities, seed and seedlings and animal fodder made available.

Two of the main requisites for formulating a detailed policy were an extensive survey of water resources and a soil survey. The work of the Ministry of Agriculture and Fisheries in soil analysis was supplemented by two important projects undertaken by Durham University. It was found that large scale developments would not be possible unless new water resources were discovered, since the falajes cannot support further large scale cultivation. Thus, in 1979, two supplementary irrigation schemes were being considered. One plan was to dig wells to the depth of 300–400 metres, where there were known reservoirs of water. The other scheme was to build re-charge dams to trap rainwater which, until then, had run to waste down the sides of Oman's main mountain ranges.

Though much of the effort after 1970 was devoted to increasing the number of experimental farms, establishing improved extensions services, increasing the use of improved strains, dealing with plant diseases and generally improving and building up on traditional methods of agriculture, this was not the whole story. A deliberate attempt was made to introduce entirely new concepts in order to maximise the revenue from Oman's natural products. One such scheme was the establishment of date processing factories at Nizwa and Rostaq in the Interior. They were built at a cost of U.S. $1.5m. and each was capable of handling about two thousand tons of dates a year. It was indicative of the new liberal thinking which predominated in Oman by the mid-1970s that half the employees of these factories were women,

233

a situation which would have appeared unthinkable only a few years previously. Utilisation of domestic resources was furthered with the establishment at Nizwa of a factory to handle tinned lime juice, tomato paste, date biscuits and other palm products. A citrus fruit centre, which could be expanded into a canning plant, was established at Sohar. Sugar mills were planned for Nizwa and Saham, while poultry projects were undertaken in both public and private sectors. Poultry farming was largely confined to eggs, with one farm producing 50,000 per day by 1980.

Most farms are plots of four or five acres. Wheat growing is heavily subsidized to raise production to 10% of internal requirements. In 1979 there were 50,000 cattle, mostly in the southern region of Dhofar. Together with goats and camels, livestock came to 341,000 head, and the target for 1980 was 522,000. By the late 1970s research was beginning to produce better quality sheep and goats with heavier body-weight. In the south also experiments were carried out in stock breeding, including the crossing of the small but sturdy

Dhofari strain with Sindhi, East African and Friesian bulls, and growing the fodder on the plain to sustain the herds. Likewise a dairy scheme was started near Salala. A further development introduced by the Dhofar Development Department was a slaughter-house, the object of which was to provide an outlet for cash sales of superfluous beasts raised by the tribesmen of the Dhofari mountains in order to stimulate the economy. The scheme appeared promising since Dhofar is the only part of the Arabian Peninsula where cattle can be raised on a large scale and the demand for meat in the neighbouring Arab and other countries is constantly rising.

With a coastline of 17,000 km, Oman's fisheries have enormous potential. The present catch is only a tiny fraction of the abundant supplies of commercially marketable fish which recent surveys indicate.

The Government spent RO 15 million during the period of the First Plan to develop the industry. Training Omani fishermen in modern methods was a major priority, but most of the budget was used in establishing a network of

Cattle are raised on a considerable scale in the Dhofar area. With the construction of new troughs (right), their water supply is assured.

ice plants, cold stores and distribution outlets in the main population centres. In 1976, a complex with ice and fish processing plants and a 3,500 tonne cold store, three coastal trawlers, and a fleet of refrigerated trucks was opened in Muttrah. By 1979 the trawlers were bringing in about 180 tonnes of fish a month, twice the size of 1978 catches.

Joint ventures with foreign companies were considered, and in 1979 deep-sea trawling was being done by a Korean company, under contract to train Omanis and provide the Government with 30% of its catch.

Fishermen also receive essential financial aid to buy specially designed aluminium fishing-boats and other modern fishing equipment. Such assistance, together with modern cold storage and marketing facilities have enabled Oman's fishermen to increase their earnings considerably and reap a hitherto unexploited harvest.

National Television

The first television broadcasts took place in the capital area around Muscat in 1974, from transmitters erected on the heights at Qurm. By 1980 virtually the whole country was covered by transmission capability – indeed Omani television was being received clearly in the Gulf and Karachi.

Before 1970 there was no radio or television. But informing the people was to become a major function of government. By 1974–5 there was nationwide transmission in colour, and public television sets were installed in the capital and main towns. Regular programmes in north and south included local and international news, live outside broadcasts and documentaries, and feature films from other Arabic-speaking countries. A network of correspondents at key points provide a domestic news service.

In 1975 a new radio and colour television broadcasting station was completed at Salala. This, together with three relay stations, was able to cover the whole of the Dhofar region. Above and right: Folk-lore dance group in one of the television studios at Salala.

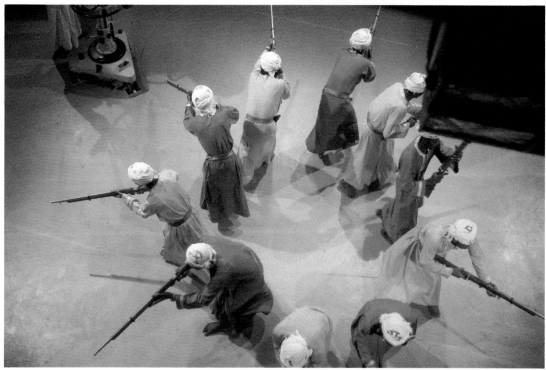

Government, Defence & Foreign Affairs

BEFORE the accession of H.M. Sultan Qaboos in July 1970, the governmental structure was simple and elementary. The Sultan exercised personal power through his Minister of the Interior, Sayyid Ahmad ibn Ibrahim, the nephew of the former Imam Azzan ibn Qais, and the *Walis* in the various districts. He also kept a close personal hold on the armed forces through a Deputy Minister of Defence and on finance through an adviser.

In September 1970 Sultan Qaboos appointed his uncle, Sayyid Tariq ibn Taimur – who had broken with his brother Sayyid Said in the early 1960s – as Prime Minister. Sayyid Tariq formed a small ministry consisting largely of distinguished Omanis who, alienated like himself, had stayed away from the country in the latter days of his brother's reign. Sayyid Tariq, however, resigned in December 1971, and thereafter Sultan Qaboos acted as his own Prime Minister as well as exercising direct control over defence and finance. He also retained direct control over foreign affairs which became increasingly important as Oman gradually broke out of its isolation from the mainstream of Arab and world events. A Minister of State for Foreign Affairs was soon appointed and, as Oman's overseas commitments grew, this office became increasingly significant. The Sultan's policies were proclaimed in a series of important speeches, particularly those made at official cele-

brations of the Sultan's Birthday and National Day in November. Policy statements were broadcast on the Omani Radio which rapidly grew from its very small beginnings in 1970, and publicised in the papers, which appeared for the first time a few months after the Sultan's accession.

Laws and Decrees

LAWS and decrees issued by the Sultan constitute the laws of the land. International treaties, agreements and charters signed or approved by the Sultan become law from the date of their publication in the Official Gazette. A legal directorate revises draft laws before they are signed, and gives legal advice on other matters referred to it by various departments.

As the complexities of the modern government which the Sultan had determined to give the country grew, more Ministers were appointed, and by 1979 there were, in addition to the Ministries of Foreign Affairs and Defence, and the Directorate of Public Finance, Ministries of Royal Diwan Affairs; of the Interior; Land and Municipal Affairs; Aqwaf and Islamic Affairs; Social Affairs and Labour; Justice; Commerce and Industry; Communications; Health; Education; Information and

H.M. Sultan Qaboos and King Khalid of Saudi Arabia discuss international affairs.

Sultan Qaboos's new palace is a happy marriage of traditional and modern styles and techniques. It is a symbol of Oman's renaissance and stability of government. Like Oman herself, it stands proudly above the old, yet harmonises with it.

The Structure of Government

☼ MINISTRIES OF WHICH
H.M. THE SULTAN HOLDS
THE PORTFOLIO

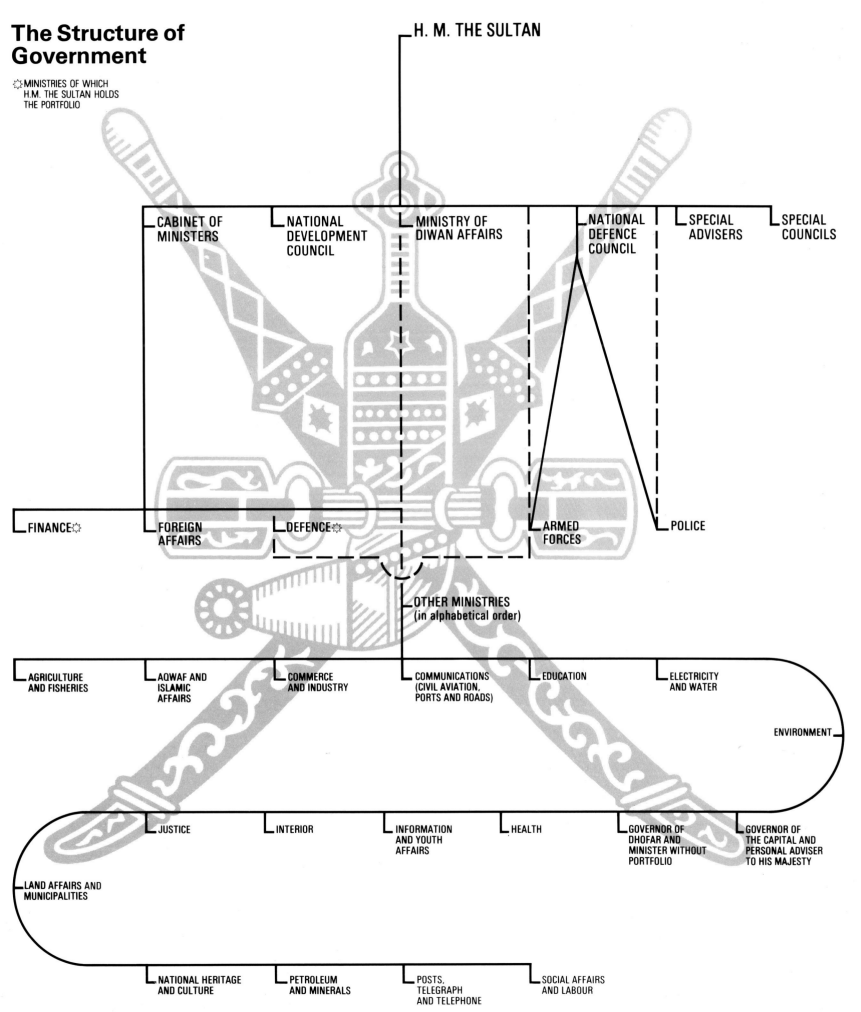

H. M. THE SULTAN

CABINET OF MINISTERS

NATIONAL DEVELOPMENT COUNCIL

MINISTRY OF DIWAN AFFAIRS

NATIONAL DEFENCE COUNCIL

SPECIAL ADVISERS

SPECIAL COUNCILS

FINANCE☼

FOREIGN AFFAIRS

DEFENCE☼

ARMED FORCES

POLICE

OTHER MINISTRIES
(in alphabetical order)

AGRICULTURE AND FISHERIES

AQWAF AND ISLAMIC AFFAIRS

COMMERCE AND INDUSTRY

COMMUNICATIONS (CIVIL AVIATION, PORTS AND ROADS)

EDUCATION

ELECTRICITY AND WATER

ENVIRONMENT

JUSTICE

INTERIOR

INFORMATION AND YOUTH AFFAIRS

HEALTH

GOVERNOR OF DHOFAR AND MINISTER WITHOUT PORTFOLIO

GOVERNOR OF THE CAPITAL AND PERSONAL ADVISER TO HIS MAJESTY

LAND AFFAIRS AND MUNICIPALITIES

NATIONAL HERITAGE AND CULTURE

PETROLEUM AND MINERALS

POSTS, TELEGRAPH AND TELEPHONE

SOCIAL AFFAIRS AND LABOUR

Youth Affairs; National Heritage and Culture; Agriculture and Fisheries; Petroleum and Minerals; Posts, Telegraph and Telephone; Electricity and Water; Youth; and Environment. In addition the Governor of the Capital and the Governor of Dhofar, under each of whom there was a considerable local administrative structure, each held ministerial rank. Another of the Sultan's uncles, Sayyid Fahr ibn Taimur, was Deputy Minister of Defence. Ministers were generally members of the Al bu Said family, or the sons of prominent merchants who had been educated abroad.

The appointment of Ministers was in the hands of the Sultan but, once invested with authority, Ministers had considerable discretion to appoint the staff and subordinate bodies required to carry out the duties laid on the ministry, although terms of service and general supervision of public service personnel were in the hands of the Ministry of Diwan Affairs. Ministries were required to submit a report annually to enable achievements to be compared with goals and effort to be appraised in the context of the Government's overall social, political and economic priorities. All projects involving expenditure of more than 0·5 million Omani Riyals had to be submitted to the Development Council, though detailed control of each ministry's expenditure was exercised through the annual budget and accounts.

Co-ordination of policies was achieved by various means. First the Council of Ministers met regularly under the presidency of the Sultan. Second, the Ministry of the Affairs of the Sultan's Diwan co-ordinated relations between the different ministries and the Cabinet Office, and in the Sultan's absence this Minister would preside. It also checked and published laws, audited State accounts and supervised the administration of tribal affairs. Third, there was a National Defence Council to co-ordinate the activities of the armed forces and police, of which the Sultan is Commander-in-Chief. Finally, the Development Council planned objectives and general policies for economic development, and supervised the various efforts of the different ministries and departments contributing to the current Development Plan.

The Ministry of Aqwaf (Religious Endowments) and Islamic Affairs was responsible for safe-guarding the Muslim faith and its spiritual values. It ran a number of religious institutes and Quran schools, notably the Islamic Training Institute at Watayah in the capital area, where religious teachers were trained. The Ministry built a number of mosques throughout the Sultanate and provided them with khatibs (preachers) and imams. Its many other duties included administering religious lands, property and libraries, publishing periodicals and booklets on religious topics and organising celebrations on religious occasions.

There were also a number of specialized councils under the chairmanship of the Sultan and comprising members of the Council of Ministers and selected others. These included the Development Council to facilitate planning by drawing together the strands of government, and the Councils for Defence, Agriculture, Fisheries and Industry, and Financial Affairs. The Council for Financial Affairs would lay down the financial policy of the State and draw up the national budget. Amongst other things its responsibility was to study the financial allocations for economic development projects approved by the Development Council.

There were several levels of administration. First, the central government and all its organs; secondly, the regional governments in the capital area and in Dhofar; thirdly, the 46 Walis of the Wilayat who were directly responsible to the Minister of the Interior and who exercised governmental control in the traditional fashion; fourthly, a number of municipalities with councils which were established in the more important towns. Another important development towards popular participation in Government was the formation, in 1979, of committees on matters of public importance.

Defence

A glance at a map immediately reveals the strategic importance of Oman. With Iran it controls the entrance to the Straits of Hormuz, through which a tanker passes about once in every twelve minutes. Port Qaboos at Mutrah is the only modern harbour between Karachi and Aden, and Oman has a thousand miles of coastline on the Indian Ocean. Thus the stability of Oman is a vital interest for her neighbours and indeed all the states in the area.

It is, therefore, not surprising that attempts should have been made to subvert the country, and an opportunity to do this arose from the rebellion which had broken out in the south in 1965. This was initially an indigenous Dhofari revolt against the restrictive policies of Sultan Said and led by the Dhofar Liberation Front. However, the direction of the revolt was taken over in 1968 by groups with revolutionary aims and contacts with communist and extreme socialist states. Their aims were clearly and succinctly stated in their title – the People's Front for the Liberation of Oman and the Arabian Gulf, (P.F.L.O.A.G.), even though they dropped ". . . and the Arabian Gulf" in 1974. They were given support and sanctuary by the People's Democratic Republic of Yemen which enabled them to operate from bases outside the country.

Sultan Qaboos, who had been hopeful that with his accession the rebellion would come to an end, offered an amnesty to the Dhofari rebels, and for some months the Sultan's Armed Forces (S.A.F. – the army) concentrated nearly as much on attempting to persuade the rebels of the benefits of peace under his rule, which were now available to the whole country, as on fighting. Unfortunately his magnanimity was not rewarded and the rebels intensified their activities, posing a threat to Salala itself in 1971. It became necessary to strengthen the S.A.F. and the Sultan of Oman's Air Force (S.O.A.F.), and to acquire helicopters and transport aircraft. Over the next year or two forces were organised into a formidable army, an increasingly sophisticated air force and an expanding navy (S.O.N. – the Sultan of Oman's Navy). With this increase in strength the Sultan's forces gradually gained a stronger hold on the mountain areas of the south and the rebels were pushed further and further from Salala and the coastal towns.

Military means alone could not win the day for the Government and consequently large sums of money were allocated at the same time to civil development in the south. A small port was created at Raysut; Salala airfield was expanded, and improved by being given a hard top; roads were pushed out from Salala, where a hospital was established, power installed and building on a considerable scale stimulated; agriculture was developed on the plain and schools and clinics were opened. The

Artillery at Izki (above). *Of all the Arabian armies, the Sultan's Armed Forces have the greatest battle experience. Early drill training for new recruits* (right).

sting in the charges made by the rebels that the Government had failed to provide for the welfare of the people was drawn when government control of the mountain areas increased and schools, clinics, trading facilities and water supplies were installed there as well.

Despite this two-pronged attempt to solve the problem in the south the rebel P.F.L.O.A.G. made two attempts to start a second front in northern Oman, one in 1972 and the other in 1974. Both were

totally abortive and swiftly nipped in the bud by the armed forces, but both attempts were aimed at alleviating the Government's intensifying pressure on the rebels in Dhofar.

The rebellion had caused as much as 50 per cent of Oman's national budget to be devoted to defence, but this did not inhibit the development which was quickly bringing Oman into the modern

Oman had the first women police in Arabia. Equipped with stylish uniforms, they are carefully trained in how to exercise authority with grace but firmness.

Nonetheless, the Sultan's forces, despite increases in strength, lacked sufficient numbers to dominate the whole of the wild and extensive mountains of the south, even though the country's outer defences had been extended in 1972 to Sarfit on the Oman–People's Democratic Republic of Yemen boundary near Hauf and to Habarut. The arrival of Iranian and Jordanian troops in 1973 and 1974 to supplement the help already being given by British officers serving in the Sultan's forces was, therefore, particularly welcome. The dual policy of military dominance and civil development together with the help of Oman's allies brought final victory in December 1975, although important members of the opposition had been coming over to the Sultan and receiving clemency for some time. This was a remarkable victory over a Marxist-dominated movement, succoured from outside.

Police (facing page) *and army* (above left) *pursued a policy of civil development alongside that of military dominance during the war in Dhofar. They still do.*

Omani Air Force Strikemasters fly out on active operations (middle right). *With the Jaguar* (above) *Oman has the strongest air defence strike power in the region.*

243

The Strategic Role

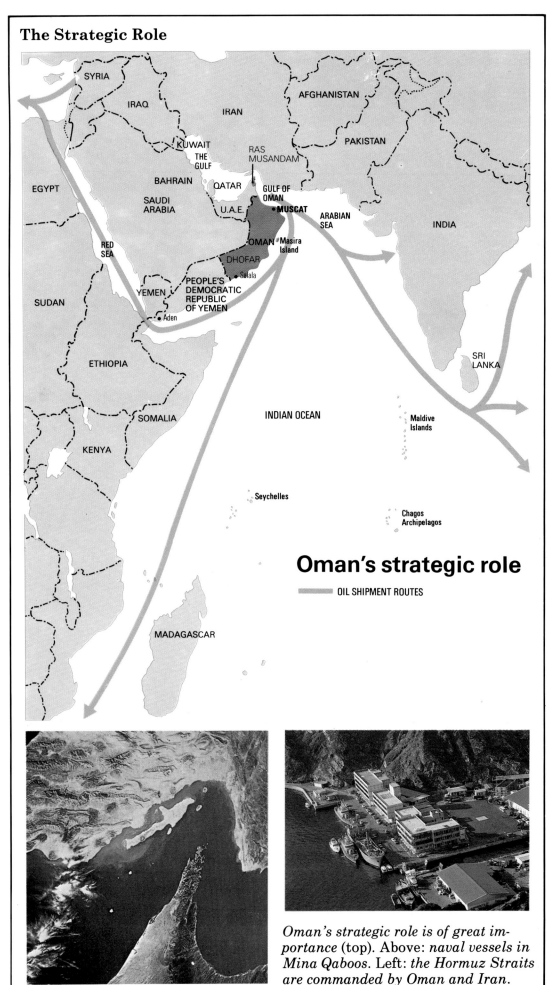

Oman's strategic role

— OIL SHIPMENT ROUTES

Oman's strategic role is of great importance (top). Above: *naval vessels in Mina Qaboos*. Left: *the Hormuz Straits are commanded by Oman and Iran.*

world. On the positive side, Oman built up the military strength which its strategic position required. The army grew from three regiments and a total strength of 4,000 in 1970 to eight infantry regiments, an artillery regiment, an armoured car squadron, and strong and efficient ancillary services in 1979. The air force grew from a small force with Provost and Beaver aircraft in 1970 to a sophisticated force, equipped with Jaguar and Hunter aircraft and radar, and with a flying and technical school planned for Masira.

Similarly the navy grew from two armoured *dhows* in 1970 to a fleet more worthy of Oman's traditional naval might: three corvettes, including the flagship *Al Said*, seven fast patrol boats, four coastal patrol and three landing craft, and a training vessel, with a manpower strength of 500 in 1979, two auxiliary store ships and more support ships on order, including minesweepers and anti-submarine helicopters.

During the period of expansion, great attention was also paid to increasing the number of Omani officers, who until the end of Sayyid Said's reign had not been permitted to hold any rank above that of Lieutenant. By 1974 100 officers each year were being commissioned from the ranks, particularly those who had distinguished themselves in battle in the south or by direct entry. Initial training was at the S.A.F. Training Regiment, and many received further training abroad, particularly in the United Kingdom, some of the officers going to Sandhurst, and in Jordan. Thus Omanis are playing an increasingly important role in maintaining the stability of the area.

Relations with other Countries

UNTIL 1970 Oman stood very much out of the mainstream of Arab and foreign affairs generally. The predominant position which the country had enjoyed in the area until the middle of the nineteenth century had been lost and indeed forgotten. The Sultanate had consular relations only with Britain and India, and even official visits between Oman and the neighbouring countries were of rare occurrence. The Sultanate had no representation at the United Nations and "the question of Oman" had remained inscribed at the U.N. since 1960, coming up for yearly discussion as the dissident Imam and his supporters kept the issue of the Omani Imamate alive.

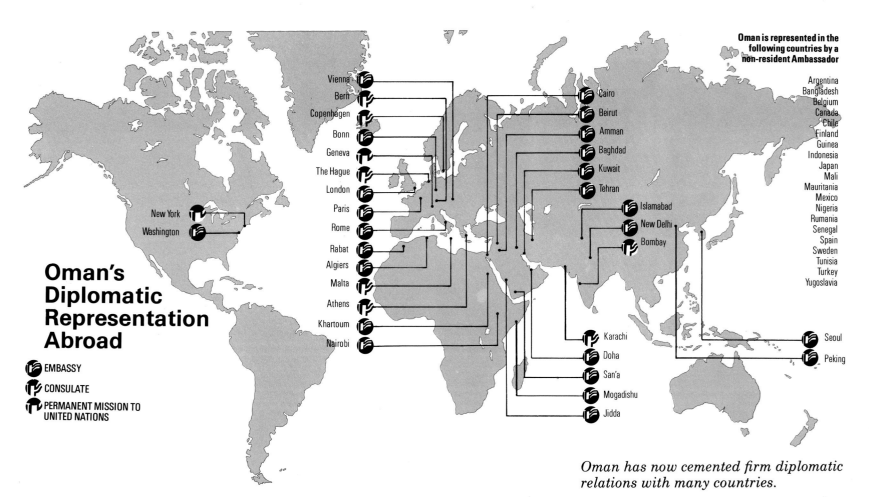

Oman's Diplomatic Representation Abroad

Vienna
Bern
Copenhagen
Bonn
Geneva
The Hague
London
Paris
Rome
Rabat
Algiers
Malta
Athens
Khartoum
Nairobi

New York
Washington

Cairo
Beirut
Amman
Baghdad
Kuwait
Tehran
Islamabad
New Delhi
Bombay

Karachi
Doha
San'a
Mogadishu
Jidda

Seoul
Peking

Oman is represented in the following countries by a non-resident Ambassador

Argentina
Bangladesh
Belgium
Canada
Chile
Finland
Guinea
Indonesia
Japan
Mali
Mauritania
Mexico
Nigeria
Rumania
Senegal
Spain
Sweden
Tunisia
Turkey
Yugoslavia

EMBASSY
CONSULATE
PERMANENT MISSION TO UNITED NATIONS

Oman has now cemented firm diplomatic relations with many countries.

After Sultan Qaboos succeeded his father in 1970, he and his Government determined to remedy this unsatisfactory state of affairs. The Sultan, therefore, announced an amnesty, proclaiming that "rebels would be permitted to return". Talib, the brother of the exiled Imam Ghalib, was even offered a ministerial post, though he rejected it. In February 1971 an Omani goodwill mission, which included several former members of the Oman Rebel Movement, was sent to visit the Arab capitals where the missions made a good impression. The Imamate issue was, however, a major stumbling block, as many Arab countries had accorded formal recognition to the Imamate and there were Imamate offices in several Arab capitals. The Sultan made it plain that the Imam Ghalib was free to return to Oman and would be accorded a religious dignity, but the offer was not accepted and the Imam remained in Saudi Arabia.

In 1971, Sayyid Tariq ibn Taimur, the Sultan's uncle, who was then Prime Minister, applied for Omani membership of the Arab League and the United Nations, and in October both applications succeeded. In December 1971, the Sultan paid a highly successful state visit to Saudi Arabia and, returning with full Saudi Arabian recognition and support, effectively put paid to the long-standing question of the Oman Imamate.

Oman began to widen its external contacts immediately after Sultan Qaboos's accession, and diplomatic instead of consular relations were exchanged with Britain and India as well as with Pakistan in 1971. In 1972, the United States, Iran, Egypt, Saudi Arabia, Jordan and Qatar followed suit, all with resident heads of mission accredited to the Sultanate. The French and the United Arab Emirates were the next to establish resident missions. By 1979 there were over forty resident missions with accredited Ambassadors including those resident elsewhere. For its part, Oman quickly established resident missions in London, New York, Washington, Cairo, Tehran, Delhi, Islamabad and a gradually increasing number of places, so that by 1979 there were thirty resident Omani missions abroad.

From 1970 onwards Oman's relations with other Arab states gradually improved as the country's isolation was progressively ended. By the mid-1970s, relations with all the countries of the Arab world were at least warm if not definitely good, with the exception of the People's Democratic Republic of Yemen

(P.D.R.Y.), which continued to aid the guerilla campaigns of the rebel People's Front for the Liberation of Oman and the Arabian Gulf. Oman referred the matter to the Arab League, which sent a mission to Dhofar in 1973, though it was not permitted to enter the P.D.R.Y. Oman's hopes of terminating the conflict were thus not fulfilled at this stage. However, the rebellion was brought to an eventual end by late 1975, after the Sultan's forces had been considerably increased and military aid had been given by Iran and Jordan as well as Oman's oldest ally, Britain. A number of other friendly states also gave financial and other assistance in varying degrees.

After 1971, Oman gradually played an increasing part in Arab League affairs and the Sultan also attended the Non-Aligned Summit at Robat and the Islamic Summit at Lahore in 1974. Thus Oman's external relations were generally normalised, but particularly close relations were developed with the neighbouring United Arab Emirates, as well as Qatar and Bahrain, Saudi Arabia, Iran, Jordan and Egypt. Oman has once again regained the position in international affairs to which its strategic situation and its long history destined it. It has every prospect of holding it.

Chronology

BC

c.12000	Stone Age civilisation in northern Oman and Shisur in Dhofar
c.3000	Earliest pottery – Jemdet Nasr period
c.2350	Magan ships trading with Sargon of Agade in Sumer
c.2275	Magan conquered by Naram-Sin of Agade
c.2025	Shipwrights mentioned in Sumerian tablets
c.2025	Magan trading with Ibbi-Sin of Ur
c.2000	Rise of Dilmun
c.1400–1300	Connections between Oman and Luristan in Iraq
c.800–700	Invasion from south Arabia by Ya'rub, whose brother Oman may have been appointed Governor
c.700	Trading with Gulf and Babylon resumed
c.563	Oman conquered by Cyrus the Great of Persia *Falaj* system developed

AD

c.50	Omana mentioned by Roman author Pliny
c.200	Azd migration into Oman led by Malik ibn Fahm
c.230	Ardashir I, founder of Persian Sassanid dynasty, regained firm control of Oman
c.520	Khosrau I of Persia dominated Oman in rivalry with Axumites of Ethiopia for control of Arabia
c.5th to 7th centuries	Christian bishopric at Sohar
630	Amr ibn al As arrived in Oman with letter from Prophet Muhammad Conversion of Oman to Islam
c.690	Apogee of Azd (of Oman) power in Basra
c.720	Fall of Azd from power and return to Oman
8th century	Sulaiman and Said, joint rulers of Oman, went to the "land of Zanj" (east Africa) when Caliphate troops occupied Oman
751	Election of first "rightful Imam" of the Ibadhis, Julanda ibn Mas'ud
893	Oman overrun by Caliphate troops led by Muhammad ibn Nur, and civil wars
9th century	Omani voyages to China
c.929	Carmathian conquest of Oman
c.950	Sohar the greatest sea port of Islam
971	Sohar devasted by the Buyids
1064	Oman invaded by the Seljuks
c.1153–1435	Oman without Imams and ruled by the Maliks of the Nabhan
c.1100–1300	Omani dynasty ruling Qais, then the centre of Gulf trade
1250	Hormuzi suzerainty established over Omani coast
1435	Imamate restored
1497	Omani pilot, Ahmad ibn Majid, navigated Vasco da Gama from Malindi in east Africa to Calicut in India
1507	Albuquerque brought Oman under Portuguese domination
1550	Muscat attacked by Piri Rais, Captain-General of the Turkish fleet
1581	Muscat again attacked by Turks under Ali Beg
1587–88	Forts Mirani and Jalali completed in Muscat by Portuguese
1624	Nasir ibn Murshid, first Imam of the Ya'ruba dynasty, elected
1646	Treaty of Commerce between the Imam and Philip Wylde of the English East India Company
c.1650	Imam Sultan ibn Saif recovered Muscat from Portuguese
1659	Treaty between the Imam and Colonel Rainsford of the East India Company about English trading in Muscat
c.1660–70	Imam Sultan ibn Saif built fort at Nizwa
1670	Dutch East India Company rented office in Muscat
mid-17th century	Oman controlled much of east African coast
1694–98	Omanis attacked Portuguese in Bombay and east Africa
c.1675	Imam Bil'arub built fort at Jabrin
1708	Imam Sultan ibn Saif II built fort at al Hazm
1718–47	Omani civil war
1748	Ahmad ibn Said elected first Imam of Al bu Said dynasty Persians involved in civil war expelled from Oman
1756–1804	Ottoman Sultan paid *kharaj* as friendly gesture to Imams through *Wali* of Basra
1760	Treaty between Imam and Mogul Emperor Establishment of Mogul mission in Muscat in "Nawab's House"

1775 Death of Imam Said at Rostaq
1794 Sayyid Sultan obtained Hormuz, Qishm, Henjam, Bandar Abbas, Chahbar, and Gwadur; all of these except Gwadur reverted to Persia in mid-19th century
1798 *Qualnameh* negotiated between British Government in Bombay and Sayyid Sultan by Mirza Mahdi Ali Khan
1799 Napoleon addressed letter to Sayyid Sultan ibn Ahmad as Imam
1800 Captain (later General Sir John) Malcolm signed treaty between Oman and Britain
Wahhabis captured Buraimi and began series of incursions into Oman lasting until 1860s
1804–56 Reign of Sayyid Said ibn Sultan
1807 Treaty of Amity and Commerce between France and Oman (short-lived)
1809 Sayyid Said joined with British in attack on Ras al Khaima and British and Omani troops attacked Wahhabis established at Shinas
1819 Sayyid Said joined with British in further attack on Ras al Khaima against Qawasim pirates
1820 Eclipse of Qasimi power and treaties signed with Trucial States
1820–21 Omani/British expeditions against Bani bu Ali
1829 Sayyid Said took Mombasa from Omani Mazari and, making Zanzibar his second capital, concentrated on east African Empire
1833 Treaty of Amity and Commerce signed with U.S.
1840 Mission of Ahmad ibn Na'man to U.S., sent by Sayyid Said
1856 Sultanates of Oman and Zanzibar divided – confirmed by Canning award of 1862
1856–66 Reign of Sayyid Thuwaini ibn Said in Oman
1862 British and French agreed mutually to respect independence of Oman and Zanzibar
1868–71 Reign of Imam Azzan ibn Qais
1869 Fort at al Hazm taken from Ya'ruba family by Azzan and Ibrahim ibn Qais
1871–88 Reign of Sayyid Turki ibn Said
1877 Commercial declaration between Holland and Muscat

1879 Dhofar re-occupied by Sayyid Turki's troops after 50-year interlude
1888–1913 Reign of Sayyid Faisal ibn Turki
1895 Muscat occupied by dissidents led by Shaikh Salih ibn Ali of Sharqiya Hirth
1901 Muscat telegraphic cable installed (earlier cable via Suez, Aden and Muscat to Karachi had failed in mid-19th century)
1913–32 Reign of Sayyid Taimur ibn Faisal
1913 Salim ibn Rashid al Kharusi elected Imam
1920 Agreement at Seeb between Sultan Taimur and tribes of the Interior
Muhammad ibn Abdulla al Khalili elected Imam
1932–70 Reign of Sayyid Said ibn Taimur
1952 Saudis occupied Buraimi
1954–59 Rebellion of Imam Ghalib ibn Ali
1955 Buraimi re-occupied by Omanis
1958 Gwadur ceded to Pakistan by purchase
1960 "Question of Oman" first debated at U.N.
1965–75 Rebellion in Dhofar
1967 Oil first produced in commercial quantities
1970 Accession of H.M. Sultan Qaboos ibn Said
1971 Oman admitted to United Nations and Arab League; end of the "Question of Oman" at U.N. Diplomatic relations established with Britain, India and Pakistan, and later with U.S., Iran, Egypt, Saudi Arabia, France and other countries
1972 Death of Sayyid Said ibn Taimur
1975 End of rebellion in Dhofar

The Flag of Oman
Until 1970 the flag of Oman was plain red. On the succession of Sultan Qaboos a competition for the best new design was held and the present flag, featuring the colours red, white and green with the arms of Oman, was selected by His Majesty and introduced. The traditional red of the former flag was retained, white was introduced because it was not only associated with the Imamate but also signified peace and purity, and green, a colour associated with the faith of Islam, also represented Dhofar and the green cultivated areas of Oman.

Glossary

Note on transliteration

The problem of transliterating Arab names into English is difficult and controversial. The expert and the Arab speaker may well prefer that transliteration should be both completely consistent and full, with dots and apostrophes to render the various sounds of the Arabic language. I have tried to achieve consistency, except where the common English version of a particular name may be better understood, but for the eye of the general reader I have omitted most of the dots and apostrophes which stricter scholarship would demand.

Personally I have always had much sympathy with what T. E. Lawrence wrote in the preface to *Seven Pillars of Wisdom*: "The general practice of orientalists in recent years has been to adopt one of the various sets of conventional signs for the letters and vowel marks of the Arabic alphabet, transliterating Mohamed as Muhammad, muezzin as mu'edhdhin, and Koran as Qur'an or Kor'an. This method is useful to those who know what it means, but this book follows the old fashion of writing the best phonetic approximations according to ordinary English spelling. The same place name will be found spelt in several different ways . . ." I have, however, not been as inconsistent in this volume as that distinguished author.

D.H.

A

aarif	supervisor of *falaj* irrigation
abaya	cloak worn by Arab women
abra	ferry
abu futila	matchlock gun
akhmas	fifths; historical divisions of old Basra
arad	salt-bush
ashgar	sodom-apple
askar	guard
athar	share in *falaj* water depending on time allowed for watering
Awkaf (sing. Wakf)	religious or administrative trusts, e.g. of *falajes*

B

badan	small boat traditionally made with planks sewn together
baghala	large ship with carved poop
bani	tribal prefix meaning "the sons of"
banjari	silver bracelet
barasti	house of palm wood and frond construction
Bawarij	Indian pirates of ninth century AD
Bibi	noble lady
bidar	man in village community responsible for certain agricultural tasks and for distribution of the *falaj* water
birqa	mask worn by some Omani women
bisht	cloak worn over *dishdasha* (q.v.)
bum	boat with long prow

C

Caliph	successor of the Prophet Muhammad and thus head of the Islamic world

D

Daudi	*falaj* channel which never dries up, named after Sulaiman ibn Daud (Solomon, son of David)
dhabi	gazelle
dibba	lizard; tribe name
dishdasha	white robe worn by men
Diwan	the Sultan's Court administration office
djinn	spirit

F

falaj	water distribution system, under or above ground
fard	kind of date

G

ghanja	small *baghala* (q.v.)
ghayl	method of irrigation with open water channels (*falajes*) led from an open source in a *wadi*
gizail	matchlock gun

H

Hajj	pilgrimage to Mecca and the other holy places incumbent upon every Muslim
halwa	sweetmeat made of starch, brown sugar, ghee, almonds, etc., typical of Oman
harim	women's quarters in private house
haris	man in village community in charge of weeding gardens
hib	long chisel used in cultivation of palm trees
hijra	the migration of the Prophet to Medina in 622 AD
hirz	charm necklace often of oblong shape and suspended round the neck on a chain
huri	canoe made from hollowed out tree trunk

I

Ibadhism	the form of Islam most generally followed in Oman, based on the doctrine of Abdulla ibn Ibadh
Id	Muslim festival holiday
'idda	period during which a divorced woman or a widow may not contract a new marriage
Imam	spiritual and secular leader of the people who at times held a position akin to kingship; also a leader in prayer

J

jaalan	water beetle; name of tribe
jalbut	boat with upright stem and transom stern
jebel	mountain
jihad	holy war

K

kafour	kind of spiced powder used in burials
khalas	type of date
khanjar	curved dagger worn by Omani men
kharaj	tax imposed on non-Muslims
khashab	boat (general word)
khuzi	meat on top of a pile of rice
Kitman	in Ibadhi doctrine, a period when true beliefs have to be concealed for political reasons
kohl	eye shadow

L

laban	yoghourt
lahaf	headscarf worn by some Omani women
laisu	outer garment worn by some Omani women
lakh	100,000 Indian rupees
Lumi Basra	limes of Basra in Iraq
lunghi	long undergarment wrapped round the waist, loin cloth

M

madhab	school of thought or doctrine of a sect
mahr	price paid for and to prospective bride by bridegroom
majlis	room where men receive their visitors and guests
manjad	heavy silver chain worn in Southern Region
manwa	warship (deriv. from man o' war (English))
mashribiya	wooden window screen (c.f. Egyptian style)
mibsali	type of date
mihrab	niche in mosque, where an Imam stands to lead prayers, facing towards Mecca
milha	marriage commitment
minjal	toothed sickle
Mutawwa (pl. *Mutawwain*)	fervent follower of Ibadhism

N

najdi	of the Najd; incense of the best quality
neel	the indigo plant

P

pice	Indian coin
purdah	state of seclusion in which Muslim women are kept

Q

qa'ada	primary shares in *falaj* ownership
Qadhi	judge of Islamic law
qaftan	outer garment
qahwa	coffee
qanat	underground water channel similar to those in Iran
qaulnameh	form of treaty
qashani	tile decoration
qirsh	Maria Theresa dollar
qu'ad	"quietists", according to Ibadhi school of thought

R

rababa	stringed instrument
ras	cape, head
rhim	gazelle
riha	kind of spice used for burials
ru'iya	sighting of the new moon

S

sadaqa (pl. *sadaqat*)	tax; voluntary alms used for religious purposes
Sahaba	the Prophet Muhammad's companions
sambuk	boat used for pearling
samra	kind of acacia
sawga	orange-flowered plant
sha'abi	lowest quality frankincense
shaduf	mechanism for raising water by means of bucket and pulley
shahuf	"pram" boat
shai hamudh	tea-like drink made from limes
shaikh	tribal leader
shasha	boat made from palm-fronds
shatha	shawl made from two pieces of cloth joined by lace
shazri	middle quality frankincense
shher	mountain (in Jibali)
Shia	major division of Islam, whose adherents believe that only the first four Caliphs were legitimate and that the Caliphate succession should have gone to the sons of Ali ibn Abu Talib, the Prophet's cousin and son-in-law
shu'iy	small fishing boat
sils	silver decoration worn with headscarf
Sunni	orthodox Muslim
sunt	kind of acacia
suq	market place
surra	small tree

T

Tabi'	person in contact with the Prophet's companions
tahr	mountain goat, *Hemitragus Jayakari*
Tuman	currency used in Oman and Iran before and during the nineteenth century

U

Ulema	body of learned men in Islam
umma	the Muslim state

W

wa'al	mountain goat (general name for both *tahr* and ibex)
wadi	dry river valley
Wahhabism	the form of Islam, mainly confined to Saudi Arabia, deriving from the doctrine of Muhammad ibn Abdul Wahhab
Wakf	see *Awkaf*
Wali	local governor of an area
wazara	long undergarment, Omani name for *lunghi* (q.v.)
Wazir	minister
wilaya (pl. *wilayat*)	governorate

Z

zalij	faience, ornamental tile
zar	evil spirit
Zuhur	state of living openly as Muslims

Bibliography

Abdul Amir, Amin *British Interests in the Persian Gulf* E. J. Brill, Leiden, 1967
Aitchison, Charles *A Collection of Treaties . . . relating to India and Neighbouring Countries* Calcutta, 1932
Albuquerque *Commentaries* Hakluyt Society, 1964. Reprinted 1970
Allama, Syed Sulaiman Nadvi *The Arab Navigation* Lahore, 1966
Allfree, Philip S. *Warlords of Oman* Hale, 1967
(Anon.) *Note of Travel or Recollection of Majunga, Zanzibar, Muscat, Aden, Mocha and Other Eastern Ports* Salem, Mass., 1854
Azzi Robert *Oman, Land of Frankincense and Oil* in *National Geographic Magazine*, February 1973
Belgrave, Sir Charles *The Pirate Coast* Bell, 1966
Bell, Gertrude *The Arab War* London, 1940
Bent, Theodore *Muscat* in the *Contemporary Review*, December 1895
Bent, Theodore *Southern Arabia* Smith Eldon, 1900
Bertram, G. C. L. *The Fisheries of Muscat and Oman*, H.M.S.O. for the Sultanate of Oman, 1948
Bibby, Geoffrey *Looking for Dilmun* Collins, 1970
Boustead, Hugh *The Wind of Morning* Chatto & Windus, 1971
Buckingham, James Silk *Travels in Assyria, Media and Persia* Henry Colburn, 1829
Burckhardt, J. L. *Notes on the Bedouins and Wahabys* London, 1830
Busch, Briton Cooper *Britain and the Persian Gulf 1894–1914* University of California Press, 1967
Capper, James *Observations on the Passage to India* London, 1785
Corderio, Luciano *Maskat* in *Geographical Journal*, Vol. XI, No. 2, February 1898
Coupland, Reginald *East Africa and its Invaders* Oxford, 1938
Cox, Sir Percy *Some Excursions in Oman* in *Geographical Journal*, Vol. LXIII, No. 3, September 1925
Dickson, H. R. P. *Kuwait and her Neighbours* Allen & Unwin, 1956
Disputes between the Rulers of Muscat & Zanzibar Proceedings of Government Commission. Education Society Press, Bycula, 1861
Eccles, G. J. *The Sultanate of Muscat and Oman* in *Journal of the Central Asian Society*, Vol. XIV, 1927
Eilts, Hermann F. *Ahmad bin Na'aman's Mission to the US in 1840: The Voyage of Al-Sultanah to New York City* Petroleum Development (Oman) Ltd. Originally published by Essex Institute, Salem, Mass., 1962

Fenelon, K. G. *The United Arab Emirates* Longmans, 1973 (first published as *The Trucial States: A Statistical Survey* Khayats, 1967)
Firouz, Kajare *Le Sultanat d'Oman* Paris, 1914
Fraser, James B. *Journey into Khorasan* London, 1825
Freeman-Grenville, G. F. P. *The Muslim and Christian Calendars* Oxford University Press, 1963
de Gaury, Gerald *A Note on Masirah Island* in *Geographical Journal*, Vol. CXXIII, No. 4, December 1957
Geary, Grattan *Through Asiatic Turkey* London, 1878
Germain, Adrien *Quelques Mots sur l'Oman et le Sultan de Maskate* in *Bulletin de la Ste. Géographique*, October 1868
Goldsmid, Sir Frederic John *Telegraph and Travel* Macmillan, 1874
Graham, G. S. *Great Britain in the Indian Ocean* Oxford, 1967
Graves, Philip *The Life of Sir Percy Cox* Hutchinson, 1941
The Gulf: Implications of British Withdrawal Washington DC Center for Strategic and International Studies, 1969
Hamilton, Alexander *A New Account of the East Indies (1688–1723)* Edinburgh, 1727, and Argonaut Press, 1930
Handbook of Arabia Intelligence Division, War Staff Admiralty, London, 2 vols. 1916–17
Hawley, Donald *Courtesies in the Trucial States* Khayats, 1965
Hawley, Donald *The Trucial States* Allen & Unwin, 1970
Hawley, Ruth *The British Embassy in Muscat. A Short History* 1974
Hay, Sir Rupert *The Persian Gulf States* Washington Middle East Institute, 1959
Herbert, Thomas *Some Yeares Travels in Divers Parts of Asia and Afrique* London, 1638
Heude, William *A Voyage up the Persian Gulf . . .* London, 1819
Historical and other information, connected with the province of Oman, Muskat, Bahrein, and other places in the Persian Gulf. No. XXIV of Selections from the Records of the Bombay Government, Bombay, 1856
Hogarth, D. G. *The Penetration of Arabia* Alson Rivers, 1905
Holden, David *Farewell to Arabia* Faber, 1966
Hopwood, Derek (ed.) *The Arabian Peninsula* Allen & Unwin, 1972
Hourani, George *Arab Seafaring* Khayats, 1963
Hulton, Jessop *The Journal* Preston, 1844
Husain M. Al Baharna *The Legal Status of the Arabian Gulf States* Manchester, 1968

Ibn Batuta *Travels* Hakluyt Society, Vol. II, 1962

Jayakar, A. S. G. *The Shahee Dialect of Arabic* in *Journal of the Bombay Branch of the Royal Asiatic Society*, No. LVIII, Vol. XXI, 1902

Jayakar, A. S. G. *The Omanee Dialect of Arabic* in *Journal of the Royal Asiatic Society of Great Britain & Ireland*, Vol. XXI (new series), Part III, July 1889 and Part IV, October 1889

Kelly, J. B. *Sultanate and Imamate in Oman* Chatham House Memorandum, December 1959

Kelly, J. B. *Britain & the Persian Gulf 1795–1880* Clarendon Press, 1968

Kelly, J. B. *Eastern Arabian Frontiers* Faber, 1964

Keppel, George *Personal Narrative of a Journey from India to England* London, 1827

Kumar, Ravinder *India and the Persian Gulf Region* Asia Publishing House, 1965

Landen, Robert G. *Oman since 1856* Princeton University Press, 1967

Lees, G. M. *The Geology and Tectonics of Oman and parts of South Eastern Arabia* in *Geographical Journal*, Vol. LXXXIV, No. 4, 1928

Lorimer *Gazetteer*, 4 vols. 1908–1915

Low, Charles Rathbone *History of the Indian Navy (1616–1863)* London, 1877

Mansur Shaik *History of Seyd Said, Sultan of Muscat* London, 1819

Marlowe, John *The Persian Gulf in the Twentieth Century* Cresset Press, 1962

Memorial of Saudi Arabia on the Buraimi Dispute – Arbitrations for the settlement of the territorial dispute between Muscat and Abu Dhabi on the one hand and Saudi Arabia on the other. Memorial of the Saudi Arabian Government. Submitted to the arbitration tribunal, Geneva, July 1955. 3 vols., Cairo, 1955

Miles, S. B. *On the Road between Sohar and El-Bereymi* in *Journal of the Asiatic Society of Bengal*, Vol. XLVI, Part 1, 1877

Miles, S. B. *The Countries & Tribes of the Persian Gulf* Second edition, Cass, 1966

Monroe, Elizabeth *Britain's Moment in the Middle East 1914–1956* Chatto & Windus, 1963

Morris, James *Sultan in Oman* Faber, 1957

Moyse-Bartlett, M. *The Pirates of Trucial Oman* Macdonald, 1966

Nicholls, C. S. *The Swahili coast: politics, diplomacy & trade on the East African littoral 1798–1856* Allen & Unwin, 1971

Niebuhr, Carsten *Description of Arabia . . . 1774* Various editions

Omar, Umberto *Il Sultanato di Oman* Rome, 1912

O'Shea, Raymond *The Sand Kings of Oman; being the experiences of an RAF officer in the little known regions of Trucial Oman, Arabia* Methuen, 1947

Ovington, John *Voyages* Paris, 1725

Owen, R. *Away to Eden* Collins, 1959

Owen, R. *The Golden Bubble* Collins, 1957

Owen, W. F. W. *Narrative of Voyages to Explore the Shores of Africa, Arabia, Madagascar* London, 1833

Palgrave, William Giffard *Narrative of a year's journey through central and eastern Arabia 1862–63* 2 vols. Macmillan, 1868

Petroleum Development (Oman) Ltd. *A Short History of Oman from the Earliest Times* Muscat, 1972

Philby, H. St. J. B. *Arabia of the Wahhabis* London, 1928

Phillips, Wendell *Unknown Oman* Longmans, 1966

Phillips, Wendell *Oman: a history* Longmans, 1967

Pilgrim, G. T. *The Geology of the Persian Gulf and the adjoining portions of Persia and Arabia* in *Geological Survey of India*, 1908

Polo, Marco *Travels* Various editions

Roberts, Edmund *Embassy to the Eastern Ports of Cochin China, Siam and Muscat in the US Sloop of War "Peacock"* New York, 1837

Ross, E. C. *Annals of Oman* Baptist Mission Press, Calcutta, 1874

Ruete, Emily *Memoirs of an Arabian Princess* Berlin 1886, London & New York 1888, Paris 1905, New York 1907

Ruschenberger, W. S. *Narrative of a Voyage . . . including . . . an Embassy to the Sultan of Muscat and the King of Siam* London, 1838

Said Ruete, Rudolph *Said bin Sultan* Alexander Ouseley, 1929

Salil ibn Razik *History of the Imams and Sayyids of Oman from AD 661–1856:* translated from the Arabic & edited & continuing the history down to 1870 by G. P. Badger. Hakluyt Society, 1871

Saunders, Daniel *The Journal of the Sufferings . . .* Salem, Mass., 1794

Shepherd, Anthony *Arabian Adventure* Collins, 1961

Skeet, Ian *Muscat and Oman* Faber, 1974

Somerville, Vice-Admiral Boyle *The Chart-Makers* Blackwood, 1928

Stiffe, Arthur W. *Ancient Trading Centres of the Persian Gulf* in *Geographical Journal*, Vol. X, No. 6, December 1897

Thesiger, Wilfred *Arabian Sands* Longmans, 1959

Thomas, Bertram *Alarms and Excursions in Arabia* Allen & Unwin, 1931

Thomas, Bertram *Among some Unknown Tribes of South Arabia* in *Journal of the Royal Anthropological Institute*, Vol. LIX, January–June 1929

Thomas, Bertram *Arab Rule under the Al Bu Said Dynasty of Oman 1741–1937.* Raleigh Lecture on History, British Academy, Vol. XXIV, 1938

Thomas, Bertram *Arabia Felix* Jonathan Cape, 1932

Thomas, Bertram *A Journey into Rub' Al Khali* in *Geographical Journal*, Vol. LXXVII, No. 1, January 1931

Tibbetts, G. R. *Arab Navigation in the Indian Ocean Before the Coming of the Portuguese* Luzac, 1971

Townsend, John *Oman: the Making of a Modern State* Croom Helm, 1977

U.K. Memorial on the Buraimi Dispute – Arbitration concerning Buraimi under the common frontier between Abu Dhabi and Saudi Arabia. Memorial submitted by the Government of the United Kingdom of Great Britain and Northern Ireland, 2 vols., London, 1955

Villiers, Alan *Sons of Sindbad* Hodder & Stoughton, 1940

Wellsted, J. R. *Travels in Arabia* 2 vols. John Murray, 1838

Wellsted, J. R. *Travels to the City of the Caliphs, along the Shores of the Persian Gulf and the Mediterranean* 2 vols. London, 1840

Wheatley, Paul *The Golden Khersonese* University of Malaya Press, 1961

Whitelock, H. H. *An Account of Arabs who inhabited the coast between Ras al Khaimah and Abu Thabee in the Gulf of Persia, generally called the Pirate Coast* Tr. Bombay Geographical Society, 1835

Wilkinson, J. C. *The Organisation of the Falaj Irrigation System in Oman* School of Geography, University of Oxford, 1974

Wilkinson, J. C. *A Sketch of the Historical Geography of the Trucial Oman down to the Beginning of the Sixteenth Century* in *Geographical Journal*, Vol. CXXX, No. 3, September 1964

Williamson, Andrew *Sohar & Omani Seafaring in the Indian Ocean* P.D.(O.) Ltd., Muscat, 1973

Wilson, Sir Arnold T. *The Persian Gulf* Clarendon Press, 1928

Wingate, Reginald *Not in the Limelight* Hutchinson, 1959

Zwemer, Rev. S. M. *Three Journeys in Northern Oman* in *Geographical Journal*, Vol. XIX, 1902

Zwemer, Rev. S. M. *Arabia, the Cradle of Islam* London and Edinburgh, 1900

Index

252